Lecture Notes in Computer Science   11435

Commenced Publication in 1973
Founding and Former Series Editors:
Gerhard Goos, Juris Hartmanis, and Jan van Leeuwen

More information about this series at http://www.springer.com/series/7412

Constantino Carlos Reyes-Aldasoro ·
Andrew Janowczyk · Mitko Veta ·
Peter Bankhead · Korsuk Sirinukunwattana (Eds.)

Digital Pathology

15th European Congress, ECDP 2019
Warwick, UK, April 10–13, 2019
Proceedings

 Springer

Editors
Constantino Carlos Reyes-Aldasoro (iD)
Electrical Engineering
City, University of London
London, UK

Andrew Janowczyk
Case Western Reserve University
Cleveland, OH, USA

Mitko Veta (iD)
Eindhoven University of Technology
Eindhoven, The Netherlands

Peter Bankhead (iD)
University of Edinburgh
Edinburgh, UK

Korsuk Sirinukunwattana
University of Oxford
Oxford, UK

ISSN 0302-9743   ISSN 1611-3349 (electronic)
Lecture Notes in Computer Science
ISBN 978-3-030-23936-7   ISBN 978-3-030-23937-4 (eBook)
https://doi.org/10.1007/978-3-030-23937-4

LNCS Sublibrary: SL6 – Image Processing, Computer Vision, Pattern Recognition, and Graphics

This Springer imprint is published by the registered company Springer Nature Switzerland AG
The registered company address is: Gewerbestrasse 11, 6330 Cham, Switzerland

Preface

Since its beginning in Heidelberg in 1992, the European Congress on Digital Pathology has been a biannual not-for-profit meeting of representatives from academia, industry, and clinical practice. Attendees at ECDP share a common interest in developing and applying new technologies to advance the field of pathology, which in the early years focused primarily on the scanning and remote viewing of histopathological images. However, as the use of telepathology has become widespread, the emphasis of the congress has increasingly moved into the application of image analysis and artificial intelligence techniques to maximize the meaningful information that can be extracted from tissue samples.

The 15th European Congress on Digital Pathology was held at Warwick University during April 10–13, 2019, with the theme "Accelerating Clinical Deployment." This marked the transition of ECDP into becoming an annual event, reflecting the rapidly expanding nature of the field. This growth has arisen through the widespread recognition that the latest developments in deep learning, when combined with accumulated knowledge of the past 30 years, are capable of solving problems that previously seemed intractable – and that one of the most pressing questions is how to translate these advances into the clinic.

ECDP 2019 was also the first time the congress invited both (a) clinical abstracts and (b) technical research papers focused on computational methods, reflecting the cross-disciplinary nature of the field. The program comprised oral presentations from pathologists and informaticians across a broad range of topics, in addition to a workshop entitled Machine Learning for Pathologists and special session on Digital Pathology in the Developing World. Together these demonstrate the recognition that digital pathology can have a truly global impact in benefiting patients – but achieving this requires effective communication across disciplines, cultures, and geographies. ECDP plays a unique role in promoting that communication.

This volume of *Lecture Notes in Computer Science* covers only the technical research papers submitted to the conference since the clinical abstracts were handled as abstracts and not full papers. The technical panel of the conference received 31 paper submissions. All these papers were peer-reviewed by an average of three reviewers and after a discussion, the Technical Program Committee selected 11 papers for oral and 10 papers for poster presentations. We believe that the papers selected for the proceedings and published in this volume represent the current state of the art in this dynamic field, and highlight the progress being made in tackling the real-world challenges of pathology.

Finally, we wish to thank the organizers of ECDP 2019, the presenters, and the attendees for making the congress a success.

April 2019

Peter Bankhead
Andrew Janowczyk
Constantino Carlos Reyes-Aldasoro
Korsuk Sirinukunwattana
Mitko Veta

Organization

Congress Chairs

Nasir Rajpoot (Congress President) — University of Warwick, UK

David Snead (Co-chair) — University Hospitals Coventry and Warwickshire, UK

Technical Program Chairs

Peter Bankhead — University of Edinburgh, UK

Andrew Janowczyk — Case Western Reserve University, USA

Constantino Carlos Reyes-Aldasoro — City, University of London, UK

Korsuk Sirinukunwattana — University of Oxford, UK

Mitko Veta — Eindohven University of Technology, The Netherlands

Program Committee

Amit Sethi — Indian Institute of Technology Bombay, India

Angel Cruz-Roa — University of the Llanos, Columbia

Cefa Karabag — City, University of London, UK

Cris Luengo — Flagship Biosciences, Inc., USA

David Edmundo Romo Bucheli — National University of Colombia, Colombia

Derek Magee — University of Leeds, UK

Francesco Bianconi — University of Perugia, Italy

Francesco Ciompi — Radboud University, The Netherlands

Geert Litjens — Radboud University, The Netherlands

George Lee — Bristol-Myers Squibb, USA

German Corredor — National University of Colombia, Colombia

Gloria Bueno — University of Castilla - La Mancha, Spain

James Monaco — Inspirata, Inc., USA

Jeffrey Nirschl — University of Pennsylvania, USA

Jose Alonso Solis-Lemus — City, University of London, UK

Jun Xu — Nanjing University of Information Science and Technology, China

Kevin Smith — KTH Royal Institute of Technology in Stockholm, Sweden

Lee Cooper — Emory University, USA

Marinus Bastiaan van Leeuwen — Philips Research, The Netherlands

Mario Kreutzfeldt — University of Geneva, Switzerland

Contents

Computer-Assisted Diagnosis and Prognosis

Image Datasets and Virtual Staining

Bringing Open Data to Whole Slide Imaging

Sébastien Besson[1], Roger Leigh[1], Melissa Linkert[2],
Chris Allan[2], Jean-Marie Burel[1], Mark Carroll[1], David Gault[1],
Riad Gozim[1], Simon Li[1], Dominik Lindner[1], Josh Moore[1],
Will Moore[1], Petr Walczysko[1], Frances Wong[1],
and Jason R. Swedlow[1,2(✉)]

[1] Department of Computational Biology, School of Life Sciences,
University of Dundee, Dundee DD1 5EH, UK
jrswedlow@dundee.ac.uk
[2] Glencoe Software, Inc., 800 5th Avenue, #101-259, Seattle,
WA 98104, USA

Abstract. Faced with the need to support a growing number of whole slide imaging (WSI) file formats, our team has extended a long-standing community file format (OME-TIFF) for use in digital pathology. The format makes use of the core TIFF specification to store multi-resolution (or "pyramidal") representations of a single slide in a flexible, performant manner. Here we describe the structure of this format, its performance characteristics, as well as an open-source library support for reading and writing pyramidal OME-TIFFs.

Keywords: Whole slide imaging · Open file format · Open data · OME-TIFF

1 Introduction

Digital Pathology is a rapidly evolving field, with many new technologies being introduced for developing and using biomarkers [1, 2], imaging [3], and feature-based image analysis [4–7], most notably using various approaches to machine and deep learning [8, 9]. As is often the case in fields that cross research science and clinical practice, this transformation has been supported by rapid technology development driven both by academia and industry. A full ecosystem of open and commercial tools for preparing and scanning slides and analysing the resulting data is now evolving. These are starting to deliver advanced, innovative technologies that, at least in some cases, can evolve into defined products suitable for use in clinical laboratories.

During similar phases in the fields of radiology, genomics, structural biology, electron and light microscopy, and many others, one of key developments that helped accelerate development was the appearance of common, defined and open methods for writing, reading, and sharing data. Each of these fields has taken different approaches to defining open data formats, and the approaches taken in different fields have had different levels of adoption. Digital Pathology, despite the rapid growth and potential of

---

S. Besson, R. Leigh and M. Linkert—These authors contributed equally to this work.

C. C. Reyes-Aldasoro et al. (Eds.): ECDP 2019, LNCS 11435, pp. 3–10, 2019.
https://doi.org/10.1007/978-3-030-23937-4_1

the field has not yet developed and adopted a mature open format that supports the wide range of data types that have emerged (with more on the horizon).

Since 2002, OME has built open software specifications and tools that accelerate and scale access to large, multi-dimensional datasets. OME's OME-TIFF [10], Bio-Formats [11] and OMERO [12] are used in 1000 s of academic, industrial and clinical laboratories worldwide managing access to imaging data and also for publishing imaging data on-line [13, 14], In this report, we present an open, flexible data format based on accepted imaging community standards that supports all the whole slide imaging (WSI) modalities we are aware of today and can expand to support many of the emerging data types that are likely to appear in the near future. Critically, we provide open source, liberally licensed software for reading, writing and validating the format, freely available documentation and specifications, open build systems that anyone can monitor for development, and open, versioned example files for use in development and benchmarking experiments. Finally, we embed the format writer in a library that supports conversion from some of the dominant WSI proprietary file formats (PFFs).

2 State and Support of WSI Formats

The field of Digital Pathology has not yet adopted an open, supported, implemented data format for storing and exchanging WSI generated by acquisition scanners. The absence of such a format means that WSI in Digital Pathology uses PFFs, making the data fundamentally non-exchangeable, not available for long-term archiving, submission with regulatory filings or on-line publication. As more research funders and scientific journals adopt the principle that research data should be Findable, Accessible, Interoperable and Reproducible (FAIR) [15], this situation ultimately prevents the field of Digital Pathology from complying with emerging trends and regulations in research science and also inhibits further innovation as exemplar datasets are not available to technology developers. Technologies like deep learning require large, diverse datasets that realistically can only be assembled by combining datasets from multiple centres and/or clinics. Cohort datasets written in incompatible PFFs slow the development of new tools and waste precious resources (usually public funding) on converting incompatible data- a process that is error-prone and often leads to data loss.

Moreover, as each new WSI scanner arrives on the market, a new data format is introduced to the community. Manufacturers update their formats at arbitrary times, further expanding the number of versions of these proprietary file formats (PFFs).

To deal with this explosion of WSI PFFs, software translation libraries have emerged that read data stored across many formats into a common open representation using a unified application programming interface (API). As of today, the two most established libraries used in the WSI domain are OpenSlide, a C-based library developed at Carnegie Mellon University [16] and Bio-Formats, a Java-based library developed by the OME Consortium [11]. Both have been developed by academic groups as open source projects. Many open-source and commercial tools in turn rely on the continued availability of these low-level libraries as a way to seamlessly access WSI data independently of its format. When reusing these libraries is not possible, commercial entities end up rewriting their own internal translational library allowing to achieve the same goal: reading WSI data independently of the format (e.g., https://free. pathomation.com/). Table 1 lists common types of WSI formats including their main manufacturer, their extension as well as their support in open-source libraries.

Table 1. List of common Proprietary File Formats (PFFs) used in the Whole Slide Imaging (WSI) domain alongside open-source libraries OpenSlide and Bio-Formats.

Manufacturer	File format extension	Support in open-source libraries
Aperio	.tiff	OpenSlide, Bio-Formats
Aperio	.svs, .afi	OpenSlide, Bio-Formats
Hamamatsu	.vms	OpenSlide, Bio-Formats
Hamamatsu	.ndpi, .ndpis	OpenSlide, Bio-Formats
Leica	.scn	OpenSlide, Bio-Formats
Mirax	.mrxs	OpenSlide
PerkinElmer	.qptiff	Bio-Formats
Philips	.tiff	OpenSlide
Sakura	.svslide	OpenSlide
Trestle	.tif	Bio-Formats, OpenSlide
Ventana	.bif, .tif	OpenSlide
Zeiss	.czi	Bio-Formats

It may appear that OpenSlide and Bio-Formats provide a convenient solution to the large and growing number of WSI PFFs. However, as shown in Table 1, no single implementation has a full coverage for the complete set of proprietary formats. Second, the burden of maintaining and expanding such libraries mainly remains the responsibility of the projects that build the libraries, as they reverse engineer each new PFF released by commercial manufacturers. The absence of prior discussion between manufacturers and community software developers involves constantly keeping up with the creation of new variants or new proprietary formats. Finally, data stored using these proprietary file formats remains fundamentally non-exchangeable between two researchers due to the absence of agreed-upon specification.

In response, we have embarked on a project to build a truly extensible, flexible, metadata-rich, cross-platform, open WSI data format for Digital Pathology.

3 Towards an Open WSI File Format

The Digital Imaging and Communications in Medicine (DICOM) working group published an official release (Supplement 145) in September 2010 specifically designed to provide a standard specification for WSI data [17]. Conversion tools for generating DICOM-compliant files have been proposed [18], but community adoption of this format is limited. A key point is that the DICOM process only provides a data specification and leaves it to other entities to build reference implementations for the community. Delivering cross-platform, versioned, supported software that can be used across a broad community with many different use cases and applications is challenging and requires substantial dedicated resources. Moreover, DICOM supports private attributes and classes that can limit opportunities for implementing interoperability.

A separate issue with DICOM Suppl. 145 specification is the lack of software libraries for efficient reading and writing of the format for I/O intensive data processing, e.g., training of convolutional neural networks and other advanced learning applications. High performance software libraries that can contend with the large data volumes collected in WSI studies are essential for the routine use of large training sets and the development of new deep learning-based approaches in Digital Pathology.

An alternative approach is to build an open format based on known, established standards that are widely supported by communities and both open and commercial software and is proven to be useful for computational workflows. For example, the Tagged Image File Format (TIFF) specification is widely used as a binary vessel for image data storage (https://www.loc.gov/preservation/digital/formats/fdd/fdd000022. shtml). Since 2005, the OME Consortium has released OME-TIFF, a variant that complies with the TIFF specification, but adds OME's flexible imaging metadata model to the TIFF header [10]. As the OME metadata model includes support for imaging metadata, region of interest annotations, and a flexible key-value store [19], the format has been used to support many different imaging modalities in research, industrial and commercial settings (https://docs.openmicroscopy.org/latest/ome-model/ome-tiff/). Open source reader and writer implementations in Java and C++ are available [11, 20], along with a large number of example files (https://downloads.openmicroscopy.org/ images/OME-TIFF/).

Given the interoperability of TIFF, it is no surprise that many PFFs have adopted the TIFF layout as a convenient way to store WSI data. Some libraries (OpenSlide, VIPS) use a so-called tiled multi-resolution TIFF format where each resolution is stored as a separate layer within a multi-page TIFF. A direct advantage of this approach is its great simplicity. However, while it applies well to single-plane RGB pyramidal images, this approach does not immediately support multi-channel data from fluorescence WSI, multiplexed data from cyclic immunofluorescence [2] and mass spectrometry-based CODEX data [3] or a through-focus series ("Z-stack"). Finally, each of these approaches, while TIFF-based is yet another PFF.

An alternative layout is to extend the TIFF specification to store reduced resolutions internally and refer to them from each layer using a specific tag SubIFD. This approach is also compatible with standard TIFF tools like libtiff (http://www.libtiff.org/) and commercial tools like Adobe Photoshop. It also allows flexibility to store new multi-plexed data, or any other extensions available in the TIFF specification. In 2018, OME proposed the usage of this strategy as an extension of its OME-TIFF specification to be able to generate exchangeable pyramidal images (https://openmicroscopy.github.io/ design/OME005/). In addition to the interoperability with other tools, this updated OME-TIFF format makes it possible to store and exchange multi-dimensional pyramidal images, so multiplexed data, through-focus Z-series and several others are supported [11]. Finally, OME's flexible metadata schemes support multiple WSI pyramidal images as well as typical ancillary images generated by WSI scanners, e.g., barcodes, macro images of the full slide, all as part of an OME-TIFF file.

A key design requirement is that this updated form of OME-TIFF is backwards compatible with existing software that reads OME-TIFF. Following discussion and feedback on the proposed approach, an update to OME-TIFF readers and writers was released that and fulfilled these requirements and several others.

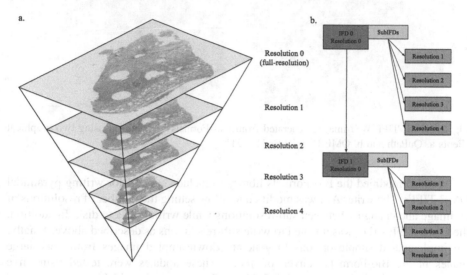

Fig. 1. a. Pyramidal image with five levels of resolution. Resolution 0 is the full-resolution plane while resolutions 1 to 4 are reduced along the X and Y dimensions using a consistent downsampling factor. b. In the updated OME-TIFF specification, this data is supported by storing metadata for sub-resolutions using the TIFF SubIFDs extension tag.

4   Implementations and Results

Figure 1 presents a graphical representation on how WSI data is stored in an OME-TIFF file. SubIFDs are used to indicate the location of sub-resolution tiles. Any software that implements the TIFF specification can be updated to read and write the file format. To demonstrate this, we modified the Bio-Formats library to read sub-resolutions from OME-TIFF files containing sub-resolution tiles. Test files were manually generated from public domain TIFF-based WSI PFFs to comply with the specification described above. These sample files were validated under two separate separate libraries that use Bio-Formats as a plug-in library, OMERO, a client-server data management application and QuPath, a desktop WSI data analysis application [12, 21]. In both cases, updating the version of Bio-Formats enabled the software to read and display the updated OME-TIFF files. We validated the number of detected images including WSI, macro and label images and the number of sub-resolutions for each image, the metadata associated with each image and finally the pixel values for regions of each sub-resolution. The updated Bio-Formats library correctly passed all image parameters via metadata requests to the Bio-Formats API and properly delivered all tiles for rendering and display (Fig. 2).

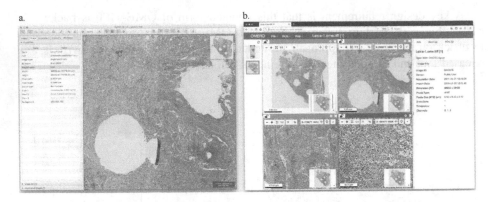

Fig. 2. OME-TIFF WSI images generated from Bio-Formats 6 visualized using two graphical clients a. QuPath and b. OMERO.iviewer [12, 21].

We also modified the Bio-Formats library to include support for writing pyramidal OME-TIFFs. The writer API was modified to allow setting the number of resolutions of an image and changing between sub-resolutions while writing data to disk. In addition, the OME-TIFF writer was updated to write sub-resolutions as described above. Finally, we implemented simple options to generate downsampled images from very large planes in the Bio-Formats conversion tools. These updates were tested using five different datasets: a selection of brightfield and fluorescent pyramidal images expressed in the main WSI PFFs supported by Bio-Formats (see Table 1), a collection of large single-plane TIFF files from the Human Protein Atlas project published in the Image Data Resource [14, 22], a synthetic image with 1400 Z-stacks, a multi-channel fluorescence image and a large electron-microscopy published in EMPIAR [23]. We converted all these datasets into OME-TIFFs using the command-line Bio-Formats tools and validated them as described above.

Table 2. List of resources publicly available for testing and validating the open OME-TIFF file format with support for multi-resolution.

Name	Description	URL
OME-TIFF	Format specification	https://docs.openmicroscopy.org/latest/ome-model/ome-tiff/specification.html
OME-TIFF	Public WSI samples	https://docs.openmicroscopy.org/latest/ome-model/ome-tiff/data.html#sub-resolutions
Bio-Formats 6	Binaries and API documentation	https://www.openmicroscopy.org/bio-formats/downloads/
Bio-Formats 6	Technical documentation	https://docs.openmicroscopy.org/latest/bio-formats6/

All of these functions have been built into and released as reference implementations that support the updated OME-TIFF formats (see Table 2) that include OME-TIFF samples for all the modalities described above, software libraries and documentation. The source code allowing to reproduce the data generation and validation is available at https://doi.org/10.5281/zenodo.2595928.

5 Discussion

We have developed an updated specification and implementation for OME-TIFF, an open image data format by adding support for multi-resolution tiles alongside existing capability for multiplexed, multi-focus and multi-timepoint images. Multi-resolution capability is important as it makes OME-TIFF usable as an exchange and/or transport format for WSI data. We have built and released example files, documentation and open source reference software implementations to ease OME-TIFF adoption by software developers and also research and clinical users.

Our goal in this work is not to declare a single data standard, but rather to build an open, supported WSI data format that is as flexible as possible, supports a wide range of metadata and binary data from many different applications, and can support the range of current and emerging domains using whole slide imaging. We have successfully tested the format across several different applications. We expect that the release of the updated OME-TIFF specification and open source software will enable the community to test the use of the format in many other domains and evaluate the utility of the specification and software. This will likely lead to several updates that steadily improve the utility and performance of OME-TIFF.

The reference implementation of the updated OME-TIFF has been developed in Java and integrated into the open-source Bio-Formats library [11]. For manufacturers, C++ and C# are usually the language of choice for writing software that drives commercial software for WSI acquisition. In addition to the Java-based library, the OME Consortium has built and released OME Files, a C++ reference implementation for reading and writing open OME formats [20] which we aim to update in the near future.

Acknowledgements. This work was funded by grants from the BBSRC (Ref: BB/P027032/1, BB/R015384/1) and the Wellcome Trust (Ref: 202908/Z/16/Z).

References

1. Udall, M., et al.: PD-L1 diagnostic tests: a systematic literature review of scoring algorithms and test-validation metrics. Diagn. Pathol. **13**, 12 (2018)
2. Lin, J.-R., et al.: Highly multiplexed immunofluorescence imaging of human tissues and tumors using t-CyCIF and conventional optical microscopes. Elife **7**, 31657 (2018)
3. Goltsev, Y., et al.: Deep profiling of mouse splenic architecture with CODEX multiplexed imaging. Cell **174**, 968–981.e15 (2018)
4. Leo, P., et al.: Stable and discriminating features are predictive of cancer presence and Gleason grade in radical prostatectomy specimens: a multi-site study. Sci. Rep. **8**, 14918 (2018)
5. Beig, N., et al.: Perinodular and intranodular radiomic features on lung CT images distinguish adenocarcinomas from granulomas. Radiology **290**, 783–792 (2018). https://doi.org/10.1148/radiol.2018180910

6. Awan, R., et al.: Glandular morphometrics for objective grading of colorectal adenocarcinoma histology images. Sci. Rep. **7**, 16852 (2017)
7. Sirinukunwattana, K., et al.: Novel digital signatures of tissue phenotypes for predicting distant metastasis in colorectal cancer. Sci. Rep. **8**, 13692 (2018)
8. Janowczyk, A., Madabhushi, A.: Deep learning for digital pathology image analysis: a comprehensive tutorial with selected use cases. J. Pathol. Inform. **7**, 29 (2016)
9. Bejnordi, B.E., et al.: Diagnostic assessment of deep learning algorithms for detection of lymph node metastases in women with breast cancer. JAMA **318**, 2199–2210 (2017)
10. Goldberg, I.G., et al.: The Open Microscopy Environment (OME) Data Model and XML file: open tools for informatics and quantitative analysis in biological imaging. Genome Biol. **6**, R47 (2005)
11. Linkert, M., et al.: Metadata matters: access to image data in the real world. J. Cell Biol. **189**, 777–782 (2010)
12. Allan, C., et al.: OMERO: flexible, model-driven data management for experimental biology. Nat. Methods **9**, 245–253 (2012)
13. Burel, J.-M., et al.: Publishing and sharing multi-dimensional image data with OMERO. Mamm. Genome **26**, 441–447 (2015)
14. Williams, E., et al.: The image data resource: a bioimage data integration and publication platform. Nat. Methods **14**, 775–781 (2017)
15. Wilkinson, M.D., et al.: The FAIR Guiding Principles for scientific data management and stewardship. Sci Data **3**, 160018 (2016)
16. Goode, A., Gilbert, B., Harkes, J., Jukic, D., Satyanarayanan, M.: OpenSlide: a vendor-neutral software foundation for digital pathology. J. Pathol. Inform. **4**, 27 (2013)
17. Singh, R., Chubb, L., Pantanowitz, L., Parwani, A.: Standardization in digital pathology: supplement 145 of the DICOM standards. J. Pathol. Inform. **2**, 23 (2011)
18. Marques Godinho, T., Lebre, R., Silva, L.B., Costa, C.: An efficient architecture to support digital pathology in standard medical imaging repositories. J. Biomed. Inform. **71**, 190–197 (2017)
19. Li, S., et al.: Metadata management for high content screening in OMERO. Methods **96**, 27–32 (2016)
20. Leigh, R., et al.: OME Files-an open source reference library for the OME-XML metadata model and the OME-TIFF file format. bioRxiv, 088740 (2016)
21. Bankhead, P., et al.: QuPath: open source software for digital pathology image analysis. Sci. Rep. **7**, 16878 (2017)
22. Uhlén, M., et al.: Proteomics. Tissue-based map of the human proteome. Science **347**, 1260419 (2015)
23. Iudin, A., Korir, P.K., Salavert-Torres, J., Kleywegt, G.J., Patwardhan, A.: EMPIAR: a public archive for raw electron microscopy image data. Nat. Methods **13**, 387–388 (2016)

PanNuke: An Open Pan-Cancer Histology Dataset for Nuclei Instance Segmentation and Classification

Jevgenij Gamper[1(✉)], Navid Alemi Koohbanani[1,3], Ksenija Benet[2], Ali Khuram[4], and Nasir Rajpoot[1,2]

[1] University of Warwick, Coventry, UK
J.Gamper@warwick.ac.uk
[2] University Hospital Coventry-Warwickshire, Coventry, UK
[3] The Alan Turing Institute, London, UK
[4] University of Sheffield, Sheffield, UK

Abstract. In this work we present an experimental setup to semi automatically obtain exhaustive nuclei labels across 19 different tissue types, and therefore construct a large pan-cancer dataset for nuclei instance segmentation and classification, with minimal sampling bias. The dataset consists of 455 visual fields, of which 312 are randomly sampled from more than 20K whole slide images at different magnifications, from multiple data sources. In total the dataset contains 216.4K labeled nuclei, each with an instance segmentation mask. We independently pursue three separate streams to create the dataset: detection, classification, and instance segmentation by ensembling in total 34 models from already existing, public datasets, therefore showing that the learnt knowledge can be efficiently transferred to create new datasets. All three streams are either validated on existing public benchmarks or validated by expert pathologists, and finally merged and validated once again to create a large, comprehensive pan-cancer nuclei segmentation and detection dataset PanNuke.

Keywords: Computational pathology · Instance segmentation · Instance classification · Histology dataset

1 Introduction

Analysis of nuclear features, that being categorical or appearance related, shape or texture, density or nucleus-to-cytoplasm ratio have been shown to not only be useful in cancer scoring, but also in discovering bio-markers that may predict treatment effectiveness [1,2,5,14]. For example, nuclear shape and textural features have been shown to be useful in recurrence prediction, while inferred nuclear categories may help in detecting different tissue structures within the tissue [8,12]. It has also been demonstrated that extracted nuclear shape features can help stratify patients in prostate cancer patients [13].

J. Gamper and N. Alemi Koohbanani—Equal contribution.

© Springer Nature Switzerland AG 2019
C. C. Reyes-Aldasoro et al. (Eds.): ECDP 2019, LNCS 11435, pp. 11–19, 2019.
https://doi.org/10.1007/978-3-030-23937-4_2

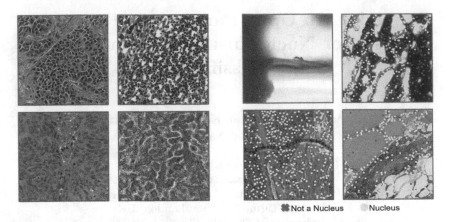

Fig. 1. Left: A sample of 4 visual fields from [11] dataset. Right: A selection of 4 visual fields randomly sampled from 27k WSIs, with an output of a detector trained on the dataset on the left overlaid. It is clear that nuclei are detected even where there are artifacts, burnt tissue, or blur. To each of the detected points a classifier can then be applied that is able to classify Non-Nucleus class

While the importance of nuclei category and features are clear, it is still vague how much data we need to ensure that any deep learning model is reliable for such tasks in medical applications. Nevertheless, it is conspicuous from commercial and academic practices that the larger and more diverse the dataset is, the more likely we are to produce a model that captures as much of the true data distribution as possible. The community has taken great steps in creating open datasets to develop algorithms for nuclei segmentation and classification [11]. However, these datasets are generally limited in size or provide only sparse nuclei labeling. For example, [11] consists of only 30 visual fields, while sparse labeling [15] prevents end-to-end training on a whole image. Moreover, various artifacts found in a whole slide image (WSI), are inherently found in clinical routine, but are commonly excluded from publicly available datasets.

Therefore, we argue that currently available data in Digital Pathology provide partially realistic environment, with *cherry-picked* visual fields as compared to the conditions where algorithms could be applied and are therefore likely to be prone to sampling bias. This has already been demonstrated in a validation study[1] of deep learning models applied to radiology images in practice where model performance dropped significantly in a real-world environment. Consequently, when creating PanNuke dataset, we employ random sampling of visual fields from 27,724 H&E WSIs and do not screen out visual fields purposely to preserve the natural distribution of visual fields variability.

We set it as our aim to obtain as diverse dataset of nuclei types as possible in H&E images with the most reliable annotations. For that, we need to overcome three main challenges: (*i*) Very little ground truth, and no ground truth at all

---

[1] http://archive.rsna.org/2018/18014765.html.

for some tissue types (*ii*) The ground truth itself is not reliable [3,4], especially for such ambiguous task as nuclei types (*iii*) Nuclei types within a tissue are context-dependent.

In summary, **our main contributions are:** (*i*) We demonstrate how important it is to create datasets that match the distribution of data in a clinical setting (*ii*) We propose a semi-automatically obtained nuclei instance segmentation and classification dataset PanNuke, that has been verified by domain experiments.

2 Materials

PanNuke is created via ensembling of multiple model combinations with already existing public data for nuclei classification/segmentation. In this regard, to produce the proposed dataset new visual fields have been randomly sampled from 19 different TCGA tissue types and other internal datasets for prostate, colon, ovarian, breast and oral tissue. Below we describe the publicly datasets that were used for training segmentation, detection and classification models.

For the initial segmentation model, we used the existing annotated datasets by Kumar [11] and CPM17 [18]. Kumar dataset has annotations for 16 images of 7 different tissue types (liver, prostate, kidney, breast, stomach, colorectal and bladder) stained with H&E and the patch size is 1024×1024. The CPM dataset consists of 32 images of lung tissue with rough image size of 600×600. Both of these dataset are extracted from The Cancer Genome Atlas (TCGA) repository.

Table 1. Initial data for nuclei classification

	Type of nuclei						
	Epithelial	Inflam	Malignat	Necrotic	Str	Non-nuclei	Total
MonuSeg	836	1,698	5,927	0	906	0	9,367
Colon Nuclei	7,544	6,003	4,685	2,547	4,468	0	25,247
SPIE	0	2,139	9,802	0	0	0	11,941
Nuclei Attribute	0	0	0	0	0	500	500
Total	8,380	9,840	20,414	2,547	5,374	500	47,055

We trained nuclei detection model using 4 datasets: Kumar dataset (16 images), CPM2017 dataset (64 images), visual fields extracted from TCGA labelled by ourselves (15 images) and the Bone Marrow dataset (11 images) [9]. For Kumar and CPM17 dataset, instance-wise segmentation is provided, and so we take the centroid, of each object as the locations of nuclei.

Classification labels and their source datasets are described in Table 1. The MonuSeg dataset originally comes only with instance segmentation masks, however a selection of images has been annotated internally by two expert pathologists and a trainee. Unlike the common annotation procedure, a detection model is first utilised to find centroids of nuclei and afterwards detected nuclei are classified by experts which is more precise and less exhausting for experts. Colon

Nuclei is an internal dataset for colon nuclei classification. A big majority of breast malignant nulcei label annotations have been sourced from a recent cellularity scoring competition by SPIE[2]. Since we are interested in detecting false positive nuclei detection or segmentation, we add an additional Non-Nucleus category, which is derived from the Nuclei Attribute dataset released in [12].

3   Methods

We followed three pathways to obtain our final validated dataset. These three pathways are segmentation, detection and classification. In order to incorporate the context, crucial to nuclei classification, we merged detection and classification into one model after a sufficient amount of data has been collected. These models are described in Sects. 3.1, 3.2, 3.3 and 3.4 respectively.

Primary reason for ensembling separate type of models trained on public datasets, is to evaluate the performance of each type in a more realistic environment. For example, in Fig. 1 we illustrate the performance of a detector trained on a public dataset applied to randomly sampled visual fields that are part of PanNuke. Clearly, burnt, blurred or poorly stained tissue should not be identified as nuclei, and therefore not contribute to the downstream analysis. However, detector trained on a public dataset does indeed detect these parts as nuclei, the same argument applies to the segmentation models. Identification of these model failures and quantification of model uncertainty serve as primary tools in creating PanNuke.

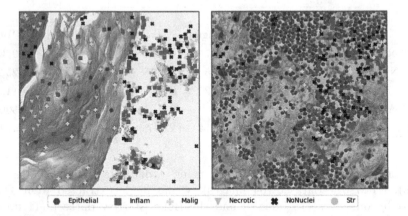

Fig. 2. Two visual fields with most uncertain classification results according to the model trained on the data in Table 1. Visual field on the left has been sampled from oral tissue, and testicular tissue on the right

---

[2] https://spie.org/conferences-and-exhibitions/medical-imaging/grand-challenge-2019.

For uncertainty quantification in classification and segmentation pathways, we employ mutual information, which captures epistemic, model uncertainty [6]. Generally, there are two types of uncertainty - epistemic and aleatoric, also known as reducible and irreducible. The reason we focus our attention on epistemic uncertainty is that it could be reduced by adding more data, or in our case annotated examples, while aleatoric uncertainty would most likely point to noisy examples that are likely to be hard to annotate by expert pathologists.

Likewise, for classification, we use mutual information to select visual fields in order to verify annotation or re-annotate regions where the model fails to predict correctly. In Fig. 2, the two most uncertain classification visual fields are depicted. As can be seen visual fields contain large white space and a large number of red blood cells which are confusing for the model. These are usually not included in public datasets, however they are very frequent in the real data. Similar to the segmentation approach, the two most uncertain visual fields per tissue are selected and re-annotated which are afterward employed for fine-tunig the model.

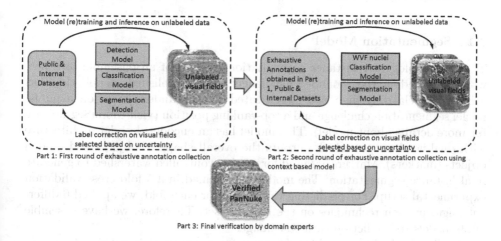

Fig. 3. An overview of data collection for the proposed large-scale pan-cancer nuclei segmentation and detection in histology images

After performing several re-annotations and re-training rounds for both segmentation and classification, the final dataset is created by ensembling detection and refined segmentation models. Namely, taking the intersection between the two and applying a refined classifier to the centroids of the instance segmentation masks. Figure 3 shows a high-level schematic diagram of our proposed approach for collecting large instance-wise annotations for visual fields sampled from H&E histology WSIs[3].

---

[3] For the final statistics for the dataset as well as the verified ground truth refer to https://jgamper.github.io/PanNukeDataset/.

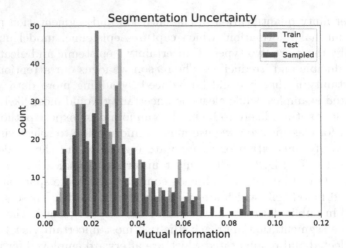

Fig. 4. By performing 5-fold cross-validation, we are able to obtain uncertainty estimates for training as well as for testing and newly sampled visual fields

3.1 Segmentation Model

The methodology for instance segmentation consists of an ensemble of a network proposed in the MonuSeg Challenge[4], an unpublished model, that has achieved a relatively high AJI (Aggregated Jaccard Index) score on a public nuclei segmentation challenge and a top-ranking position (visit MonuSeg website for more details about model). This model has an encoder-decoder architecture with dual-head output which outputs the overall shape of objects and eroded objects (markers). Markers are used for marker-controlled watershed to generate final instance segmentation. The models are trained in a 5-fold cross-validation experimental setup. For predicting the output for each fold, we applied 6 different augmentation techniques on the test dataset. Therefore, we have ensemble of 30 models to predict on each test image.

As discussed above, to identify cases for re-annotation within the newly extracted visual fields, we use the mutual information measure described above. A distribution of model uncertainties for test and training data of the model as well as for the newly extracted visual fields is depicted in Fig. 4. We re-annotate the data from the longer tail and add it to the training data.

3.2 Detection Model

Overall, the detection network is trained using 106 images of different tissue types with 5-fold setup and 6 test augmentation techniques. Hence, ensemble of 30 predictions are used to estimate the location of nuclei. Among all successful detection networks [10,15,16], We adopt the same procedure as [19] due to it's

---

[4] https://monuseg.grand-challenge.org/.

robustness and simplicity to construct our labels for training our network. The network architecture for this model is the same as segmentation model.

3.3 Classification Model

For nuclei classification, we create an ensemble of four 18 layer residual networks [7]. The networks are based on the selection of patch training sizes - 64×64 or 32×32, and training with manifold mixup or without [17]. Every patch has a nucleus to be classified at the centre of the patch, detected either by the segmentation or detector models described above.

To balance out the classes, while training each model we employ weighted sampling. Therefore under-represented patches are sampled more often to balance distribution of nuclei classes in each batch during training our network. The test set classification performance (accuracy) for four models ranged from 85% to 92% on held out validation data from public datasets.

3.4 Whole Visual Field Nuclei Classification Model

After finalizing the first round of collecting exhaustive annotations (around 10% percent of the dataset), we identified that a large portion of nuclear labels depends on the surrounding tissue, i.e. context. Therefore, unlike the classification model described in the previous section, we trained a network that predicts labels for all nuclei in the visual field as compared to per patch based model in 3.3. In 3, Part 2 we use this model as a Whole Visual Field (WVF) classification model.

The same network structure as in 3.1 was considered, however the target labels consist of six channels correspond to six nuclei types. For each nuclei position on the image a circle with radius of 8 pixel was considered. We used cross-entropy as an objective function. For test time, detection map generated by detection network was utilized to locate each nuclei, these locations were matched on prediction map of classification network to attain the nuclear labels.

4   Conclusion

In this paper, we have proposed an approach for semi-automatically collecting large amount of annotations from H&E histology images which is a main step for constructing robust prediction models. To this end, we develop PanNuke: a nuclei instance segmentation and classification dataset with the world's largest collection of annotations so far. The diversity and natural distribution of the real-world data is preserved by randomizing the process without removing any clinically valuable images. As a follow up, we will release a highly optimised end-to-end robust and efficient nuclei classification and segmentation model. We will additionally release patch-based classifier optimised as part of the process described in this work. We believe such a classifier, due to the variety of seen nuclei, might prove to be useful for unsupervised nuclei classification in other tissue types such as Bone Marrow, Meningioma, etc.

References

1. Beck, A.H., et al.: Systematic analysis of breast cancer morphology uncovers stromal features associated with survival. Sci. Transl. Med. **3**(108), 108ra113 (2011)
2. Chang, H., et al.: Invariant delineation of nuclear architecture in glioblastoma multiforme for clinical and molecular association. IEEE Trans. Med. Imaging **32**(4), 670–682 (2013)
3. Elmore, J.G., et al.: Diagnostic concordance among pathologists interpreting breast biopsy specimens. Jama **313**(11), 1122–1132 (2015)
4. Elmore, J.G., Wells, C.K., Lee, C.H., Howard, D.H., Feinstein, A.R.: Variability in radiologists' interpretations of mammograms. N. Engl. J. Med. **331**(22), 1493–1499 (1994)
5. Filipczuk, P., Fevens, T., Krzyzak, A., Monczak, R.: Computer-aided breast cancer diagnosis based on the analysis of cytological images of fine needle biopsies. IEEE Trans. Med. Imaging **32**(12), 2169–2178 (2013)
6. Gal, Y.: Uncertainty in deep learning. University of Cambridge (2016)
7. He, K., Zhang, X., Ren, S., Sun, J.: Deep residual learning for image recognition. In: Proceedings of the IEEE Conference on Computer Vision and Pattern Recognition, pp. 770–778 (2016)
8. Javed, S., Fraz, M.M., Epstein, D., Snead, D., Rajpoot, N.M.: Cellular community detection for tissue phenotyping in histology images. In: Stoyanov, D., et al. (eds.) OMIA/COMPAY -2018. LNCS, vol. 11039, pp. 120–129. Springer, Cham (2018). https://doi.org/10.1007/978-3-030-00949-6_15
9. Kainz, P., Urschler, M., Schulter, S., Wohlhart, P., Lepetit, V.: You should use regression to detect cells. In: Navab, N., Hornegger, J., Wells, W.M., Frangi, A.F. (eds.) MICCAI 2015. LNCS, vol. 9351, pp. 276–283. Springer, Cham (2015). https://doi.org/10.1007/978-3-319-24574-4_33
10. Koohababni, N.A., Jahanifar, M., Gooya, A., Rajpoot, N.: Nuclei detection using mixture density networks. In: Shi, Y., Suk, H.-I., Liu, M. (eds.) MLMI 2018. LNCS, vol. 11046, pp. 241–248. Springer, Cham (2018). https://doi.org/10.1007/978-3-030-00919-9_28
11. Kumar, N., Verma, R., Sharma, S., Bhargava, S., Vahadane, A., Sethi, A.: A dataset and a technique for generalized nuclear segmentation for computational pathology. IEEE Trans. Med. Imaging **36**(7), 1550–1560 (2017)
12. Lee, G., Veltri, R.W., Zhu, G., Ali, S., Epstein, J.I., Madabhushi, A.: Nuclear shape and architecture in benign fields predict biochemical recurrence in prostate cancer patients following radical prostatectomy: preliminary findings. Eur. Urol. Focus **3**(4–5), 457–466 (2017)
13. Lu, C., et al.: Nuclear shape and orientation features from H&E images predict survival in early-stage estrogen receptor-positive breast cancers. Lab. Investig. **98**(11), 1438 (2018)
14. Sethi, A., Sha, L., Deaton, R.J., Macias, V., Beck, A.H., Gann, P.H.: Abstract lb-285: computational pathology for predicting prostate cancer recurrence (2015)
15. Sirinukunwattana, K., Raza, S.E.A., Tsang, Y.W., Snead, D.R., Cree, I.A., Rajpoot, N.M.: Locality sensitive deep learning for detection and classification of nuclei in routine colon cancer histology images. IEEE Trans. Med. Imagingg **35**(5), 1196–1206 (2016)
16. Tofighi, M., Guo, T., Vanamala, J.K., Monga, V.: Deep networks with shape priors for nucleus detection. In: 2018 25th IEEE International Conference on Image Processing (ICIP), pp. 719–723. IEEE (2018)

17. Verma, V., et al.: Manifold mixup: Learning better representations by interpolating hidden states (2018)

18. Vu, Q.D., et al.: Methods for segmentation and classification of digital microscopy tissue images. arXiv preprint arXiv:1810.13230 (2018)

19. Zhou, Y., Dou, Q., Chen, H., Qin, J., Heng, P.A.: SFCN-OPI: detection and fine-grained classification of nuclei using sibling FCN with objectness prior interaction. In: Thirty-Second AAAI Conference on Artificial Intelligence (2018)

Active Learning for Patch-Based Digital Pathology Using Convolutional Neural Networks to Reduce Annotation Costs

Jacob Carse[✉] and Stephen McKenna

CVIP, School of Science and Engineering, University of Dundee,
Dundee DD1 4HN, Scotland, UK
{j.carse,s.j.z.mckenna}@dundee.ac.uk

Abstract. Methods to reduce the need for costly data annotations become increasingly important as deep learning gains popularity in medical image analysis and digital pathology. Active learning is an appealing approach that can reduce the amount of annotated data needed to train machine learning models but traditional active learning strategies do not always work well with deep learning. In patch-based machine learning systems, active learning methods typically request annotations for small individual patches which can be tedious and costly for the annotator who needs to rely on visual context for the patches. We propose an active learning framework that selects regions for annotation that are built up of several patches, which should increase annotation throughput. The framework was evaluated with several query strategies on the task of nuclei classification. Convolutional neural networks were trained on small patches, each containing a single nucleus. Traditional query strategies performed worse than random sampling. A K-centre sampling strategy showed a modest gain. Further investigation is needed in order to achieve significant performance gains using deep active learning for this task.

Keywords: Active learning · Image annotation · Deep learning · Nuclei classification

1 Introduction

Modern deep learning algorithms have been shown to improve performance for tasks such as classification, segmentation and detection in digital pathology. However, deep learning algorithms require large annotated datasets from which to build high performing models. This requirement for data has been identified as a key challenge for using deep learning algorithms for digital pathology [12] and medical image analysis [5]. There are several approaches to tackling this problem which include semi-supervised learning, weakly supervised learning, active learning, and their combinations. This paper focuses on the use of active learning to aid in annotation collection for patch-based digital pathology image analysis.

© Springer Nature Switzerland AG 2019
C. C. Reyes-Aldasoro et al. (Eds.): ECDP 2019, LNCS 11435, pp. 20–27, 2019.
https://doi.org/10.1007/978-3-030-23937-4_3

Active learning is a type of machine learning which hypothesises that having a learning algorithm select the data it uses to train itself can reduce the amount of data needed for training. Active learning is used within modern applications to reduce the quantity of annotations needed. Annotating only the data selected by the learning algorithm reduces the overall cost of building an effective model. In a pool-based scenario, the learning algorithm has access to a large pool of unannotated data. Over multiple iterations, the learning algorithm selects data to be annotated and added to the training data [9].

Active learning algorithms use query strategies to select the data to be annotated. There are numerous query strategies available with the most popular methods being based on uncertainty. Uncertainty sampling is a simple query strategy that samples data based on a model's predictions for the unannotated data.

While these methods have been shown to work well with many traditional learning algorithms, this is not the case when working with deep learning algorithms. There are several reasons for this. Firstly, deep learning algorithms jointly learn feature representations and classifiers/regressors. Selecting only difficult examples to train the model leads to learnt features that are not representative, decreasing the quality of the model [13]. Secondly, traditional query strategies are used to select a single data point. It has been shown that deep learning algorithms work better with batch updates and so require a query strategy to select an optimal batch and not just the top ranked points [8]. Thirdly, the softmax output from a classifier trained using deep learning algorithms does not represent the model's uncertainty well, which is commonly used to sample unannotated data [4].

A standard approach for using learning algorithms for digital pathology is to use patches from larger images. This allows the images to be input to learning algorithms such as convolutional neural networks (CNNs) more efficiently and removes the necessity of annotating very large images. When using patch-based methods that use small patches, for tasks such as nuclei detection and classification, using active learning to select patches for annotation can be detrimental for annotation collection. This is due to small patches being time consuming and tedious to annotate. Small patches may also not include enough context for accurate annotation.

To address these issues, this paper modifies query strategies so that tasks which rely on small patches can efficiently use active learning and ease the effort needed from expert annotators. Methods were tested using the CRCHistoPhenotypes dataset for nuclei detection and classification [10].

2   Related Work

Since the rise in popularity of deep learning, numerous active learning query strategies have been proposed. Some are simple alterations to existing active learning query methods, such as Cost-Effective Active Learning (CEAL) [13]. In this algorithm, predictions are made for all the unannotated data and a batch is then selected from the data with the highest uncertainty. In addition to this, the most confident predictions are also added to the training data with their predicted label. This increases the overall size of the training dataset without any extra annotation cost, adding data which is easier to classify so that the model can learn more representative features during training. Other methods seek to alter the deep learning algorithms so that traditional active learning query strategies can be used. Using Bayesian deep learning algorithms to produce more accurate uncertainty metrics is an example of this [4].

The Core-Set query strategy [8] focuses on selecting a batch of unannotated data that can be used for both learning representative features and optimising the classifier. This is done by treating the problem as a cover problem and using a mixed integer programming heuristic to minimise the covering radius of the data. Another query strategy for deep learning uses adversarial attacks to estimate the decision boundaries of the model and selects the data closest to the decision margins [3]. These query strategies achieve state of the art results when working with CNNs, demonstrating how active learning has potential for working with deep learning algorithms.

The popularity of deep learning inspired multiple applications in digital pathology [5]. These rely on availability of large annotated datasets such as the CRCHistoPhenotypes dataset [10]. Application of deep learning algorithms is limited by dataset availability. Despite this, numerous advances in digital pathology have been made using deep learning, for example in nuclei detection and classification [10], organ segmentation [1] and classification of diseases [7].

The expense of annotating large quantities of data has led researchers to investigate how active learning might be applied to digital pathology problems. Cosatto *et al.* [2] used active learning to collect 10,000 nuclei annotations which were then used to train a machine learning model for nuclear grading. Yang *et al.* [14] developed an active learning framework for digital pathology segmentation, specialised for that task.

3   Proposed Methods

Patch-based methods are common within digital pathology and medical image analysis more generally. However, applying active learning to these methods can be tedious, especially in systems that use small patches. Small patches can be difficult to annotate in isolation. Even if their spatial visual context in provided to the annotator, continually having to reassess context for each annotation can be inefficient and frustrating. We propose a region-based alternative that requests annotations over regions containing multiple small patches. Working with larger regions eases the effort needed from the annotator and can lead to an improved annotation collection throughput. This alteration allows for a learning algorithm to be trained with the small patches and only treats the data as regions when querying the unannotated data.

The proposed query strategy makes a simple modification to how an existing query strategy works. An overview of this can be seen in Algorithm 1 where S

is an existing query strategy. This algorithm is called at the end of each active iteration, once a model has been trained on the currently available annotations. It extracts all the patches from each unannotated region and make predictions on each patch. These predictions are then averaged to create a prediction for the overall region. Once all the regions have predictions, these predictions can be used within an active learning query strategy. An example of this would be using entropy uncertainty sampling where an uncertainty value for each region would be calculated and sampled. However, this approach can also be applied to more complex query strategies such as core-set sampling, by solving the K-centre problem for the region predictions rather than feature representations for individual data points.

4   Experiments

A nuclei classification task was chosen to investigate the effectiveness of using region-based active learning within digital pathology. This task used the CRCHistoPhenotypes dataset which consists of 22,444 annotated nuclei from 100 H&E stained histology images [10]. Coordinates for each nucleus along with their corresponding classifications have been annotated in this dataset. Each cropped histology image was split into 2,500 100×100 pixel regions from which 30×30 pixel patches were extracted for each nucleus. Augmentation was used during training, each patch being augmented by having a Gaussian blurring filter applied, and by horizontal and vertical flipping.

This experiment used a simple CNN inspired by the architecture used in the nuclei classification benchmark for the CRCHistoPhenotypes dataset [10]. It consisted of two convolutional layers, one with 36 filters with a size of 4×4 and the other with 48 filters with a size of 3×3, both of which were followed

---

Algorithm 1. Alteration to query strategy for region-based active learning

---

Input : θ are the trained weights for the learning algorithm,
δ is the learning algorithm,
U is the set of unannotated data,
n is the batch to be selected,
S is the query strategy that will be used.

Output: U' which is a sampled set from U

1 **RegionQueryStrategy** θ, δ, U, n, S
2   **foreach** *region r in U* **do**
3          $P \leftarrow \text{ExtractPatches}(r)$ extract patches from region
4          $O \leftarrow \delta(\theta, P)$ makes predictions on extracted patches
5          $O' \leftarrow \text{Average}(O)$ average predictions
6          $Y := Y + O'$ append region average to array of averages
7   **end**
8      $U' \leftarrow S(Y, n)$ select regions to query using the query strategy
9   **return** U'

---

by max pooling layers with a filter size of 2×2. These layers were followed by two fully connected layers with 1200 neurons and 512 neurons respectively. This architecture is summarised in Table 1. Each hidden layer used ReLU activation functions and the two fully connected layers used dropout for regularisation [11]. Dropout was also used to adapt the CNN into a Bayesian CNN.

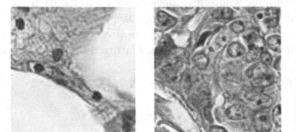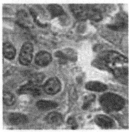

Fig. 1. Three example regions from the CRCHistoPhenotypes dataset [10] with multiple nuclei that will be extracted into patches and augmented.

The training environment is constantly changing between iterations as the dataset expands. The Adadelta training algorithm for gradient decent was chosen as the CNN's training optimiser [15]. Adadelta requires no manual tuning of learning rate as it adapts based on the training gradients, making it ideal for active learning tasks. To ensure that the model has been trained after each active iteration and that overfitting have been avoided, an early stopping method was used. The early stopping method chosen compares the generalisation loss (Eq. 1) and training progression (Eq. 2) and will stop training before overfitting [6]. Generalisation loss is calculated by comparing the validation loss for each epoch $L_{val}(t)$ against the minimum validation loss across all epochs. The

Table 1. The Convolutional Neural Network architecture for nuclei classification used in the region-based active learning experiments.

Convolutional neural network architecture for nuclei classification		
Type	Filter dimensions	Input/output dimensions
I		$30 \times 30 \times 3$
C	$4 \times 4 \times 1 \times 36$	$26 \times 26 \times 36$
M	2×2	$12 \times 12 \times 36$
C	$3 \times 3 \times 36 \times 48$	$10 \times 10 \times 48$
M	2×2	$5 \times 5 \times 48$
F	$5 \times 5 \times 48 \times 1200$	1×1200
F	$1 \times 1 \times 512 \times 512$	1×512
F	$1 \times 1 \times 512 \times 4$	1×4

training progression value is calculated by analysing the training losses $L_{tr}(t)$ over a batch of recent epochs of size k.

$$GL(t) = 100 \cdot \left(\frac{L_{va}(t)}{\min_{t' \leq t} L_{va}(t')} - 1 \right) \tag{1}$$

$$P_k(t) = 1000 \cdot \left(\frac{\sum_{t'=t-k+1}^{t} L_{tr}(t')}{k \cdot \min_{t'=t-k+1}^{t} L_{tr}(t')} - 1 \right) \tag{2}$$

Experiments tested the region-based modification combined with a range of query strategies. These query strategies included several more basic methods which will be used specifically to act as baselines for the other query strategies, built specifically for deep learning algorithms. These basic query strategies are random, least confident uncertainty, margin uncertainty and entropy uncertainty sampling. The other query strategies tried were K-Centre sampling (solved using a greedy approximation), Core-Set sampling [8] and Bayesian active learning by disagreement (BALD) sampling using Bayesian neural networks [4].

In each experiment, all available data were initially treated as unannotated; two randomly selected regions were then used to form the initial annotated training set. After each active iteration, two regions were selected from the unannotated regions to be added to the training set. This was continued for 50 iterations meaning that 102 regions out of 2,500 formed the final training set in each experiment. Each experimental setting was run five times with different random seeds (different weight initialisation and initial annotated patches).

5   Results

Table 2 gives the test accuracy and loss (averaged over the five runs) after 50 iterations for each of the query strategies. These results were obtained on a single, unchanging test set. Notably, only K-Centre sampling achieved a higher average accuracy than a random sampling strategy. Core-set sampling accuracy was very similar to that of random sampling. The other query strategies were all worse than simply adopting random sampling. Figures 2 and 3 show the test accuracy and loss for each strategy after each iteration.

For comparison, a fully supervised CNN trained on a much larger training set of 2,500 annotated regions achieved an accuracy of 68.53% and a loss of 1.111. Training using the K-Centre query strategy achieved an accuracy of 61.41% and a loss of 1.137 using 4% of the annotations.

Table 2. The accuracy and loss for each model trained with different query strategies over 50 iterations resulting in a total of 102 annotated regions.

Query strategy	Random	Least confident	Margin	Entropy	K-Centre	Core-set	BALD
Accuracy	58.25%	48.92%	45.84%	32.37%	61.41%	57.33%	48.23%
Loss	1.154	1.243	1.268	1.39	1.123	1.157	1.247

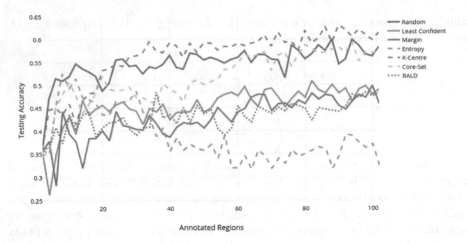

Fig. 2. Test accuracy across active iterations.

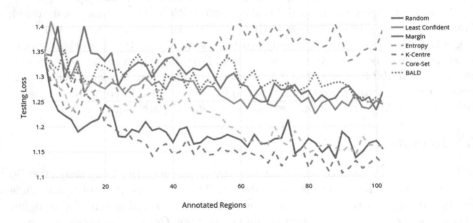

Fig. 3. Test loss across active iterations.

6   Conclusion

This paper proposed a mechanism for applying deep active learning to patch-based systems with specific focus on its application to nuclei classification. The results clearly showed that the traditional active learning query strategies performed poorly. Active learning methods tailored to deep CNNs are needed. Reducing annotation overheads and thus the cost of developing deep learning systems for digital pathology and medical image analysis can allow those with less access to resources to work on a range of problems. Methods such as active learning have great potential but further work is needed in order to achieve significant gains on tasks such as that investigated here.

References

1. BenTaieb, A., Hamarneh, G.: Topology aware fully convolutional networks for histology gland segmentation. In: Ourselin, S., Joskowicz, L., Sabuncu, M.R., Unal, G., Wells, W. (eds.) MICCAI 2016. LNCS, vol. 9901, pp. 460–468. Springer, Cham (2016). https://doi.org/10.1007/978-3-319-46723-8_53
2. Cosatto, E., Miller, M., Graf, H.P., Meyer, J.S.: Grading nuclear pleomorphism on histological micrographs. In: 19th International Conference on Pattern Recognition, pp. 1–4 (2008)
3. Ducoffe, M., Precioso, F.: Adversarial active learning for deep networks: a margin based approach. In: Proceeding of Machine Learning Research, vol. 80 (2018)
4. Gal, Y., Islam, R., Ghahramani, Z.: Deep Bayesian active learning with image data. Proc. Mach. Learn. Res. **70**, 1183–1192 (2017)
5. Litjens, G., et al.: A survey on deep learning in medical image analysis. Med. Image Anal. **42**, 60–88 (2017)
6. Prechelt, L.: Early stopping—but when? In: Montavon, G., Orr, G.B., Müller, K.-R. (eds.) Neural Networks: Tricks of the Trade. LNCS, vol. 7700, pp. 53–67. Springer, Heidelberg (2012). https://doi.org/10.1007/978-3-642-35289-8_5
7. Schaumberg, A.J., Rubin, M.A., Fuchs, T.J.: H&E-stained whole slide image deep learning predicts SPOP mutation state in prostate cancer. In: BioRxiv BioRxiv:064279 (2018)
8. Sener, O., Savarese, S.: Active learning for convolutional neural networks: a core-set approach. In: International Conference on Learning Representations (2018)
9. Settles, B.: Active learning. Synth. Lect. Artif. Intell. Mach. Learn. **6**(1), 1–114 (2012)
10. Sirinukunwattana, K., Raza, S.E.A., Tsang, Y.W., Snead, D.R.J., Cree, I.A., Rajpoot, N.M.: Locality sensitive deep learning for detection and classification of nuclei in routine colon cancer histology images. IEEE Trans. Med. Imaging **35**(5), 1196–1206 (2016)
11. Srivastava, N., Hinton, G., Krizevsky, A., Sutskever, I., Salakhutdinov, R.: Dropout: a simple way to precent neural networks from overfitting. J. Mach. Learn. Res. **15**(1), 1929–1958 (2014)
12. Tizhoosh, H.R., Pantanowitz, L.: Artificial intelligence and digital pathology: challenges and opportunities. J. Pathol. Inform. **9**, 38 (2018)
13. Wang, K., Zhang, D., Li, Y., Zhang, R., Lin, L.: Cost-effective active learning for deep image classification. IEEE Trans. Circuits Syst. Video Technol. **27**(12), 2591–2600 (2017)
14. Yang, L., Zhang, Y., Chen, J., Zhang, S., Chen, D.Z.: Suggestive annotation: a deep active learning framework for biomedical image segmentation. In: International Conference on Medical Image Computing and Computer-Assisted Intervention, pp. 399–407 (2017)
15. Zeiler, M.: ADADELTA: an adaptive learning rate method. arXiv preprint arXiv:1212.5701 (2012)

Patch Clustering for Representation of Histopathology Images

Wafa Chenni[1], Habib Herbi[2], Morteza Babaie[3], and Hamid R. Tizhoosh[3,4(✉)]

[1] Pierre and Marie Curie University, Paris, France
[2] Sorbonne University, Paris, Ile-de-France, France
[3] Kimia Lab, University of Waterloo, Waterloo, Canada
[4] Vector Institute, Toronto, Canada
tizhoosh@uwaterloo.ca

Abstract. Whole Slide Imaging (WSI) has become an important topic during the last decade. Even though significant progress in both medical image processing and computational resources has been achieved, there are still problems in WSI that need to be solved. A major challenge is the scan size. The dimensions of digitized tissue samples may exceed 100,000 by 100,000 pixels causing memory and efficiency obstacles for real-time processing. The main contribution of this work is representing a WSI by selecting a small number of patches for algorithmic processing (e.g., indexing and search). As a result, we reduced the search time and storage by various factors between (50%–90%), while losing only a few percentages in the patch retrieval accuracy. A self-organizing map (SOM) has been applied on local binary patterns (LBP) and deep features of the KimiaPath24 dataset in order to cluster patches that share the same characteristics. We used a Gaussian mixture model (GMM) to represent each class with a rather small (10%–50%) portion of patches. The results showed that LBP features can outperform deep features. By selecting only 50% of all patches after SOM clustering and GMM patch selection, we received 65% accuracy for retrieval of the best match, while the maximum accuracy (using all patches) was 69%.

1 Introduction

The advances in digital image processing and machine learning for digital pathology are showing practical results. The advantage of such techniques is the ability to assist pathologists for higher accuracy and efficiency. Such algorithms lead to more reliable diagnosis by presenting computer-based second opinions to the clinician [22]. Digital Pathology (DP) uses Whole Slide Imaging (WSI) as a base for diagnosis. Unlike the traditional pathology workflow in which the tissue samples are inspected under a microscope and stored in physical archives, WSI enables the digitization of glass slides to very high-resolution digital images (slides/scans). The introduction of such technologies has led to the development of countless methods combining machine learning and image processing to support the diagnostic workflow which is labour-intensive, time costly, and

C. C. Reyes-Aldasoro et al. (Eds.): ECDP 2019, LNCS 11435, pp. 28–37, 2019.
https://doi.org/10.1007/978-3-030-23937-4_4

subject to human errors [4]. The digitization of the biopsy samples has simplified parts of the analysis, however, it has also introduced several challenges. There are only a few public digital datasets available for machine-learning purposes [27]. In addition, the existing datasets are generally unlabeled because of the tedious and costly nature of the manual delineation of regions of interest in digital images. Moreover, DP methods suffer from the image imperfections caused by the presence of artifacts and the absence of accurate methods for tissue (foreground) extraction [17]. Content-based image retrieval (CBIR) is considered as a practical solution for processing unlabeled data. Retrieving similar cases from pathology archives alongside their treatment records may help pathologists to write their reports much more confidently. Finally, the requirements of WSI for memory usage and computational power is problematic for IT infrastructures of hospitals and clinics. Therefore, it is desired to have solutions that make the image processing more memory efficient and computationally less expensive. This paper addresses the reduction of data dimensionality by clustering images with in order to provide a compact representation of the scans for algorithmic processing. Our techniques are developed under the constraint of working with unlabeled data, a constrained that is motivated by the reality of the clinical workflow.

2   Related Works

Tissue examination under a microscope reveals important information to render accurate diagnosis and thus, provide effective treatment for different diseases [8]. DP offers several opportunities and also presents challenges to the image processing architectures [15]. Presently, only a small fraction of glass slides are digitized [20], but even if WSI was more widely available, there are a number of technical issues that would need to be addressed for their effective usage. One of the main challenges is data management and storage [8]. Most importantly, the large dimensions of the WSI files require a large amount of memory and a expensive computational power.

Content-Based Image Retrieval (CBIR) is an approach to find images with similar visual content to a query image by searching a large archive of images. This is helpful in medical imaging and DP databases where text annotations alone might be insufficient to precisely describe an image [25,29]. In order to retrieve similar images, a proper feature representation is needed [12]. In CBIR, accuracy and fast search for similar images from large datasets are important. Therefore, various techniques for dimensionality reduction of features are used to speed up CBIR systems [6]. Some of these techniques include principal component analysis (PCA), compact bilinear pooling [30] and fast approximate nearest neighbor search [16]. Image subsetting methods [1,2] have been used to choose a small region of the whole slide images for computational analysis while reducing the size of the image for a better tissue representation. Other image subsetting algorithms use sparsity models for multi-channel representation and classification, and expectation maximization by logistic regression [11,26]. Generally, the

$20x$ magnification is commonly used for many diagnostic tasks [18,24]. As well, dividing the whole slides into small patches (or tiles) of 256×256 to 1000×1000 pixels is a common strategy to overcome the large dimensionality of the WSI data [21,23]. This approach results in thousands of patches that should be analyzed individually. Low-resolution approaches are considerably faster, however, they may loose the local morphology. One possible solution is regional averaging where a region is not considered region of interest (ROI) unless it extends over multiples patches. On the other hand, this can cause missing small ROIs such as small or isolated tumors. Another solution would be to analyze the complete image on low resolution and then refine this result on high-resolution patches by using a registration on each patch [14]. In this manner, the local morphology is taken into account. However, one major downside is the significantly longer run time. In this work, We propose unsupervised learning using handcrafted and deep features, followed by patch selection through Gaussian mixture models, to provide a more compact representation of the digital slides for image indexing and search purposes.

3   Materials and Methods

Dataset and Data Preparation – We used the KimiaPath24 dataset to evaluate our experiments. This dataset contain 24 WSIs. The slides show diverse organs and tissue types with different texture patterns [5]. The glass slides were captured by a digital scanner in bright field using a 0.75 NA lens[1]. The dataset contains 1325 test images (patches) of size 1000×1000 pixels ($0.5\,\mathrm{mm} \times 0.5\,\mathrm{mm}$) from all 24 cases. Figure 1 shows some example patches (the dataset can be downloaded online[2]).

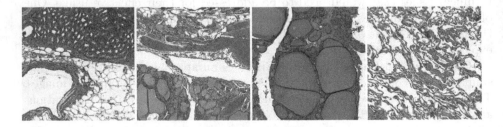

Fig. 1. Sample patches from KimiaPath24 dataset.

All training and test patches are down-sampled from 1000×1000 pixels to 250×250 pixels in order to be more easily processed by for the feature extraction. We patched WSIs without overlap and then we removed all patches with high background homogeneity (more than %99) [5]. As a result, we created 27,055

---

[1] TissueScope LE scanner by Huron Digital Pathology.

[2] http://kimia.uwaterloo.ca/kimia_lab_data_Path24.html.

training patches from 24 WSIs. The presented dataset comprising of diverse body parts may be suitable for intra-class search operations such as metastasis and floater detection.

Methodology – Figure 3 illustrates our approach. We divided the whole slide image into many patches, extract features, cluster the patches and then selected a subset of patches to represent the scan. We applied image search to verify the accuracy loss as a consequence of data reduction. We have performed search by extracting same features from the test set and then compared them against features from all training cases by calculating the Euclidean distance as a measure of (dis)similarity. The most similar patch is considered to be the output of the CBIR system.

Convolutional Neural Networks (CNN) can learn general features that are not specific to the dataset or task [13]. The deeper layers are more specific to the task of the network. Many results indicate that extracted features from CNNs (deep features) are highly discriminative [3]. These features are extracted from different layers of the CNN depending on the degree of specificity of the feature [9]. Usually, the features are extracted from the last layer before the classification layer which allows getting the most specific and high abstraction features that can be used for another task (dimensionality reduction, unsupervised learning, etc.). In this work, we used all 4096 outputs of the last layer before the classification layer in the VGG16 network, a pre-trained network model with 16 layers [9,10]. The second feature extraction method is a handcrafted method that uses the LBP algorithm (local binary patterns) [19,28]. The obtained feature vectors are histograms of uniform and rotation-invariant patterns. The LBP vector is a concatenation of two vectors. The first one has a radius parameter of 3 pixels and 24 pixels to consider resulting in 26 bins. The second one has a radius parameter of 1 pixel and 8 pixels to consider set to 8 resulting in 10 bins. The concatenated histogram will be of 36 dimensions (bins) for each patch.

All patches of a scan are represented by two different sets of features for comparison, namely deep features and LBP histograms. We then train SOM to cluster each patch. We do not know how many clusters each scan may contain. Hence, each scan is split into a given number of clusters found by the SOM algorithm. The range of number of clusters found by SOM was between 10 and 20. Parameter tuning is performed to shed light on variance and map size (see Fig. 2). We used GMMs [7] for patch selection. The number of representatives for each cluster is investigated from range 10% to 50% of the total number of the patches. It is important to point out that the deep features have a large feature vector (more than 4000 elements). Therefore, we used PCA to reduce the dimensionality of deep features. We kept 95% of the variance for each vector which yielded a new feature vector of 1078 elements. We also experimented with random patch selection which provided slightly worse results compared to GMMs.

While trying to minimize the number of clusters and maximize the variance ratio, we observed that these two parameters are positively correlated. Figure 2

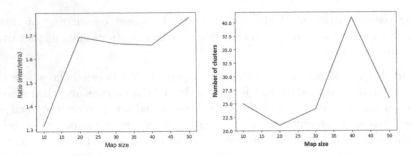

Fig. 2. SOM parameters: The effect of map size on ratio and number of clusters; Left: variance ratio versus map size. Right: the number of clusters versus the map size.

shows the variation of these two parameters versus the map size. We can see that with an increasing ratio, the number of clusters is reaching large numbers. Based on empirical knowledge, a desirable number of clusters would be less than 30. We can see that 20 may be regarded as a suitable value for the map size as it provides a good compromise between the number of clusters and the inter-/intra-variance ratio. It is important to point out that changing the SOM's learning rate did not have much impact. With these values, we are able to cluster 18 clusters per scan on average. Some of the clusters contain few patches (less than 1% of the total number of patches). We merged such clusters with the closest cluster (using Euclidean distance) resulting in a smaller number of clusters. In case of important clusters removed by merging, GMM may still select those patches. However, one must keep in mind that main purpose of the CBIR systems is generally recognizing dominant tissue patterns and not detecting minute cellular details. The latter is a subject for detection and segmentation algorithms.

4   Results

LBP descriptor outperformed deep features 3 times out of 4. Other (deeper) networks may perform better, however, they also require more resources. The LBP histogram has 36 bins while the VGG16 feature vector length is 1078 (after application of PCA). Figure 4 shows two examples for sample patches that SOM groups together using deep features. Figure 5 illustrates two sets of patches selected by GMMs from SOM clusters. The accuracy calculation aims to compare the performance of the proposed method for image retrieval using LBP and deep features separately by comparing it to the accuracy obtained using the training data set (27,055 patches). We have used the KimiaPath24 guidelines to calculate the **patch-to-scan accuracy** η_p, **whole-scan accuracy** η_W and the total accuracy η_{total}. LBP's performance improved with the increase of selected data whereas for VGG16 features the performance only improved with the increase of selected data in the case of random selection. Indeed, with

GMM selection, performance decreased with more data. This might be due to the length of VGG feature vectors. Figure 6 gives a general overview of the performances evaluation while Table 1 reports all accuracy measurements (_r and _g are indicate random selection and GMM selection, respectively).

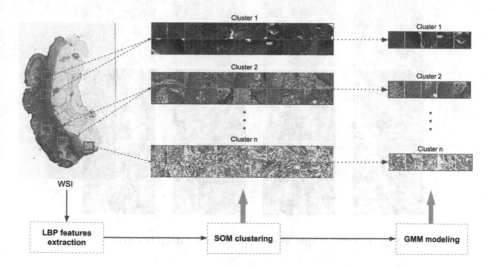

Fig. 3. SOM clustering and GMM patch selection.

Table 1. Retrieval accuracy for VGG16 and LBP features with the GMM patch selection.

GMM selection	Features	Feature length	η_p	η_w	η_{total}
10%	LBP	36	58.41	58.03	33.7
10%	VGG	1078	59.32	61.47	36.46
15%	LBP	36	60.38	60.87	36.75
15%	VGG	1078	57.28	57.91	33.17
20%	LBP	36	60.98	61.82	37.7
20%	VGG	1078	57.28	59.51	34.08
30%	LBP	36	63.54	63.27	40.21
30%	VGG	1078	57.96	58.72	34.03
40%	LBP	36	64.83	64.98	42.13
40%	VGG	1078	61.58	64.01	39.42
50%	LBP	36	65.28	64.30	41.98
50%	VGG	1078	61.13	63.33	38.71
100%	LBP	36	69.13	69.40	47.98
100%	VGG	1078	63.25	66.19	41.86
100%	LBP [5]	555	66.11	62.52	41.33

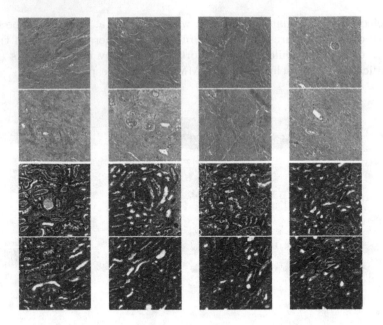

Fig. 4. Two sample SOM clusters using deep features.

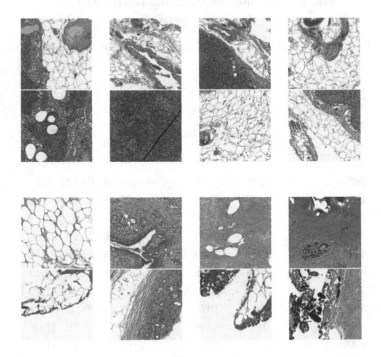

Fig. 5. Two sample GMM patch selection.

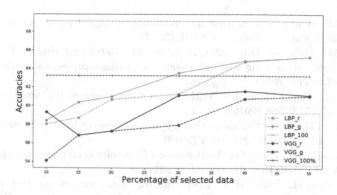

Fig. 6. Evolution of performance of our methods versus percentages of reduced data. Note that the underscore '100%' means that the entire training data set has been used.

5 Conclusions

Performance of both LBP and deep features generally drops as a result of patch selection, a fact that can be considered during the algorithm design. However, the run time and memory requirements can be considerably reduced which can be an advantage in dealing with large WSI archives. For CBIR systems in histopathology, retrieval of similar images is a major challenge because of the enormous size of the archives. The results of our experiments showed that for the algorithmic purposes such as image search the size of the image indexing (i.e., feature calculation) can be drastically reduced while keeping the relevant information and characteristics of each scan. Keeping **50%** of the patches and using LBP descriptor and GMM selection reduces the index size and, expectedly, the computational requirements by 50% and reaches a CBIR accuracy of **65%** (for the first match) only **4%** less than feature extraction for the entire data.

References

1. Adiga, U., Malladi, R., Fernandez-Gonzalez, R., de Solorzano, C.O.: High-throughput analysis of multispectral images of breast cancer tissue. IEEE Trans. Image Process. **15**(8), 2259–2268 (2006)
2. Aiad, H.A., Abdou, A.G., Bashandy, M.A., Said, A.N., Ezz-Elarab, S.S., Zahran, A.A.: Computerized nuclear morphometry in the diagnosis of thyroid lesions with predominant follicular pattern. Ecancermedicalscience **3**, 146 (2009). can-3-146[PII]
3. Ali Sharif Razavian, Hossein Azizpour, J.S.S.C.: CNN features off-the-shelf: an astounding baseline for recognition (2014)
4. AlZubaidi, A.K., Sideseq, F.B., Faeq, A., Basil, M.: Computer aided diagnosis in digital pathology application: review and perspective approach in lung cancer classification. In: 2017 Annual Conference on New Trends in Information and Communications Technology Applications (NTICT), pp. 219–224. IEEE (2017)

5. Babaie, M., et al.: Classification and retrieval of digital pathology scans: a new dataset. In: CVMI Workshop@ CVPR (2017)
6. Babaie, M., Tizhoosh, H.R., Zhu, S., Shiri, M.: Retrieving similar X-ray images from big image data using Radon barcodes with single projections. arXiv preprint arXiv:1701.00449 (2017)
7. Chan, S.H., Zickler, T.E., Lu, Y.M.: Demystifying symmetric smoothing filters. CoRR abs/1601.00088 (2016)
8. Cooper, L.A.D., et al.: Digital pathology: data-intensive frontier in medical imaging. Proc. IEEE **100**(4), 991–1003 (2012)
9. Garcia-Gasulla, D., et al.: On the behavior of convolutional nets for feature extraction. J. Artif. Intell. Res. **61**, 563–592 (2017)
10. Han, S., Mao, H., Dally, W.J.: Deep compression: compressing deep neural networks with pruning, trained quantization and Huffman coding. arXiv preprint arXiv:1510.00149 (2015)
11. Hou, L., Samaras, D., Kurc, T.M., Gao, Y., Davis, J.E., Saltz, J.H.: Patch-based convolutional neural network for whole slide tissue image classification. In: Proceedings of the IEEE Conference on Computer Vision and Pattern Recognition, pp. 2424–2433 (2016)
12. Khatami, A., Babaie, M., Khosravi, A., Tizhoosh, H.R., Nahavandi, S.: Parallel deep solutions for image retrieval from imbalanced medical imaging archives. Appl. Soft Comput. **63**, 197–205 (2018)
13. LeCun, Y., Haffner, P., Bottou, L., Bengio, Y.: Object recognition with gradient-based learning. In: Forsyth, D.A., Mundy, J.L., di Gesú, V., Cipolla, R. (eds.) Shape, Contour and Grouping in Computer Vision. LNCS, vol. 1681, pp. 319–345. Springer, Heidelberg (1999). https://doi.org/10.1007/3-540-46805-6_19
14. Lotz, J., et al.: Patch-based nonlinear image registration for gigapixel whole slide images. IEEE Trans. Biomed. Eng. **63**(9), 1812–1819 (2016)
15. Madabhushi, A., Lee, G.: Image analysis and machine learning in digital pathology: challenges and opportunities. Med. Image Anal. **33**, 170–175 (2016)
16. Marshall, B.: A brief history of the discovery of *Helicobacter pylori*. In: Suzuki, H., Warren, R., Marshall, B. (eds.) Helicobacter pylori, pp. 3–15. Springer, Tokyo (2016). https://doi.org/10.1007/978-4-431-55705-0_1
17. Moriya, T., et al.: Unsupervised pathology image segmentation using representation learning with spherical k-means. In: Medical Imaging 2018: Digital Pathology, vol. 10581, p. 1058111. International Society for Optics and Photonics (2018)
18. Stathonikos, N., Veta, M., Huisman, A., van Diest, P.J.: Going fully digital: perspective of a Dutch academic pathology lab. J. Pathol. Inform. **4**, 15 (2013)
19. Ojala, T., Pietikäinen, M., Harwood, D.: A comparative study of texture measures with classification based on featured distributions. Pattern Recogn. **29**(1), 51–59 (1996)
20. Onega, T., et al.: Digitized whole slides for breast pathology interpretation: current practices and perceptions. J. Dig. Imaging **27**, 642–648 (2014)
21. Pitiot, A., Bardinet, E., Thompson, P., Malandain, G.: Piecewise affine registration of biological images for volume reconstruction. Med. Image Anal. **10**, 465–83 (2006)
22. Robboy, S.J., Altshuler, B.S., Chen, H.Y.: Retrieval in a computer-assisted pathology encoding and reporting system (CAPER). Am. J. Clin. Pathol. **75**(5), 654–661 (2016)
23. Roberts, N., et al.: Toward routine use of 3D histopathology as a research tool. Am. J. Pathol. **180**(5), 1835–1842 (2012)

24. Al-Janabi, S., Huisman, A., Jonges, G.N., ten Kate, F.J., Goldschmeding, R., van Diest, P.J.: Whole slide images for primary diagnostics of urinary system pathology: a feasibility study. J. Pathol. Inform. **3**(4), 91–96 (2014)
25. Sridhar, A., Doyle, S., Madabhushi, A.: Content-based image retrieval of digitized histopathology in boosted spectrally embedded spaces. J. Pathol. Inform. **6**(1), 41 (2015)
26. Srinivas, U., Mousavi, H.S., Monga, V., Hattel, A., Jayarao, B.: Simultaneous sparsity model for histopathological image representation and classification. IEEE Trans. Med. Imaging **33**(5), 1163–1179 (2014)
27. Tizhoosh, H., Babaie, M.: Representing medical images with encoded local projections. IEEE Trans. Biomed. Eng. **65**(10), 2267–2277 (2018)
28. Topi, M., Timo, O., Matti, P., Maricor, S.: Robust texture classification by subsets of local binary patterns. In: 15th International Conference on Pattern Recognition, ICPR, vol. 3, pp. 935–938, September 2000
29. Yang, L., et al.: A boosting framework for visuality-preserving distance metric learning and its application to medical image retrieval. IEEE Trans. Pattern Anal. Mach. Intell. **32**, 30–44 (2010)
30. Zhang, X., Liu, W., Dundar, M., Badve, S., Zhang, S.: Towards large-scale histopathological image analysis: hashing-based image retrieval. IEEE Trans. Med. Imaging **34**(2), 496–506 (2015)

Virtually Redying Histological Images with Generative Adversarial Networks to Facilitate Unsupervised Segmentation: A Proof-of-Concept Study

Michael Gadermayr[1,2]([✉]), Barbara M. Klinkhammer[3], and Peter Boor[3]

[1] Salzburg University of Applied Sciences, Salzburg, Austria
Michael.Gadermayr@fh-salzburg.ac.at
[2] Institute of Imaging and Computer Vision, RWTH Aachen University,
Aachen, Germany
[3] Institute Pathology, University Hospital Aachen,
RWTH Aachen University, Aachen, Germany

Abstract. Approaches relying on adversarial networks facilitate image-to-image-translation based on unpaired training and thereby open new possibilities for special tasks in image analysis. We propose a methodology to improve segmentability of histological images by making use of image-to-image translation. We generate virtual stains and exploit the additional information during segmentation. Specifically a very basic pixel-based segmentation approach is applied in order to focus on the information content available on pixel-level and to avoid any bias which might be introduced by more elaborated techniques. The results of this proof-of-concept trial indicate a performance gain compared to segmentation with the source stain only. Further experiments including more powerful supervised state-of-the-art machine learning approaches and larger evaluation data sets need to follow.

Keywords: Histology · Adversarial networks · Segmentation ·
Kidney · Unsupervised · Tubuli · Glomeruli

1 Motivation

State-of-the-art digital whole slide scanners generate large amounts of digital histological image data. To exploit the availability of huge data, image analysis in this field has recently gained significant importance. Fully-automated image analysis applications mostly consist of either segmentation [2,4] or classification [1,6,11]. For both tasks, convolutional neural networks exhibit the state-of-the-art method. Here, we focus on the segmentation of histological whole slide images.

For segmentation applications in histology, fully-convolutional networks [2,4] yielded excellent performances. However, these methods require typically large amounts of annotated (i.e. manually segmented) training data. Such training

© Springer Nature Switzerland AG 2019
C. C. Reyes-Aldasoro et al. (Eds.): ECDP 2019, LNCS 11435, pp. 38–46, 2019.
https://doi.org/10.1007/978-3-030-23937-4_5

data needs to be collected for each individual task, which constitutes a significant burden for the deployment of deep networks especially for specific tasks with are not done very frequently. Further challenges arise if the underlying distribution between training and testing data is dissimilar, which could be introduced by various aspects, such as inter-scanner variability, inter-subject variability, dye variations, different staining protocols or pathological modifications [5]. While variability in color can be effectively compensated [9], other types require either training data covering all possible variability or dedicated domain adaptation approaches. Unsupervised segmentation techniques theoretically do not require any annotated training data, however, such approaches are often either hand-crafted for very specific tasks and/or show clearly lower performance compared to the latest supervised methods.

Recently, generative adversarial networks, making use of the so-called cycle consistency loss [12] (cycleGANs), were introduced. These architectures facilitate highly realistic image-to-image translation [7,8,12] from one domain to another related domain. The core idea consists of the cycle-consistency loss, which allows a training of these models without any supervision and without the requirement of corresponding pairs. These approaches only need two sets of images referring to two different domains (such as two different staining protocols). In this work, we investigate the applicability of image-to-image translation for converting images from one stain to another stain. Specific stains partly show image content which cannot be determined based on image information obtained from other stains. Consequently, e.g. a "fake" Col3 (collagen type 3) image might not be perfectly identical compared to the corresponding real (i.e. conventionally stained) Col3 image. However, this is not required for the considered application scenarios, as we focus on general segmentation tasks only. The information required for segmenting the regions-of-interest are definitely available in all investigated stains. However, automated segmentation is not a trivial task. Basic pixel-based methods, such as clustering and thresholding mostly do not yield reasonable outcomes or at least exhibit high dependency of the underlying stain.

Contributions: We propose and investigate a method to facilitate segmentation tasks by generating virtual stains. Artificial stains are obtained with a generative adversarial network relying on the cycle-consistency loss and are further merged with the original input image. With the obtained "augmented" images, we perform experiments with very basic pixel-based unsupervised segmentation approaches. The aim of this work is not to achieve the highest segmentation scores, but to obtain reasonable scores with methods which are easy to adapt and without any problem specific pre- and post-processing. Surely, neural networks trained on large image data exhibit better performance, but training data generation is often not economically efficient. Additionally, the rather basic setting allows to assess whether the idea of merging real and fake images is effective in principle. Evaluation is performed on four segmentation tasks in renal histopathology. Particularly, we segment glomeruli, tubuli, nuclei in glomeruli and nuclei in tubuli.

2   Methods

The proposed method consists of three stages (Fig. 1): in the first stage, image-to-image translation is applied in order to augment the available image data. Based on an original (e.g. PAS stained) input image, further virtual stains (e.g. Col3, ...) are computationally generated. In the second stage, all available data is aggregated and prepared for facilitating a final segmentation. In the third stage, an unsupervised pixel-based technique is applied to obtain a segmentation output.

Stage 1: For training the image-to-image translation models, we need a set of training patches P_s showing the stain corresponding to the image to be segmented (denoted as source domain stain S_s). For each of the other n considered stains S_i ($1 \leq i \leq n$), a further set of training patches P_i is required. Based on this data, image translation models are trained for each stain-combination $(S_s, S_1), (S_s, S_2), ..., (S_s, S_n)$. For details see Sect. 2.1.

Stage 2: After training the image translation models, the input images are translated to each of the virtual stains. For each input image, we obtain a set containing n images with dimensionality $p \times q \times c$, where p and q refers to the image dimensionality and c is the number of color channels (typically $c = 3$). Together with the original input image, these images are concatenated along their third dimension resulting in one single $p \times q \times ((n+1) \cdot c)$ images. Next, the pixels of the obtained multi-channel image are interpreted as vectors. To obtain a decorrelation of information, principal component analysis is performed as a last step of data preparation. Thereby we obtain e.g. one channel highlighting the violet hematoxilin and another channel highlighting the red eosin content in case of processing an H&E patch.

Stage 3: In order to avoid an introduction of any supervision, we perform simple vector quantization, specifically k-means clustering. The labels obtained for each vector are finally interpreted as a label map. To determine the optimal number of clusters depending of the segmentation task, exhaustive search is performed. We

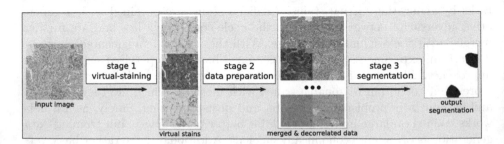

Fig. 1. The proposed approach consists of three stages: in the virtual-staining phase (stage 1), the image data is augmented by generating a set of fake images for different stains. In stage 2, the images are merged and the channels are decorrelated. In stage 3, unsupervised segmentation is performed

optimize the segmentation score (F_1-score) in a leave-one-out cross-validation. Although we are aware that thereby a certain degree of supervision is introduced, we are confident that choosing this number can be easily performed by a medical expert if visually inspecting the output label maps. As we investigate five settings only (between 2 and 6 clusters), only five label maps need to be investigated manually.

2.1 Stain-Translation Model

For training the stain-translation cycleGAN model, first patches are extracted from the source stain P_s as well as from a target stain P_i. Training patches with a size of 512×512 pixels are extracted from the original WSIs. For each data set, we extract 1500 of these patches at random positions in the WSIs (as long as 50% of the patch shows kidney tissue). Because due to the large size of the WSIs in the range of gigapixels, a holistic processing of complete images (without patch extraction) is not feasible.

With these patches, a cycleGAN based on the GAN-loss $\mathcal{L}_{GAN}$, the cycle-loss $\mathcal{L}_{cyc}$ as well as the identity loss $\mathcal{L}_{id}$ is trained [12] (with corresponding weights $w_{id} = 1, w_{cyc} = 1, w_{GAN} = 1$). Apart from a U-Net based generator network [10], the standard configuration based on the patch-wise CNN discriminator is utilized [12])[1]. Training is performed for 50 epochs. Learning rate is set to 10^{-5}. For data augmentation, random flipping and rotations (0, 90, 180, 270°) are applied.

2.2 Evaluation Details

This proof-of-concept study investigates WSIs showing renal tissue of mouse kidney. Images are captured by the whole slide scanner model C9600-12, by Hamamatsu with a 20× objective lens. As suggested in previous work [4], the second highest resolution is used for both segmentation and stain-translation. We consider a scenario where WSIs dyed with periodic acid Schiff (PAS) are available for training the segmentation model. As virtual stains, we consider Acid Fuchsin Orange G (AFOG), cluster of differentiation 31 (CD31) and a stain focused on highlighting Collagen III (Col3). The data sets used for training the image translation models consist of 12 WSIs for each of the stains PAS, AFOG, Col3 and CD31. Five further PAS images are employed for evaluation only.

For evaluating the final segmentation performance, 5 patches (which are not used for training) are manually annotated. As annotation of the fine structures is extremely time-consuming, we manually labeled only a fraction of the patches.

For quantitative evaluation, the F_1-score (which is similar to the Dice similarity coefficient) is employed as common practice in case of segmentation tasks.

---

[1] We use the provided PyTorch reference implementation [12].

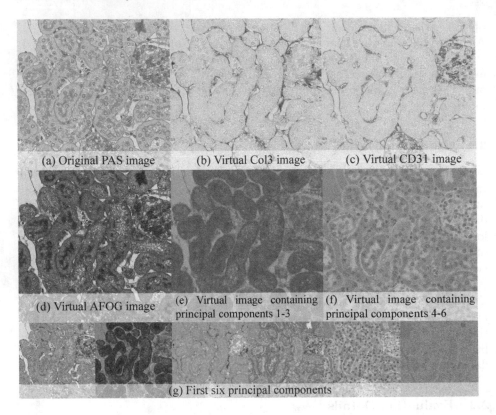

(a) Original PAS image   (b) Virtual Col3 image   (c) Virtual CD31 image

(d) Virtual AFOG image   (e) Virtual image containing principal components 1-3   (f) Virtual image containing principal components 4-6

(g) First six principal components

Fig. 2. Qualitative results of the virtual staining approach. The subfigures (b)–(d) show virtual stains corresponding to the original input image (a). The color-channels in subfigures (e) and (f) indicate the principal components after the principal component analysis of the merged images. The six channels are individually shown in subfigure (g). (Color figure online)

3   Results

Figure 2 shows qualitative results of the image translation process. The subfigures (b)–(d) show virtual stains corresponding to the original input image (a). The color-channels in subfigures (e) and (f) indicate the first six principal components after the principal component analysis of the merged images. Each of the first six channels are individually shown in subfigure (g).

Figure 3 shows qualitative results of the segmentation approach: Each subfigure shows a specific task and each column indicates the data used for segmentation. The first column corresponds to a segmentation of original PAS images. Columns 2–4 correspond to a processing of single virtually stained images and the last column corresponds to the segmentation based on the merged images collecting information of the original input images and all virtually stained images. We notice a clear impact of the stain domain on the resulting segmentation

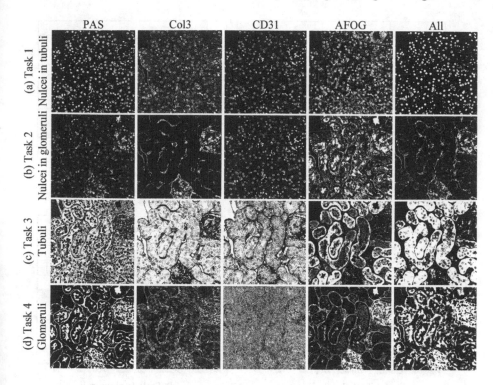

Fig. 3. Qualitative results of the segmentation approach: Each row (subfigure) shows a specific task and each column indicates the data used for segmentation. The first column corresponds to a segmentation of original image data. Column 2–4 correspond to single virtual stains and the last column corresponds to the segmentation based on the merged images

output. There is also not one single stain (Column 1–4) which exhibits the best results for each of the four task.

Quantitative segmentation scores are provided in Fig. 4. Each subplot shows the F_1-score obtained when segmenting the original PAS images, the virtual images (Col3, CD31 and AFOG) as well as the merged image (All). The proposed approach (All) corresponds to the best median scores for each segmentation task. Segmenting the virtual stains without merging all available information leads to improvements compared to a segmentation of original PAS data in one setting ((c), CD31).

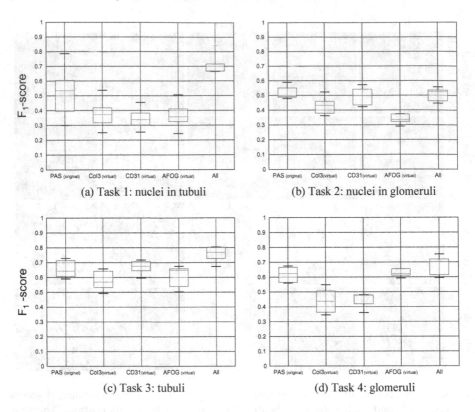

(a) Task 1: nuclei in tubuli

(b) Task 2: nuclei in glomeruli

(c) Task 3: tubuli

(d) Task 4: glomeruli

Fig. 4. Quantitative results for the four different segmentation tasks. Each subplot shows the F_1-score obtained when segmenting the original PAS images, the virtual images (Col3, CD31 and AFOG) as well as the merged images 'All'

4   Discussion

Making use of unpaired image-to-image translation, we propose a methodology to facilitate unsupervised segmentation of histological images.

We notice that image translation models based on generative adversarial networks are able to generate realistic virtually stained image material. Certainly, our experimental setting does not allow to make statements on the difference between virtual and corresponding real images. For such an evaluation, perfect corresponding pairs and a perfect alignment of these pairs would be obligatory.

However, as we focus on general segmentation tasks, we do not necessarily need perfect reconstructions of real images. Instead we focus on facilitating a segmentation by augmenting the information available in the images. The augmentation is obtained by translating the images to different domains (stains) and finally merging all available stains in one virtual image.

Based on the qualitative as well as the quantitative results, we notice that the additional information helps for various segmentation tasks. Anyway, without considering neighborhood information, the considered segmentation tasks are highly challenging. E.g. a segmentation of tubuli is highly challenging based on PAS data because the color inside these structures is not homogeneous and can be similar to other structures (white, purple). A discrimination based on color information is simplified in case of a translation to the CD31 stain which shows a higher degree of homogeneity. If making use of all available information, the segmentation output can be improved even further as shown by the qualitative as well as the quantitative results. In general, we do not notice an increase of accuracy for the single virtual stainings. Obviously, PAS exhibits a good stain for general-purpose segmentation approaches in kidneys. Based on this observation, it is even more interesting, that a combination of all available information still leads to improvements. Apparently, it is effective to add (uncorrelated) features even though the single features are not highly discriminative.

The selection of WSIs for the specific stains for training the image translation model was performed randomly. We expect that a more intelligent selection of well suited (e.g. high contrast) images might improve segmentation performance even further due to intra-slide variability in color and structure.

In future work, the effect of the proposed stain-augmentation method on state-of-the-art supervised techniques need to be investigated. On the one hand, it might be argued that segmentation networks are highly powerful and non-linear methods which are able to learn the underlying task similar to human, independent of the underlying stain. On the other hand, it was shown that even deep fully-convolutional networks show different segmentation performance for different stains [3].

To conclude, we proposed a methodology to facilitate unsupervised segmentation of histological images by making use of an image translation approach. We showed that image translation not only allows a generation of realistic "fake" images, but is also capable of facilitating segmentation scenarios. For all of the four considered segmentation tasts, improvements were obtained compared to a straight-forward processing of the original input data. Although we only investigated a basic unsupervised approach, we expect improvements for other more elaborated segmentation techniques such as deep fully-convolutional networks which need to be investigated in future.

References

1. Barker, J., Hoogi, A., Depeursinge, A., Rubin, D.L.: Automated classification of brain tumor type in whole-slide digital pathology images using local representative tiles. Med. Image Anal. **30**, 60–71 (2016)
2. BenTaieb, A., Hamarneh, G.: Topology aware fully convolutional networks for histology gland segmentation. In: Ourselin, S., Joskowicz, L., Sabuncu, M.R., Unal, G., Wells, W. (eds.) MICCAI 2016. LNCS, vol. 9901, pp. 460–468. Springer, Cham (2016). https://doi.org/10.1007/978-3-319-46723-8_53
3. Gadermayr, M., Appel, V., Klinkhammer, B.M., Boor, P., Merhof, D.: Which way round? A study on the performance of stain-translation for segmenting arbitrarily dyed histological images. In: Frangi, A.F., Schnabel, J.A., Davatzikos, C., Alberola-López, C., Fichtinger, G. (eds.) MICCAI 2018. LNCS, vol. 11071, pp. 165–173. Springer, Cham (2018). https://doi.org/10.1007/978-3-030-00934-2_19

4. Gadermayr, M., Dombrowski, A.K., Klinkhammer, B.M., Boor, P., Merhof, D.: CNN cascades for segmenting sparse objects in gigapixel whole slide images. Comput. Med. Imaging Graph. **71**, 40–48 (2019)
5. Gadermayr, M., Eschweiler, D., Jeevanesan, A., Klinkhammer, B.M., Boor, P., Merhof, D.: Segmenting renal whole slide images virtually without training data. Comput. Biol. Med. **90**, 88–97 (2017)
6. Hou, L., Samaras, D., Kurc, T.M., Gao, Y., Davis, J.E., Saltz, J.H.: Patch-based convolutional neural network for whole slide tissue image classification. In: Proceedings of the International Conference on Computer Vision (CVPR 2016) (2016)
7. Isola, P., Zhu, J.Y., Zhou, T., Efros, A.A.: Image-to-image translation with conditional adversarial networks. In: Proceedings of the International Conference on Computer Vision and Pattern Recognition (CVPR 2017) (2017)
8. Johnson, J., Alahi, A., Fei-Fei, L.: Perceptual losses for real-time style transfer and super-resolution. In: Leibe, B., Matas, J., Sebe, N., Welling, M. (eds.) ECCV 2016. LNCS, vol. 9906, pp. 694–711. Springer, Cham (2016). https://doi.org/10.1007/978-3-319-46475-6_43
9. Macenko, M., et al.: A method for normalizing histology slides for quantitative analysis. In: Proceedings of the IEEE International Symposium on Biomedical Imaging: From Nano to Macro (ISBI 2009), pp. 1107–1110 (2009). https://doi.org/10.1109/ISBI.2009.5193250
10. Ronneberger, O., Fischer, P., Brox, T.: U-Net: convolutional networks for biomedical image segmentation. In: Navab, N., Hornegger, J., Wells, W.M., Frangi, A.F. (eds.) MICCAI 2015. LNCS, vol. 9351, pp. 234–241. Springer, Cham (2015). https://doi.org/10.1007/978-3-319-24574-4_28
11. Sertel, O., Kong, J., Shimada, H., Catalyurek, U.V., Saltz, J.H., Gurcan, M.N.: Computer-aided prognosis of neuroblastoma on whole-slide images: classification of stromal development. Pattern Recognit. **42**(6), 1093–1103 (2009)
12. Zhu, J.Y., Park, T., Isola, P., Efros, A.A.: Unpaired image-to-image translation using cycle-consistent adversarial networks. In: Proceedings of the International Conference on Computer Vision (ICCV 2017) (2017)

Virtualization of Tissue Staining in Digital Pathology Using an Unsupervised Deep Learning Approach

Amal Lahiani[1,2(✉)], Jacob Gildenblat[3], Irina Klaman[1], Shadi Albarqouni[2], Nassir Navab[2], and Eldad Klaiman[1]

[1] Pathology and Tissue Analytics, Pharma Research and Early Development, Roche Innovation Center Munich, Penzberg, Germany
amal.lahiani@roche.com
[2] Computer Aided Medical Procedures, Technische Universität München, Munich, Germany
[3] DeePathology.ai, Ra'anana, Israel

Abstract. Histopathological evaluation of tissue samples is a key practice in patient diagnosis and drug development, especially in oncology. Historically, Hematoxylin and Eosin (H&E) has been used by pathologists as a gold standard staining. However, in many cases, various target specific stains, including immunohistochemistry (IHC), are needed in order to highlight specific structures in the tissue. As tissue is scarce and staining procedures are tedious, it would be beneficial to generate images of stained tissue virtually. Virtual staining could also generate in-silico multiplexing of different stains on the same tissue segment. In this paper, we present a sample application that generates FAP-CK virtual IHC images from Ki67-CD8 real IHC images using an unsupervised deep learning approach based on CycleGAN. We also propose a method to deal with tiling artifacts caused by normalization layers and we validate our approach by comparing the results of tissue analysis algorithms for virtual and real images.

Keywords: Virtual staining · Multiplexing · Unsupervised deep learning · Histopathology

1 Introduction

In the field of pathology, staining types determine which parts or targets in the tissue are highlighted with specific colors. Tissue staining materials and procedures can be time consuming, expensive, and typically require special expertise. These limitations usually reduce the number of examinations and stainings performed on a sample. This can limit clinicians' ability to obtain all relevant information from a patient biopsy. In many cases information exists in the stained

C. C. Reyes-Aldasoro et al. (Eds.): ECDP 2019, LNCS 11435, pp. 47–55, 2019.
https://doi.org/10.1007/978-3-030-23937-4_6

slide image about targets and objects not specifically targeted by the stain. For example, pathologists have the ability to identify lymphocytes in a Hematoxylin and Eosin (H&E) image [11] even without directly staining them for lymphocyte specific markers. This fact motivated the research in the direction of generating virtually stained slides from other modalities [2,4,7,8,13]. Recently, supervised deep learning based methods have been applied in the task of virtual staining generation [1,3,6,14]. As supervised training methods are based on coupled pairs of aligned images, all the aforementioned methods require additional accurate registration steps between dataset image pairs.

In this work we propose to virtually generate FAP-CK stained slide images from Ki67-CD8 stained slide images. These input and output stainings were chosen for several reasons. First, information about tumor characteristics in FAP-CK could be encoded in the form of proliferation and tumor infiltrating lymphocytes in Ki67-CD8. Furthermore, Ki67-CD8 is one of the classical Immunohistochemistry (IHC) stainings used in histopathology while FAP-CK is a new duplex IHC protocol allowing to characterize tumor and to advance research in the direction of drug development. Additionally, generating virtual FAP-CK stained slide images from Ki67-CD8 allows the creation of a virtual multiplexed brightfield image, i.e. having 4 target stains on the same whole slide coordinate system, which is technically challenging using classical staining methods. In this paper, we present an unsupervised deep learning method based on Cycle-Consistent Adversarial Networks (CycleGAN) [17]. This allows avoiding the slide registration process for training datasets and facilitates dealing with variability present in sets of slide images due to different lab protocols, scanners and experiment conditions. We further present a method aimed at reducing the tiling artifact caused by tile-wise processing of large images, a common problem in image style transfer encountered when high resolution testing images can not fit into memory [16]. Finally, we validate the results of our method by comparing quantification of tumor cells and FAP in virtual slides with a real stained slide taken from the same tissue block.

2   Methodology

2.1   Dataset

We selected a subset of whole slide images (WSI) of Colorectal Carcinoma metastases in liver tissue from biopsy and surgical specimen from our internal pathology image database. All the slides were chosen following a review of tissue, staining and image quality. The training dataset includes 20 images: 10 from Ki67-CD8 stained slides and 10 from FAP-CK stained slides, each from different patients. As high resolution whole slide histology images contain billions of pixels with 20x magnification and hardware memory is limited, it is necessary to tile the image into smaller segments for analysis and when possible use lower magnification. For these reasons, slides were tiled into overlapping 512×512 images at 10x magnification. The reduced magnification allows to have enough

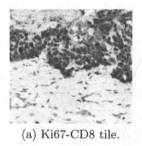

(a) Ki67-CD8 tile.   (b) FAP-CK tile.

Fig. 1. Ki67-CD8 and FAP-CK example tiles.

contextual information in the input which is needed in order to learn a meaningful feature set in the model while at the same time facilitates dealing with the computational memory limits [12]. The tiling yielded 17025 tiles from Ki67-CD8 slides and 17812 tiles from FAP-CK slides. In order to test the performance of our method, we selected 10 pairs of Ki67-CD8/FAP-CK slides from the same tissue block. The training and testing images were taken from different patients. Figure 1 shows examples of Ki67-CD8 and FAP-CK tiles.

2.2 Network Architecture and Inference

In order to map images from one staining to the other, we used a CycleGAN [17] based method which allows to learn transforms between domain spaces without the need to use paired registered image datasets. As generator networks we used ResNet architectures [9] with 11 residual blocks. The ResNet architecture used as a generator has a receptive field of 207×207 pixels, roughly corresponding to 190×190 microns on the $10x$ magnification image of the tissue. This receptive field size allows enough contextual information from the surroundings of the target pixel in the input to find meaningful histology features for the prediction of the virtual stain on the output image. Due to the CycleGAN memory burden, we were not able to fit more than one 512×512 RGB image per batch during training per GPU (Nvidia P100). In order to distribute the training on multiple GPUs and accelerate the learning process, we implemented the stochastic synchronous ADAM algorithm [5] and used the pytorch distributed computing library which allowed us to use 12 GPUs concurrently.

In order to overcome the memory bound hardware limitations, inference of the trained network on the testing slides was also done tilewise. The tile output is then merged back in order to obtain a virtual whole slide image. This inference workflow yielded whole slide images containing tiling artifacts. As style transfer networks give better and more realistic results when instance normalization layers are used [15], these layers were introduced in the CycleGAN architecture. Instance normalization layers are applied at test time as well, making the value of any output pixel depends not only on the network parameters and the receptive field area in the input but also on the statics of the input tile image. Let's assume that:

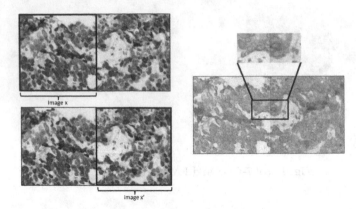

Fig. 2. (right) Tiling effect in adjacent output tiles. (left) Image x and x' correspond to 2 adjacent input tiles from a whole slide image. The green and red circles correspond to 2 adjacent pixels belonging to the same cell nucleus but to different input tiles. (Color figure online)

$$y = g(x),$$

where x, y and g correspond to an input tensor, an output tensor and an instance normalization layer respectively. Let $x \in \mathbb{R}^{T \times C \times W \times H}$ be a tensor containing a batch of T images and x_{tijk} the $tijk^{th}$ element, where j and k correspond to spatial dimensions, i corresponds to the feature channel and t corresponds to the batch index. In this case, g can be expressed as:

$$y_{tijk} = g(x_{tijk}) = \frac{x_{tijk} - \mu_{ti}}{\sqrt{\sigma_{ti}^2 + \varepsilon}}$$

where μ_{ti} and σ_{ti}^2 are the mean and variance of the input tile. If we consider 2 adjacent pixels x_{tijk} and x'_{tijk} with similar values on the edges of two adjacent input tiles x and x' having very different statistics, the instance normalization functions g and g' applied to these two pixels will be completely different. This results in a tiling artifact in the generated whole slide image as adjacent output tiles might have significantly different pixel values on their borders (Fig. 2).

With instance normalization it is possible to use the same running mean and variance values for all the tiles at inference time in a way similar to inference with batch normalization. This approach indeed yielded output images without the tiling artifact. However, the resulting output at inference was of lower quality and had very faint colors. This effect can be explained by the fact that the training datasets are quite variable and containing both tissue and background, this makes the running mean and variance locally irrelevant. We propose a solution to the tiling artifact problem by using overlapping tiles during inference. Our solution is based on using a smaller input size of 128×128 instead of 512×512 and on using a sliding window for the instance normalization function statistics, allowing to have a smooth transition in the statistic values when deploying on 2

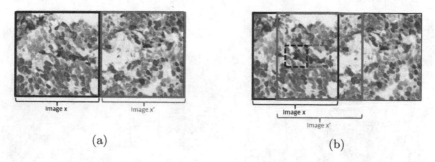

(a)   (b)

Fig. 3. Image (a) corresponds to the inference performed on 2 adjacent slides using the classical method. Image (b) corresponds to the new inference approach. The solid and dotted line squares correspond to the sliding window considered and the effective tile used for inference respectively.

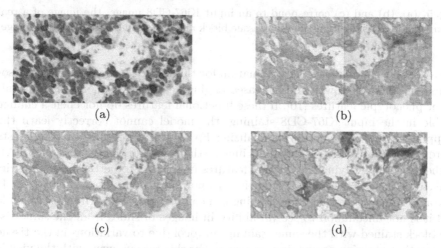

(a)   (b)

(c)   (d)

Fig. 4. Effect of the new inference approach. (a) corresponds to 2 adjacent tiles from the input Ki67-CD8 image. (b) and (c) show to the corresponding image area in the output virtual FAP-CK image using the classical inference method and the proposed solution respectively. (d) shows a corresponding area from a real FAP-CK image from the same tissue block.

adjacent slides (Fig. 3). Using this approach, we manage to substantially reduce the tiling artifact (Fig. 4).

3   Results and Validation

Visual assessment of the generated images shows that the results are visually similar to the real staining of a slide from the same tissue block (Fig. 5).

We notice that in several cases FAP (purple connective tissue in FAP-CK images) expression is different between the real and virtual images (Fig. 6). The localisation of FAP is generally successful however the patterns and the amounts

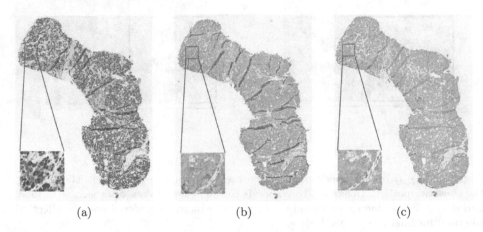

(a)   (b)   (c)

Fig. 5. (a), (b) and (c) correspond to an input Ki67-CD8 image, the image of a real stained FAP-CK slide from the same tissue block and the virtual FAP-CK slide image.

are not always matching. One explanation for this effect can be that FAP is associated with tumor growth and increased angiogenesis rather than with anatomical or phenotypic features [10]. If these functional features do not elicit a change visible in the input Ki67-CD8 staining, the model cannot correctly learn the mapping. The model success in localizing FAP, even if not flawlessly, suggests there are visual features in the input images that indicate the expression of FAP in the tissue. Identifying these visual features might lead to better FAP stain virtualisation as well as to new insights into tumor microenvironment anatomies. It is worthwhile to note that slide staining is a complex process with many variable and it is not uncommon to see variability in images of slides from the same tissue block stained with the same staining protocol due to variations in the tissue preparation, staining or imaging processes. For this reason, even with the visible difference in FAP expression in our virtual slides compared to the real stained slides, the results could still prove practically useful in some cases. Obtaining a virtual image which is slightly different from the real one should be acceptable as long as the pathological interpretations of both of them are similar.

We validate our results on a dataset of 10 testing paired images of slides from the same tissue block using an automatic algorithm for CK^+ and FAP cells detection. The algorithm was developed and validated using real FAP-CK images. The results include CK^+ cell densities and FAP densities in real and virtual whole slide images. We verify that the difference between results on real and virtual stained slides is not one sided, meaning that our mapping algorithm does not consistently over-generate or under-generate CK or FAP.

In order to visualize the difference between these densities we compute the absolute relative difference between the results obtained in the real and virtual slides (Fig. 7). Analysis of the results shows a median absolute relative difference of 8% with 0.016 variance between CK densities in real and virtual slides. This was also confirmed by our expert pathologist who evaluated real and virtual

(a) real FAP-CK tile.   (b) Virtual FAP-CK tile.

Fig. 6. FAP expression differences in real and virtual images.

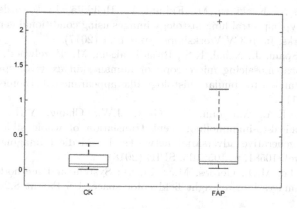

Fig. 7. Boxplot representation of the absolute relative difference between real and corresponding virtual slides for CK^+ cell densities (left side) and FAP cell densities (right side).

paired slides and reported high correlation in CK expression. For FAP, we report a median of 14% with a variance of 0.466, reflecting a substantially higher variability than for CK. Our expert pathologist also confirmed this observation and mentioned that FAP features are completely not visible for pathologists in Ki67-CD8 staining. This observation is very interesting for our research and allows us to discover the limitations of simulation methods when biological constraints are present.

4   Conclusions

We propose to use an unsupervised deep learning method based on CycleGAN in order to virtually generate FAP-CK from Ki67-CD8 tissue stained images. Instance normalization used with the CycleGAN architecture helps the network learn a more realistic mapping between the stainings but introduces a tiling artifact in the merged testing set whole slide images. We significantly reduce this artifact by using a new inference approach based on overlapping tiles to create smooth transitions in the instance normalization layers. We validate our method using a test dataset of Ki67-CD8 input images for which a real FAP-CK images from the same tissue blocks were generated.

In the next steps, we plan to use additional input stainings and compare the results to our current results in order to define biological constraints to the success of stain virtualization. We also plan to replace the instance normalization module in the CycleGAN with an improved normalization element that reduces the titling effect during inference.

References

1. Bayramoglu, N., Kaakinen, M., Eklund, L., Heikkilä, J.: Towards virtual H&E staining of hyperspectral lung histology images using conditional generative adversarial networks. In: ICCV Workshops, pp. 64–71 (2017)
2. Bini, J.M., Spain, J., Nehal, K.S., Rajadhyaksha, M., Hazelwood, V., DiMarzio, C.A.: Confocal mosaicing microscopy of human skin ex vivo: spectral analysis for digital staining to simulate histology-like appearance. J. Biomed. Opt. **16**(7), 076008 (2011)
3. Burlingame, E.A., Margolin, A., Gray, J.W., Chang, Y.H.: Shift: speedy histopathological-to-immunofluorescent translation of whole slide images using conditional generative adversarial networks. In: Medical Imaging 2018: Digital Pathology, vol. 10581, p. 1058105. SPIE (2018)
4. Can, A., Bello, M.O., Gerdes, M.J., Li, Q.: System and methods for mapping fluorescent images into a bright field color space. US Patent 8,269,827 18 Sept 2012
5. Chen, J., Pan, X., Monga, R., Bengio, S., Jozefowicz, R.: Revisiting distributed synchronous SGD. arXiv preprint arXiv:1604.00981 (2016)
6. Christiansen, E.M., et al.: In silico labeling: predicting fluorescent labels in unlabeled images. Cell **173**(3), 792–803 (2018)
7. Gareau, D.S.: Feasibility of digitally stained multimodal confocal mosaics to simulate histopathology. J. Biomed. Opt. **14**(3), 034050 (2009)
8. Giacomelli, M.G., et al.: Virtual hematoxylin and eosin transillumination microscopy using epi-fluorescence imaging. PLoS ONE **11**(8), e0159337 (2016)
9. He, K., Zhang, X., Ren, S., Sun, J.: Deep residual learning for image recognition. In: Proceedings of the IEEE CVPR, pp. 770–778 (2016)
10. Kelly, T., Huang, Y., Simms, A.E., Mazur, A.: Fibroblast activation protein-α: a key modulator of the microenvironment in multiple pathologies. Int. Rev. Cell Mol. Biol. **297**, 83–116 (2012)
11. Kuse, M., Sharma, T., Gupta, S.: Classification scheme for lymphocyte segmentation in H&E stained histology images. In: Ünay, D., Çataltepe, Z., Aksoy, S. (eds.) ICPR 2010. LNCS, vol. 6388, pp. 235–243. Springer, Heidelberg (2010). https://doi.org/10.1007/978-3-642-17711-8_24
12. Lahiani, A., Gildenblat, J., Klaman, I., Navab, N., Klaiman, E.: Generalising multistain immunohistochemistry tissue segmentation using end-to-end colour deconvolution deep neural networks. IET Image Process. **13**(7), 1066–1073 (2019)
13. Lahiani, A., Klaiman, E., Grimm, O.: Enabling histopathological annotations on immunofluorescent images through virtualization of hematoxylin and eosin. JPI **9**, 1 (2018)

14. Rivenson, Y., Wang, H., Wei, Z., Zhang, Y., Gunaydin, H., Ozcan, A.: Deep learning-based virtual histology staining using auto-fluorescence of label-free tissue. arXiv preprint arXiv:1803.11293 (2018)
15. Ulyanov, D., Vedaldi, A., Lempitsky, V.: Instance normalization: the missing ingredient for fast stylization. arxiv 2016. arXiv preprint arXiv:1607.08022 (2016)
16. Zhu, J.Y.: Freezing instance normalization during test phase? (2017). https://github.com/junyanz/CycleGAN/issues/32. Accessed 01 Oct 2018
17. Zhu, J.Y., Park, T., Isola, P., Efros, A.A.: Unpaired image-to-image translation using cycle-consistent adversarial networks. In: ICCV (2017)

Evaluation of Colour Pre-processing on Patch-Based Classification of H&E-Stained Images

Francesco Bianconi[1,3]([⊠]), Jakob N. Kather[2],
and Constantino C. Reyes-Aldasoro[3]

[1] Department of Engineering, Università degli Studi di Perugia,
Via Goffredo Duranti 93, 06135 Perugia, Italy
bianco@ieee.org
[2] Department of Medicine III, University Hospital RWTH Aachen,
52074 Aachen, Germany
jakob.kather@nct-heidelberg.de
[3] School of Engineering and Mathematical Sciences, City,
University of London, London EC1V OHB, UK
reyes@city.ac.uk

Abstract. This paper compares the effects of colour pre-processing on
the classification performance of H&E-stained images. Variations in the
tissue preparation procedures, acquisition systems, stain conditions and
reagents are all source of artifacts that can affect negatively computer-
based classification. Pre-processing methods such as colour constancy,
transfer and deconvolution have been proposed to compensate the artifacts. In this paper we compare quantitatively the combined effect of six
colour pre-processing procedures and 12 colour texture descriptors on
patch-based classification of H&E-stained images. We found that colour
pre-processing had negative effects on accuracy in most cases – particularly when used with colour descriptors. However, some pre-processing
procedures proved beneficial when employed in conjunction with clas-
sic texture descriptors such as co-occurrence matrices, Gabor filters and
Local Binary Patterns.

Keywords: Colour · Histology · Hematoxylin · Eosin · Texture

1 Introduction

Digital Pathology has grown considerably in recent years encompassing
computer-based activities that allow for improvements and innovations in the
workflow of pathology [1]. In this domain the automated processing of tissue
samples has received increasing attention due to the potential applications in

F. Bianconi—Performed this work as an Academic Visitor at City, University of
London.

C. C. Reyes-Aldasoro et al. (Eds.): ECDP 2019, LNCS 11435, pp. 56–64, 2019.
https://doi.org/10.1007/978-3-030-23937-4_7

diagnosis [2], grading [3], identification of tissue substructures [4], prognostication and mutation prediction [5]. A number of problems, however, still limit the adoption of digital pathology on a large scale: the relatively scarce availability of large labelled datasets of histological images, the differences in the acquisition systems and/or protocol used as well as the variability in tissue preparation and/or stain reactivity [6]. The latter, in particular, can generate colour variations and artifacts that can reduce significantly the accuracy of computer-based methods. This problem has attracted much attention lately and different colour pre-processing methods have been proposed as possible solutions [7]. Still, their beneficial effects on patch-based classification of H&E-stained images are not clear, since only few studies have addressed the subject in a quantitative way [8–10]. Also, apart from [10], little has been investigated as concerns the coupled effects of colour pre-processing and the specific image descriptor used.

In this paper we present a quantitative evaluation of the effects of colour pre-processing on patch-based classification of H&E-stained images. The study is based on seven datasets of histological images from different sources, six colour pre-processing procedures and 12 colour texture descriptors.

Abbrv.	Sample images	Tissue type	Classes / Patch size
AP		Breast cancer (invasive ductal carcinoma)	Grade I ($n = 107$), II ($n = 102$) and III ($n = 91$) / 1280px × 960px
BH		Breast cancer (eight histological types)	Benign ($n = 625$) and malignant ($n = 1370$) / 700px × 460px
KM		Low and high grade colorectal cancer	Epithelium, stroma, complex stroma, debris, adipose, necrosis and background ($n = 625$ each) / 150px × 150px
LM		Lymphoma	Chronic lymphocytic leukemia ($n = 113$), follicular lymph. ($n = 139$) and mantle cell lymph. ($n = 122$) / 1388px × 1040px
NKI		Breast cancer (grades I, II and III)	Epithelium ($n = 1106$) and stroma ($n = 189$) / 100px × 100px
VGH		Breast cancer (grades I, II and III)	Epithelium ($n = 226$) and stroma ($n = 47$) / 100px × 100px
WR		Colorectal cancer	Benign ($n = 74$) and malignant ($n = 91$) / Variable

Fig. 1. Datasets used in the experiments: round-up table and sample images.

2 Materials and Methods

2.1 Image Datasets (Fig. 1)

Agios Pavlos (AP). Breast carcinoma histological images from the Department of Pathology, 'Agios Pavlos', General Hospital of Thessaloniki, Greece [11] (https://zenodo.org/record/834910) representing tissue samples from 21 patients with invasive ductal carcinoma of grade I, II and III.

BreakHis (BH). Breast carcinoma histological images from Pathological Anatomy and Cytopathology, Paraná, Brazil [12] of breast tumour from eight different histological subtypes (https://omictools.com/breakhis-tool).

Kather Multiclass (KM). Histological images of colorectal cancer from the University Medical Center Mannheim, Heidelberg University, Germany [4] (https://zenodo.org/record/53169) representing eight tissue subtypes.

Lymphoma (LM). Multi-center collection of histological images from malignant lymphoma [13] (https://ome.grc.nia.nih.gov/iicbu2008/lymphoma/index.html) organised in three classes: chronic lymphocytic leukemia, follicular lymphoma and mantle cell lymphoma.

Netherlands Cancer Institute (NKI). Tissue micro-arrays (TMAs) from a cohort of patients with breast cancer enrolled at the Netherlands Cancer Institute, Amsterdam, Netherlands [14] (https://tma.im/tma_portal/C-Path/supp.html). The dataset includes with segmentation masks from which we extracted tiles of well defined areas of epithelium and stroma.

Vancouver General Hospital (VGH). Same structure as (NKI), but here the images come from a cohort of 328 patients enrolled at Vancouver General Hospital in Canada [14] (https://tma.im/tma_portal/C-Path/supp.html).

Warwick-QU (WR). Histological images of colorectal cancer from the University Hospitals Coventry and Warwickshire, United Kingdom [15] (https://warwick.ac.uk/fac/sci/dcs/research/tia/glascontest/download/) organised in two classes (benign and malignant).

2.2 Colour Normalisation

We evaluated three colour constancy, two colour transfer and one colour deconvolution method as detailed below. The effects of each method on a set of sample images are shown in Figs. 2 and 3.

Colour Constancy. We considered chromaticity representation ('chroma' in the remainder), grey-world normalisation ('gw') and histogram equalisation ('heq') [16]. In the experiments we used Jost van de Weijer's Color Constancy Toolbox (http://lear.inrialpes.fr/people/vandeweijer/research.html) and Matlab's histeq() function respectively for 'gw' and 'heq'.

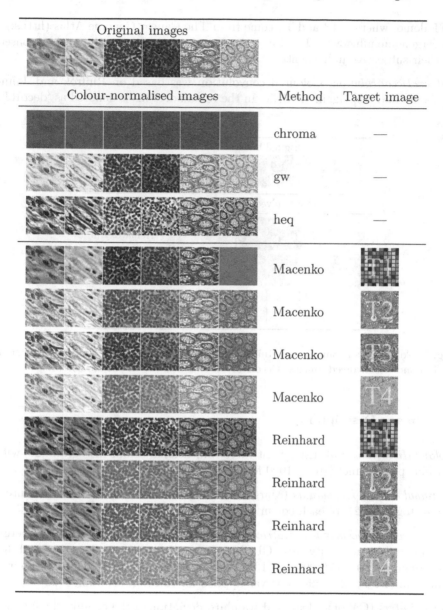

Fig. 2. Illustration of the effects of normalisation. Notice the influence of target images.

Colour Transfer. We employed Macenko's [17] and Reinhard's [18] methods using the implementation provided with Warwick's Stain Normalization Toolbox (https://warwick.ac.uk/fac/sci/dcs/research/tia/software/sntoolbox/, SNT henceforth). For each of the two approaches we used four target images, denoted in the remainder as T1, T2, T3 and T4 (Fig. 2). These are all histology images except T1, which is a colour calibration checker. As for the others, T2 is part of

SNT demo, whereas T3 and T4 come from The Cancer Genome Atlas (https://cancergenome.nih.gov/). The target images were chosen by the authors based on their subjective judgement.

Colour Deconvolution. Colour deconvolution was based on Ruifrok and Johnston's method [19], again via SNT. In the remainder this is denoted as 'decoRJ'.

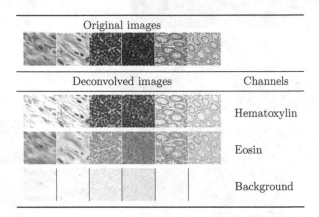

Fig. 3. Colour deconvolution via Ruifrok and Johnston's method: samples of original (RGB) and deconvolved images. Deconvolved channels are in pseudo-colours.

2.3   Image Descriptors

Colour Histogram (FullHist). Joint three-dimensional colour histogram [20] with ten bins per channel ($10^3 = 1000$ features).

Marginal Colour Histograms (MargHists). Concatenation of the three 1D intensity histograms [21] of each colour channel ($256 \times 3 = 768$ features).

Grey-Level Co-occurrence Matrices (GLCM). Contrast, correlation, energy, entropy and homogeneity from GLCM computed at distance 1px, 2px and 3px and orientation $0°$, $45°$, $90°$ and $135°$ ($5 \times 3 \times 4 = 60$ features). Discrete Fourier transform (DFT) normalisation was applied for rotation invariance [22].

Gabor Filters (Gabor). Mean and standard deviation of the magnitude of transformed images from a bank with four frequencies and six orientations ($2 \times 4 \times 6 = 48$ features). Rotation invariance was obtained via DFT normalisation.

Local Binary Patterns (LBP). Concatenation of rotation-invariant ('ri') LBP histograms computed at resolution 1px, 2px and 3px using non-interpolated eight-pixel neighbourhoods as detailed in [23].

Hybrid Methods. Marginal colour versions of Gabor, GLCM and LBP were also obtained by applying the corresponding grey-scale descriptor to each colour channel separately and concatenating the resulting features. These are indicated as 'MargGabor', 'MargGLCM' and 'MargLBP' tn the remainder.

Pre-trained Convolutional Networks. L_2-normalised output of the last fully-connected layer from the following pre-trained networks: ResNet-50 and ResNet-101 [24], VGG very deep 16 and VGG very deep 19 [25].

3   Results and Discussion

Each dataset was analysed for a combination of pre-processing and image descriptor, the accuracy being estimated via split-sample validation with stratified sampling at the image level[1]. The random subdivision into train and test set was repeated a hundred times and the results averaged. Classification was based on the 1-NN rule with L_1 distance. We used a train ratio (i.e. fraction of images used for training) $f = 1/4$ and $f = 1/8$, and the results did not show significant deviation in the overall trend. The best and second-best combinations are shown in Fig. 4. Pre-trained ResNet50/ResNet101 performed best or second-best in eight cases out of 14 (accuracy range of best configurations 71.56%–98.81%), followed by joint and marginal colour histograms (six cases, accuracy range 80.09%–98.16%). As for colour pre-processing, doing nothing was the best or second-best option in seven cases out of 14, followed by heq and chroma.

Table 1 shows the difference to the baseline (colour pre-processing vs. no colour pre-processing) by descriptor and pre-processing method. Colour pre-processing resulted in a loss of accuracy in most cases – in particular, methods that rely on colour responded negatively to colour pre-processing. Colour transfer via Macenko's and Reinhard's methods did not show a clear trend as for the effects of the target image used. Note that the non-histological target image (T1) gave better results than the histological ones (T2–T4) in some cases.

By contrast, the texture-based methods proved more resilient to colour pre-processing. In this case there was even a noticeable gain in accuracy in some combinations descriptor/pre-processing method: marginal colour texture descriptors (i.e. MargGabor, MargGLCM and MargLBP) responded positively both to 'chroma' normalisation and colour deconvolution. This suggests that texture features provide complementary information when extracted separately from each of the hematoxylin, eosin and background channels.

---

[1] Complete results available at https://drive.google.com/drive/folders/1bc1mO_RCQp pfbrCjqjWlF50YoZNLWbW4?usp=sharing.

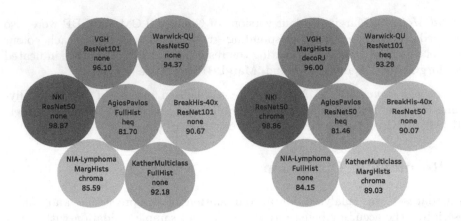

Fig. 4. Best (left) and second-best combinations (right) for each dataset. Each circle corresponds to a dataset, with its descriptor, pre-processing and accuracy. Colours reflect accuracy (brown = best, blue = worst). Results obtained for $f = 1/4$. (Color figure online)

Table 1. Effect of colour pre-processing: difference to the baseline broken down by image descriptor and colour pre-processing method. Colour reflects accuracy (brown = best, blue = worst). Values are averaged over the seven datasets; $f = 1/4$.

| | | | | | Colour pre-processing method | | | | | | | | | |
Descriptor	none	chroma	gw	heq	Macenko (T1)	Macenko (T2)	Macenko (T3)	Macenko (T4)	Reinhard (T1)	Reinhard (T2)	Reinhard (T3)	Reinhard (T4)	decoRJ	AVG
FullHist	0.00	-8.10	-3.06	-1.77	-5.84	-5.26	-6.28	-5.02	-42.65	-42.65	-42.65	-42.65	-31.50	-18.26
MargHists	0.00	0.59	-5.82	-24.50	-7.08	-4.70	-4.18	-5.05	-27.32	-28.25	-27.00	-30.20	-6.90	-13.11
Gabor	0.00	-0.42	1.16	-2.78	-2.11	-1.84	-1.68	-2.03	-2.18	-1.45	-1.66	-1.22	-0.28	-1.27
GLCM	0.00	0.96	0.52	-3.41	-0.30	-1.64	-0.16	-2.67	-1.50	-2.68	-1.02	-6.82	-2.53	-1.63
LBP	0.00	3.64	-0.36	-0.23	0.39	-0.16	0.01	-0.09	1.48	-1.12	-0.36	-0.56	-0.47	0.16
MargGabor	0.00	2.31	1.65	-0.52	2.04	-1.44	-1.73	-1.96	-1.75	-0.93	-2.42	-1.88	5.80	-0.06
MargGLCM	0.00	4.71	0.78	-1.91	2.75	-3.95	-3.11	-5.47	-0.68	-3.66	-1.32	-6.97	4.66	-1.09
MargLBP	0.00	4.40	0.40	-0.17	2.02	-0.67	-1.12	-0.81	3.70	-0.26	-0.42	-1.56	2.93	0.65
ResNet50	0.00	-2.24	-1.39	-1.32	-1.91	-2.48	-1.96	-2.31	-22.72	-25.56	-24.50	-26.41	-14.71	-9.81
ResNet101	0.00	-3.83	-0.39	-1.63	-2.93	-1.50	-1.35	-2.88	-24.64	-26.01	-25.58	-26.74	-17.31	-10.37
Vgg16	0.00	-2.93	-1.13	-1.04	-3.90	-0.87	-1.21	-1.30	-20.17	-22.79	-21.90	-23.38	-14.20	-8.83
Vgg19	0.00	-1.05	-1.14	-2.26	-1.29	-3.58	-1.75	-4.81	-19.50	-20.47	-20.06	-20.42	-12.29	-8.36
AVG	0.00	-0.16	-0.73	-3.46	-1.51	-2.34	-2.04	-2.87	-13.16	-14.65	-14.07	-15.73	-7.23	-6.00

4 Conclusions

Colour pre-processing produced a noticeable loss of accuracy in the classification of histological samples in most cases, particularly when used along with image descriptors that rely on colour. This is consistent with [10], but differs from [9]. Some pre-processing methods (i.e. chroma and decoRJ) had positive effects when coupled with certain texture descriptors, specifically MargGabor, MargGLCM and MargLBP. This is a novel finding that should be better explored and validated in future studies.

In conclusion, our results suggest that the use of colour pre-processing for patch-based classification of H&E images should be considered with care. In particular: 1) no pre-processing may provide better results than pre-processing in most cases; 2) the selection of the pre-processing procedure should always be evaluated in conjunction with the image descriptor(s) used.

Acknowledgements. This work was partially supported by the Italian Ministry of Education, University and Research (MIUR) under the Individual Funding Scheme for Fundamental Research ('FFABR 2017') and by the Department of Engineering at the University of Perugia, Italy, under the Fundamental Research programme 2018.

References

1. Griffin, J., Treanor, D.: Digital pathology in clinical use: where are we now and what is holding us back? Histopathology **70**(1), 134–145 (2017)
2. Sudharshan, P., Petitjean, C., Spanhol, F., et al.: Multiple instance learning for histopathological breast cancer image classification. Expert Syst. Appl. **117**, 103–111 (2019)
3. Jørgensen, A., Emborg, J., Røge, R., et al.: Exploiting multiple color representations to improve colon cancer detection in whole slide H&E stains. In: Stoyanov, D., et al. (eds.) Computational Pathology and Ophthalmic Medical Image Analysis. LNCS, vol. 11039, pp. 61–68. Springer, Cham (2018). https://doi.org/10.1007/978-3-030-00949-6_8
4. Kather, J., Weis, C.-A., Bianconi, F., et al.: Multi-class texture analysis in colorectal cancer histology. Sci. Rep. **6** (2016). Article no. 27988
5. Coudray, N., Ocampo, P., Sakellaropoulos, T., et al.: Classification and mutation prediction from non-small cell lung cancer histopathology images using deep learning. Nat. Med. **24**, 1559–1567 (2018)
6. Khan, A., Rajpoot, N., Treanor, D., et al.: A nonlinear mapping approach to stain normalization in digital histopathology images using image-specific color deconvolution. IEEE Trans. Biomed. Eng. **61**(6), 1729–1738 (2014)
7. Komura, D., Ishikawa, S.: Machine learning methods for histopathological image analysis. Comput. Struct. Biotechnol. **16**, 34–42 (2018)
8. Sethi, A., Sha, L., Vahadane, A., et al.: Empirical comparison of color normalization methods for epithelial-stromal classification in H and E images. J. Pathol. Inform. **7**(17) (2016)
9. Ciompi, F., Geessink, O., Bejnordi, B.E., et al.: The importance of stain normalization in colorectal tissue classification with convolutional networks. In Proceedings of the IEEE International Symposium on Biomed Imaging, Melbourne, Australia (2017)
10. Gadermayr, M., Cooper, S.S., Klinkhammer, B., Boor, P., Merhof, D.: A quantitative assessment of image normalization for classifying histopathological tissue of the kidney. In: Roth, V., Vetter, T. (eds.) GCPR 2017. LNCS, vol. 10496, pp. 3–13. Springer, Cham (2017). https://doi.org/10.1007/978-3-319-66709-6_1
11. Dimitropoulos, K., Barmpoutis, P., Zioga, C., et al.: Grading of invasive breast carcinoma through Grassmannian VLADencoding. PLoS ONE **12**(9) (2017)
12. Spanhol, F., Oliveira, L., Petitjean, C., et al.: A dataset for breast cancer histopathological image classification. IEEE Trans. Biomed. Eng. **63**(7), 1455–1462 (2016)

13. Shamir, L., Orlov, N., Mark Eckley, D., et al.: IICBU 2008: a proposed benchmark suite for biological image analysis. Med. Biol. Eng. Comput. **46**(9), 943–947 (2008)
14. Beck, A., Sangoi, A., Leung, S., et al.: Imaging: systematic analysis of breast cancer morphology uncoversstromal features associated with survival. Sci. Transl. Med. **3**(108) (2011)
15. Sirinukunwattana, K., Snead, D.R.J., Rajpoot, N.M.: A stochastic polygons model for glandular structures in colon histology images. IEEE Trans. Med. Imaging **34**(11), 2366–2378 (2015)
16. Cernadas, E., Fernández-Delgado, M., González-Rufino, E., et al.: Influence of normalization and color space to color texture classification. Pattern Recognit. **61**, 120–138 (2017)
17. Macenko, M., Niethammer, M., Marron, J., et al.: A method for normalizing histology slides for quantitative analysis. In: Proceedings of the IEEE International Symposium on Biomedical Imaging (ISBI), Boston, USA, pp. 1107–1110, June 2009
18. Reinhard, E., Ashikhmin, M., Gooch, B., et al.: Color transfer between images. IEEE Comput. Graph. Appl. **21**(5), 34–41 (2001)
19. Ruifrok, A., Johnston, D.: Quantification of histochemical staining by color deconvolution. Anal. Quant. Cytol. Histol. **23**(4), 291–299 (2001)
20. Swain, M., Ballard, D.: Color indexing. Int. J. Comp. Vis. **7**(1), 11–32 (1991)
21. Pietikainen, M., Nieminen, S., Marszalec, E., et al.: Accurate color discrimination with classification based on feature distributions. In: Proceedings of the International Conference on Pattern Recognition (ICPR)Vienna, Austria, vol. 3, pp. 833–838, August 1996
22. Bianconi, F., Fernández, A.: Rotation invariant co-occurrence features based on digital circles and discrete fourier transform. Pattern Recogn. Lett. **48**, 34–41 (2014)
23. Bianconi, F., Bello-Cerezo, R., Napoletano, P.: Improved opponent color local binary patterns: an effective localimage descriptor for color texture classification. J. Electron. Imaging, **27**(1) (2018)
24. He, K., Zhang, X., Ren, S., et al.: Deep residual learning for image recognition. In: Proceedings of Computer Vision and Pattern Recognition, Las Vegas, USA, pp. 770–778, January 2016
25. Chatfield, K., Simonyan, K., Vedaldi, A., et al.: Return of the devil in the details: delving deep into convolutional nets. In: Proceedings of the British Machine Vision Conference, Nottingham, UK, September 2014

Segmentation

Automated Segmentation of DCIS in Whole Slide Images

Nikhil Seth[1,2]($\boxtimes$), Shazia Akbar[1,2], Sharon Nofech-Mozes[2],
Sherine Salama[2], and Anne L. Martel[1,2]

[1] Department of Medical Biophysics, University of Toronto, Toronto, Canada
nikhil.seth@utoronto.ca
[2] Sunnybrook Research Institute, Toronto, Canada

Abstract. Segmentation of ducts in whole slide images is an important step needed to analyze ductal carcinoma *in-situ* (DCIS), an early form of breast cancer. Here, we train several U-Net architectures – deep convolutional neural networks designed to output probability maps – to segment DCIS in whole slide images and validate the optimal patch field of view necessary to achieve superior accuracy at the slide-level. We showed a U-Net trained at 5x achieved the best test results (DSC = 0.771, F1 = 0.601), implying the U-Net benefits from having wider contextual information. Our custom U-Net based architecture, trained to incorporate patches from all available resolutions, achieved test results of DSC = 0.759 (F1 = 0.682) showing improvement in the duct detecting capabilities of the model. Both architectures show comparable performance to a second expert annotator on an independent test set. This is preliminary work for a pipeline targeted at predicting recurrence risk in DCIS patients.

Keywords: DCIS · Segmentation · U-Net · Digital pathology · Deep learning

1 Introduction

Ductal carcinoma *in-situ* (DCIS) is a non-invasive form of breast cancer, accounting for approximately 2,500 new cases per year in Canada [1]. After breast conserving surgery (BCS) to remove the lesion, DCIS patients may undergo post-surgery radiotherapy to reduce the risk of developing local recurrences. Since prediction of absolute risk of recurrence based on traditional histopathologic evaluation is limited, it is not possible at present to identify patients with very low risk of recurrence in whom radiotherapy can be safely omitted. Improved stratification of patients into low- and high-risk recurrence groups would be of great benefit for a guidance-based treatment approach.

Histopathologic evaluation of excised tissue is an important step for planning additional treatment and understanding the underlying biology of tumors which can help to some extent estimate recurrence risk. As digital slides are becoming more accessible in practice, automation can be adopted to analyze large datasets of archived tissue. Previous work has shown quantitative features extracted from digital pathology images containing DCIS may improve prognostication [2]. Typical digitized whole slide images (WSIs) are extremely large (approximately 3–8 GB each) and have

C. C. Reyes-Aldasoro et al. (Eds.): ECDP 2019, LNCS 11435, pp. 67–74, 2019.
https://doi.org/10.1007/978-3-030-23937-4_8

information stored at several different magnifications. As such, it is impractical to extract quantitative features from an entire WSI due to computational and computer memory constraints. To efficiently extract relevant information, scalable and efficient methods are needed to accurately localize DCIS regions in WSIs. This is a non-trivial problem due to high intraclass variability within WSIs and comparatively low interclass variability between DCIS and normal ducts. This sets up a challenging segmentation problem and given recent advancements in deep learning it is possible to leverage large datasets of WSIs to overcome these issues. In this paper, we describe a fully automated pipeline for segmentation of ducts containing DCIS which encompasses convolutional neural networks (CNNs) trained on patches extracted from WSIs.

2 Materials and Methods

Dataset. Our dataset consists of 202 women who were diagnosed with DCIS between 2012/2013 and underwent BCS. Specimens were handled per routine tissue processing to produce formalin-fixed paraffin embedded tissue blocks and H&E stained sections. Representative sections were imaged in a digital slide scanner. An expert pathologist reviewed each WSI and márked annotations via a pen tool around the DCIS ducts, using the Pathcore Sedeen™ viewer [3]. These annotations served as our ground truth segmentations for training CNNs. WSIs were split into subsets for training (n = 111), hyperparameter tuning (n = 72) and testing (n = 19). An additional 10% of the training set was held out as a validation set, to monitor the CNN for early stopping.

Training. Due to computational costs associated with reading WSIs into memory, the data must be subdivided into patches for training. To account for high variability within our dataset, each patch was augmented via random rotations at either 0, 90, 180 or 270°. This augmentation increases the effective size of the training set. The CNNs are trained using the mean pixelwise cross-entropy loss function and Adam optimizer [4]. Training runs for 100 epochs, and the model with lowest validation loss from the last 10 epochs is selected as the final trained model. This training scheme allows networks sufficient training time, whilst ensuring they do not finish with a stochastically unfavourable update.

Resolution vs. Field of View. Our WSIs were formatted such that the following resolutions were available: 5x, 10x and 20x. Using a constant patch size of 256×256, patches extracted at greater resolutions will have a narrower field of view (FOV). Here we set out to determine which resolution to FOV ratio is most informative for identifying DCIS. Example patches from these different resolution patch sets can be seen in Fig. 1. Whilst there are many CNNs available in the literature, we opted to train a U-Net [5], as they have shown to be effective for segmentation tasks whilst learning complex features in a fully-automated manner. Modifications to the original U-Net architecture include using ELU activation functions and batch normalization, as they have been shown to train networks faster [6, 7]. We use padded convolutions to ensure that the output segmentation maps have the same dimensions as the input image.

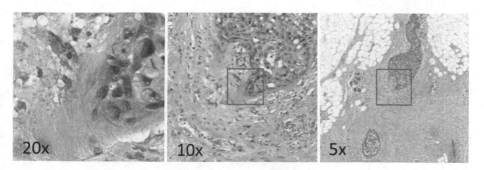

Fig. 1. Example patches from each of the three training datasets. The blue squares show the FOV of the patch one resolution step up within the context of the lower resolution patch. Patch sizes are 128 μm (20x), 512 μm (10x), 2048 μm (5x). (Color figure online)

Multi-resolution Network. In order to overcome the resolution vs. FOV trade off we also designed a novel multi-resolution network (Fig. 2). Instead of feeding only one FOV at a time, all three FOVs are treated as a single input sample, giving the network access to both high resolution details and wider contextual information. Two architectures were designed to handle multi-resolution inputs. One in which three patches were concatenated into a single nine channel image (9ch), and the second is a custom architecture (Fig. 2) that splits the U-Net down-sampling arm into three convolutional branches, one for each FOV, before recombining via concatenation and feeding into the up-sampling arm (3rm). The label images used to train these networks correspond to the high-resolution input images.

Evaluation. Patches were extracted from each WSI at the appropriate resolution to create segmentation maps during test time. They were sequentially fed through each CNN, and the outputs were stitched together to create an output probability image. Each segmentation map was thresholded to create binary DCIS masks. The ground truth masks were downsampled to evaluate the lower resolution segmentation maps. We used the following metrics to validate the performance of each CNN.

Dice Coefficient. The dice similarity coefficient is a measure of positive overlap between two binary images. It is defined as:

$$DSC = \frac{2 \cdot TP}{2 \cdot TP + FP + FN} \tag{1}$$

where TP is the number of true positive pixels in the images, FP is the number of false positive pixels, and FN is the number of false negatives. It is a similarity measure ranging from zero to one – one meaning the two images are identical. The dice coefficient is a useful metric for labels on a WSI because it does not depend on true negative values. This means that, unlike other metrics such as binary accuracy, the dice coefficient is not inflated by the high number of background pixels.

Modified F1 Score. The F1 score is the harmonic mean of precision and recall and is defined as follows:

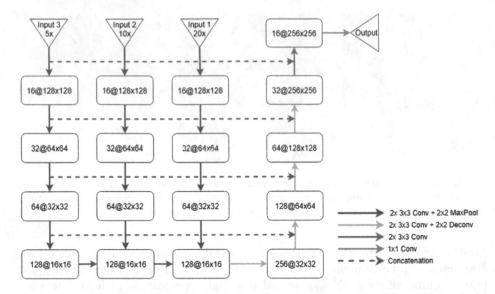

Fig. 2. Diagram of the multi-resolution U-Net (3rm). Each input is a 256×256 histology patch, and the output is a 256×256 probability map. Inputs are down-sampled separately before being combined and up-sampled.

$$F_1 = \frac{2 \cdot precision \cdot recall}{precision + recall} \qquad (2)$$

The F1 score and dice coefficient are mathematically identical. However, for the F1 score, precision and recall are calculated at the object (duct) level from a binarized DCIS mask, whereas the dice score is computed at the pixel level. As expert labels often group collections of ducts together as one region (Fig. 3), we modified precision and recall so as not to penalize multiple predicted regions within a single ground truth region. The downside is that the F1 score is no longer symmetric; swapping the predicted and ground truth images will result in a different value for the F1 score. Henceforth, all mentions of the F1 score refer to this modified version of the metric.

Post-processing. Our post-processing pipeline consisted of a thresholding operation on the probability masks, followed by a morphological opening, and finally a morphological closing. The threshold and morphological disk radius were tuned sequentially using metrics computed on the tuning set. The threshold maximizing the dice coefficient is found first. This threshold is then fixed to find the morphological radius maximizing the F1 score.

Random Parameter Search. A random search paradigm [8] was used to tune U-Net hyperparameters, whereby the parameter space is randomly sampled and used to train the model a set number of times. This allows us to set a search budget independent of the number of parameters and possible values. The search efficiency does not decrease by adding extra parameters that do not affect performance. Searched hyperparameters

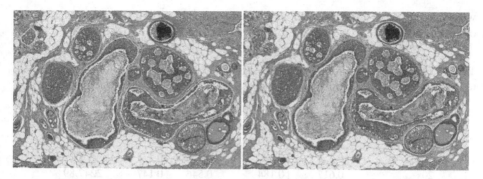

Fig. 3. Example of a group of DCIS ducts annotated independently by two different pathologists. They annotated images in two categories; definite DCIS (blue) and probable DCIS (yellow). The remainder of each image would be considered not DCIS. (Color figure online)

included depth, dilation rate, loss, optimizer, activation, dropout, regularization, pooling function and initializer. The search ran 100 times, each with a randomly sampled set of hyperparameters. Models were trained with 5-fold cross-validation.

Annotator Similarity. A second expert pathologist was asked to independently annotate all the DCIS on the held-out test set of 19 WSIs. The dice coefficient and F1 score were measured between pathologists to assess inter-observer variability in our dataset. Figure 3 shows an example of such independent paired annotations. This image illustrates the significant variability between observers. These annotator similarity comparisons serve as a benchmark for the described automated techniques.

3   Results and Discussion

Resolution Architecture Evaluation. Test results for each resolution architecture, including their post-processing pipelines, can be seen in Table 1. Each network was run on the independent test set used to compare annotators and evaluated against the annotator who created the original training labels. The 5x model achieves the greatest dice coefficient and F1 score of the single resolution networks. This implies that the segmentation quality benefits from patches with a greater FOV, as the network can make use of the wider contextual information. This makes sense considering that pathologists mostly determine which regions contain DCIS from observing WSIs at low resolution, using higher resolutions to fine tune their decisions. The 5x U-Net also offers additional benefits including decreased training and run times due to the reduced WSI size at this resolution. The 3rm multi-resolution architecture had the best F1 score out of all the U-Nets, and a dice coefficient comparable to the 5x U-Net. Thus, the 3rm network was successfully able to combine information from high and low resolutions to increase the segmentation accuracy and duct detecting capabilities of the model, however this was at the cost of significantly longer processing times. An ROC analysis, as seen in Fig. 4a, further supports the conclusion of 5x performing best with an area under the receiver operating characteristic (AUC) of 0.987. The 3rm shows slightly worse performance than the 5x model, though it is still an improvement over all the other models.

Table 1. Results for each architecture run on the test set. P-values are from Wilcoxon sign-rank tests comparing each model to the second annotator. Asterisks indicate statistical significance.

Model	Dice score	Dice P-value	F1 score	F1 P-value	Time (s)
Second annotator	0.732	N/A	0.427	N/A	N/A
5x	0.771	0.314	0.601	0.077	6.35
10x	0.558	0.009*	0.478	0.573	93.16
20x	0.617	0.184	0.546	0.147	2247.89
3rm	0.759	0.398	0.682	0.006*	3065.07
9ch	0.691	0.546	0.662	0.016*	3177.02

Comparison with Second Annotator. A Wilcoxon sign-rank test was performed to compare each models' results to the annotator similarity metrics. When comparing dice coefficients, only the 10x network was found to be significantly different (worse) than the second annotator. No other networks show statistical differences from the second annotator, implying they have comparable performance. When comparing the F1 scores, both multi-resolution models showed statistically significant improvement over the second annotator. It is important to note the small sample size of dually annotated WSIs in this test set. More labelled test data would be helpful in teasing out the performance differences between each model.

Random Search Results. The 5x U-Net was chosen for the random parameter search, due to its superior performance and drastically reduced run time. The randomly generated models were each run and evaluated on the tuning set. The AUC was calculated and averaged across all folds for each model. A series of iterative Kruskal-Wallis tests was performed on the model set. At each iteration, the test is performed. If it is significant ($p < 0.05$), the lowest mean AUC model is removed from the set. This process is repeated until the test is not significant, resulting in a set of the top models that are not significantly different from one another. The results of this analysis can be seen in Fig. 4b. The set of top models includes the base model with original hyper-parameters. Most models produced by the search did not improve on the base model, but a reasonably large group (n = 19) are shown to have not significantly different performance from the base model. This implies that the U-Net architecture is stable across small hyperparameter alterations, and the baseline hyperparameters were chosen to move forward.

Sample Output. Figure 5 shows an example of predictions generated from the 5x U-Net on an entire WSI from the test set, compared to annotations from one of the pathologists. The predicted segmentation regions are generally very close to the annotation borders, with large drops in probability marking the edges of predicted DCIS regions. Some additional ducts are detected, albeit with low probabilities. For our intended purpose of this pipeline, this result is acceptable because we want our model

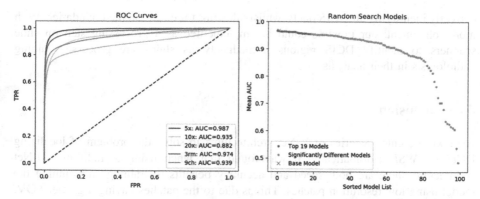

Fig. 4. a (left). ROC curves for each model, run on the testing set. The ROC analysis requires the raw probability values, and thus does not include the post-processing pipeline for each model. b (right). Models resulting from the random parameter search, sorted by mean test AUC Blue represents top set of models showing no difference from the Kruskal-Wallis test. Orange is all other models. The green x represents the model with the baseline hyperparameter set. (Color figure online)

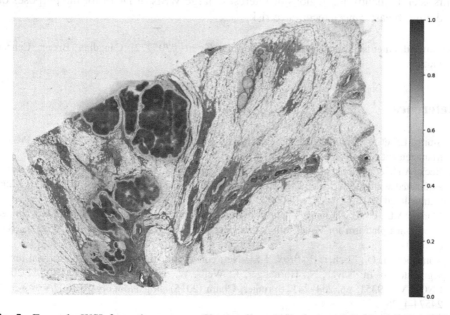

Fig. 5. Example WSI from the test set. Blue outlines indicate a pathologist labelled DCIS region. The colour overlay represents the probability map output by the 5x based model. Red indicates high probability and blue is low. Zero values are set to be transparent. (Color figure online)

to be sensitive to duct boundaries for subsequent feature extraction in stromal regions surrounding DCIS. This is achieved by optimizing the pipeline to have the best dice coefficient. Optimizing for the best F1 score would yield an algorithm suited to correctly identifying all DCIS ducts, whilst allowing for errors on the boundaries. With more refinement, our pipeline could be implemented as a processing step on slide scanners to identify DCIS regions immediately as slides are processed, aiding pathologists in their analysis.

4 Conclusion

Here we presented a series of U-Net architectures to solve the problem of localizing DCIS on WSIs automatically. It was found that when using a traditional U-Net architecture, there are both speed and accuracy benefits to training and running the model using low resolution patches. This is due to the patches having a greater FOV, giving the U-Net access to wider contextual information. Two novel multi-resolution architectures were presented, that combined patches from all three available resolutions to overcome the resolution vs. FOV trade-off. However, this comes at the expense of increased training and running times. Finally, a comparison was made between two pathologist annotators, showing that the best networks have performance comparable to the second annotator on the segmentation task. Future work will use this pipeline as a first step in identifying regions-of-interest in large WSIs of DCIS for the purposes of predicting breast cancer recurrence risk.

Acknowledgements. Canadian Cancer Society Grant #705772, Canadian Breast Cancer Federation.

References

1. Smith, L., et al.: Members of the Canadian Cancer Statistics Advisory Committee Project Management (2018)
2. Beck, A.H., et al.: Systematic analysis of breast cancer morphology uncovers stromal features associated with survival. Sci. Transl. Med. **3**(108), 108ra113 (2011). https://doi.org/10.1126/scitranslmed.3002564
3. Martel, A.L., et al.: An image analysis resource for cancer research: PIIP—pathology image informatics platform for visualization, analysis, and management. Cancer Res. **77**(21), e83–e86 (2017)
4. Ronneberger, O., Fischer, P., Brox, T.: U-Net: convolutional networks for biomedical image segmentation. In: Navab, N., Hornegger, J., Wells, W., Frangi, A.F. (eds.) MICCAI 2015. LNCS, vol. 9351, pp. 234–241. Springer, Cham (2015). https://doi.org/10.1007/978-3-319-24574-4_28
5. Clevert, D.-A., Unterthiner, T., Hochreiter, S.: Fast and accurate deep network learning by exponential linear units (ELUs). In: ICLR (2016)
6. Ioffe, S., Szegedy, C.: Batch normalization: accelerating deep network training by reducing internal covariate shift. In: ICML (2015)
7. Kingma, D.P., Ba, J.: Adam: a method for stochastic optimization. In: ICLR (2015)
8. Bengio, Y., et al.: Random search for hyper-parameter optimization. J. Mach. Learn. Res. **13**, 281–305 (2012)

A Two-Stage U-Net Algorithm
for Segmentation of Nuclei
in H&E-Stained Tissues

Amirreza Mahbod[1,2(✉)], Gerald Schaefer[3], Isabella Ellinger[1], Rupert Ecker[2],
Örjan Smedby[4], and Chunliang Wang[4]

[1] Institute for Pathophysiology and Allergy Research,
Medical University of Vienna, Vienna, Austria
amahbod@kth.se
[2] Department of Research and Development, TissueGnostics GmbH, Vienna, Austria
[3] Department of Computer Science, Loughborough University, Loughborough, UK
[4] Department of Biomedical Engineering and Health Systems,
KTH Royal Institute of Technology, Stockholm, Sweden

Abstract. Nuclei segmentation is an important but challenging task
in the analysis of hematoxylin and eosin (H&E)-stained tissue sections. While various segmentation methods have been proposed, machine
learning-based algorithms and in particular deep learning-based models
have been shown to deliver better segmentation performance. In this work,
we propose a novel approach to segment touching nuclei in H&E-stained
microscopic images using U-Net-based models in two sequential stages. In
the first stage, we perform semantic segmentation using a classification U-
Net that separates nuclei from the background. In the second stage, the
distance map of each nucleus is created using a regression U-Net. The final
instance segmentation masks are then created using a watershed algorithm
based on the distance maps. Evaluated on a publicly available dataset
containing images from various human organs, the proposed algorithm
achieves an average aggregate Jaccard index of 56.87%, outperforming
several state-of-the-art algorithms applied on the same dataset.

Keywords: Digital pathology · Tissue analysis ·
Nuclei segmentation · Deep learning · U-Net

1 Introduction

Nuclei segmentation in microscopic images of hematoxylin and eosin (H&E)-
stained tissue sections is a fundamental step required to determine nuclei count,
nuclei size and nucleus-to-cytoplasm ratio, which are in turn used for cancer
grading and determining cancer prognosis [2,4,6]. However, developing an automatic segmentation algorithm is challenging due to large variations in colour,

This research has received funding from the Marie Sklodowska-Curie Actions of the
European Union's Horizon 2020 programme under REA grant agreement no. 675228.

C. C. Reyes-Aldasoro et al. (Eds.): ECDP 2019, LNCS 11435, pp. 75–82, 2019.
https://doi.org/10.1007/978-3-030-23937-4_9

staining, texture and shape of nuclei. While various conventional image processing methods, including thresholding, morphological operations, region growing, active contour models, graph cuts, k-means clustering and probabilistic models, have been proposed, their levels of accuracy, especially for less typical cases, are inferior compared to machine learning-based algorithms due to under- or over-segmentation issues [2,4,6].

Machine learning-based algorithms and in particular fully convolutional networks (FCNs) have shown excellent performance for semantic segmentation tasks in various applications [2]. However, they are not directly applicable to nuclei segmentation which has to deal with touching objects in the same class. A number of methods have been proposed in the literature to address this issue. In the original U-Net approach [10], a customised weighted loss function was designed to assign larger weights in the separation borders. In [8], an ensemble of FCN-based methods was proposed to separate jointly segmented nuclei. While this method gave satisfying results compared to raw encoder-decoder-based models, it failed in some more challenging cases [9]. In [2,6], the problem of touching nuclei was addressed by defining a new class for nuclei boundaries and formulating the problem as a ternary segmentation task. However, this might not work well in some histological images where the boundaries are fuzzy and not well-defined. Another approach which is becoming popular for solving instance segmentation problems including nuclei segmentation in microscopic images is Mask-RCNN [3]. This multi-task algorithm is a combination of several sub-networks including region proposal network, feature pyramid network and FCN that together perform instance segmentation. Training this model usually includes tuning many hyper-parameters which makes it challenging to find an optimal performance.

A classical way to tackle the touching cell problem is to perform a distance transform on the segmentation mask followed by a watershed algorithm. Although this method has been proven to be ineffective for many largely overlapping cases, it inspired us to train a deep convolutional neural network (DNN) to infer each individual nucleus distance map directly. Unlike a distance transform from the fused segmentation contour, a DNN could utilise the image texture information to recognise the nucleus borders in the overlapping region and build distinct "dams" between overlapping nuclei. In this study, we propose a two stage nuclei segmentation algorithm, where we first train an FCN to separate the nuclei from the background and then train a second FCN to generate a distance map of individual nuclei to separate them from each other.

Although developed independently, our approach has similarities with the approach in [9] which also uses DNN-based distance map inference. However, that method is based on a single regression network while our approach, when applied on a challenging dataset of various H&E-stained tissues, shows that having an additional segmentation FCN can provide overall improved segmentation performance. Evaluation using the aggregate Jaccard index (AJI), which is sensitive to both semantic and instance segmentation performance, shows that our approach yields excellent segmentation performance and outperforms several state-of-the-art algorithms.

2   Proposed Method

An overview of our proposed method is shown in Fig. 1. In the following, we describe each stage in detail.

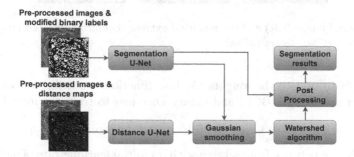

Fig. 1. Flowchart of the proposed algorithm. Only the training phase is depicted; the inference phase is similar except that no ground truth masks are fed to the model.

2.1   Pre-processing

Normalising H&E-stained images is a common approach to address staining variability. In our approach, we choose a reference image from the training data and then normalise all other images to match the staining separation vectors based on Macenko *et al.*'s method [7]. To identify an appropriate reference image, we analyse the histograms of all images. For this, we first convert the RGB images to grayscale using the standard $Y = 0.299R + 0.587G + 0.114B$ transformation where R, G and B are the red, green and blue channels of the raw image and Y is the resulting grayscale image. Then, from the grayscale images, an image whose histograms of nuclei and background areas are most different is chosen as the reference image.

Moreover, we apply colour augmentation in the training phase as suggested in [1]. Figure 2 shows an example of the extreme cases of colour augmentation for a sample training image. Besides colour augmentation, we also apply a standard augmentation scheme that performs random rotations (0, 90, 180 and 270 degrees) and random horizontal or vertical flipping. Finally, the input images are resized to 1024×1024 while intensity values are normalised to the $[0; 1]$ range.

2.2   U-Net Models

We use two deep models based on the popular U-Net architecture [10]. In the first, a standard U-Net model (referred to as segmentation U-Net in Fig. 1) is trained from scratch with four max pooling layers in the extracting path and four transpose convolutional layers in the expanding path. We use the Adam

Fig. 2. Original image (left) and the resulting extreme colour augmented images (middle and right). (Color figure online)

optimiser [5] to update the weights. As loss function, we utilise a combination of binary cross-entropy (BCE) and binary Dice loss to train the model as

$$Loss_{total} = 0.5Loss_{BCE} + Loss_{Dice}. \qquad (1)$$

We train the network from scratch with an initial learning rate of 0.001 which is dropped by a factor of 0.4 after every 80 epochs. We train the model for 240 epochs with a batch size of 2 to fit in GPU memory.

In order to obtain better instance segmentation results, we modify the provided ground-truth nuclei masks in the training phase. First, we binarise the provided ground truth. Then, we remove all touching borders using a simple image subtraction for all overlapping areas in the masks. Finally, we apply a morphological erosion operation on the masks to obtain a distinction between objects. An example of this procedure is shown in Fig. 3 for a cropped training sample. Although this modification helps the network to distinguish some touching nuclei, it does not perform well enough for more challenging cases.

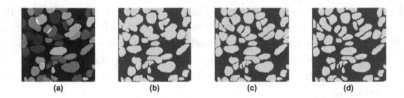

Fig. 3. Modification of ground truth (GT): (a) original GT, (b) binarised GT, (c) border removed GT, and (d) eroded GT.

Therefore, in analogy to [9], we train another U-Net model (referred to as distance U-Net in Fig. 1) based on the distance map of the provided ground truth to identify each nucleus. The structure of this network is similar to the standard segmentation U-Net model, but in this stage we train the model only for 120 epochs while the learning rate was dropped at the 60-th epoch. We use a mean squared error loss function since we try to solve a regression task in this phase.

Unlike [9], where detection and fusion of local maxima are controlled by a manually set threshold, our proposed method uses the results from both stages (segmentation U-Net results and predicted distance maps) to form the final instance segmentation masks in an automatic way. In order to obtain smoother distance maps and prevent false local maxima detection, we apply a Gaussian smoothing filter on the predicted distance maps. We hypothesise that the smoothing factor depends on the nucleus sizes in the image (i.e., applying a filter with a larger kernel for images with bigger average nucleus size). To have an estimate of the average nucleus size, we use the results from the segmentation U-Net from the first phase.

After applying the filter, we find the local maxima from the distance maps and use them as seed points for a marker-controlled watershed algorithm [11]. All these steps are performed automatically and thus we avoid the use of any manual rule to separate touching objects and perform training in an end-to-end manner.

2.3   Post-processing

We use the results of the segmentation U-Net as a mask on the derived distance map of the second U-Net to classify all background pixels as indicated in Fig. 1.

We also apply two other simple post-processing steps to improve the final segmentation results. First, we remove very small objects (<20 pixels) from the segmentation mask and, second, we fill holes in the detected objects to obtain uniformly segmented nuclei.

3   Experimental Results

We utilised the Keras framework[1] for algorithm development using a standard workstation with an Intel Core i5-6600k 3.50 GHz CPU, a single NVIDIA GTX 1070 with 8 GB memory and 16 GB of installed RAM. With this setup, the first and second training stages took around 10 and 5 h, respectively. The number of trainable parameters for the first and the second stage of the algorithm were identical at 1,941,105 for each stage.

For evaluation, we used a publicly available dataset [6] which includes 30 images of H&E-stained sections of 7 different organs (breast, liver, kidney, prostate, bladder, colon and stomach samples) obtained in 18 different hospitals, and contains about 22,000 manually annotated nuclei.

In order to evaluate the generalisation ability of the model and compare our method with three state-of-the-art algorithms [6,9,10], we split the data into training and test sets in the exact same manner as described in [6,9]. We used a subset of images from 4 organs (breast, liver, kidney and prostate) in the training phase, while the remaining images (i.e., those from bladder, colon and stomach samples and remaining images from the first 4 organs) were used for testing. No other external images were used for training.

We used the aggregate Jaccard index (AJI) suggested by [6] as our main evaluation index since it is sensitive to both semantic segmentation and instance

---

[1] https://keras.io/.

segmentation performance. In addition, we also report our results based on the average Dice score and the F1-score. While the average Dice score shows the general performance of the algorithm for semantic segmentation, the F1-score is sensitive to the object level error and thus quantifies the ability to correctly separate touching objects. However, as described in [6], AJI is a more reliable evaluation index as it is sensitive to pixel level and object level errors at the same time.

Table 1 shows the obtained quantitative results of our proposed method for all test images as well as comparative results from [6, 9, 10].

Table 1. Experimental results for all test images. For each image, we give the results, in terms of average Dice score, F1-score and AJI, for the approach from [10] but using the modified ground truth (denoted U-Net), the approach from [6] (denoted CNN3), the deep regression model from [9] (denoted DR), and our proposed algorithm. In addition, we list the average results over the test images for organs seen in the training phase (i.e., breast, liver, kidney, and prostate) and unseen in the training phase (i.e., bladder, colon, and stomach) as well as average results over all 14 test images. In each line, the best result is bolded.

organ	image	average Dice score (%)				F1-score (%)				AJI (%)			
		U-Net	CNN3	DR	Proposed	U-Net	CNN3	DR	Proposed	U-Net	CNN3	DR	Proposed
Breast	Image 1	**83.33**	68.85	N/A	83.30	82.37	74.78	77.61	**84.02**	57.57	49.74	53.34	**60.08**
	Image 2	76.24	74.76	N/A	**76.27**	69.34	**91.49**	83.80	76.46	41.34	57.96	**58.84**	52.17
Liver	Image 1	77.62	67.26	N/A	**77.63**	69.27	**85.68**	78.77	75.98	47.17	51.75	**54.46**	52.41
	Image 2	**70.58**	70.36	N/A	70.51	80.31	**94.09**	66.84	82.77	46.72	**51.48**	44.32	47.37
Kidney	Image 1	**74.88**	66.06	N/A	74.85	80.70	78.69	78.05	**83.93**	52.63	47.92	**56.48**	54.36
	Image 2	**80.68**	78.37	N/A	80.47	85.76	71.32	76.06	**86.69**	58.74	**66.72**	54.20	60.73
Prostate	Image 1	80.63	**83.06**	N/A	80.78	80.63	**87.17**	80.30	85.04	30.04	49.14	**62.73**	62.27
	Image 2	**80.43**	75.37	N/A	80.40	79.39	74.52	79.03	**87.91**	47.97	37.61	62.94	**64.05**
average (seen test organs)		**78.05**	73.01	N/A	78.03	78.47	82.21	77.56	**82.85**	47.77	51.54	55.91	**56.68**
Bladder	Image 1	84.94	**93.12**	N/A	84.79	78.11	81.84	**86.23**	79.93	59.42	54.65	**64.57**	61.02
	Image 2	75.47	63.04	N/A	**75.62**	67.17	75.06	**77.68**	72.05	44.67	49.68	**54.67**	53.07
Colon	Image 1	75.99	**76.79**	N/A	75.60	68.64	71.36	72.12	**73.68**	40.41	**48.91**	42.40	46.86
	Image 2	**79.02**	71.18	N/A	78.99	77.47	77.46	75.90	**79.68**	53.53	**56.92**	44.84	50.95
Stomach	Image 1	86.06	**89.13**	N/A	85.82	80.07	**97.81**	85.47	88.52	54.31	45.38	64.08	**64.83**
	Image 2	85.63	**89.82**	N/A	85.40	83.53	**96.09**	85.20	89.71	56.90	43.78	65.50	**66.06**
averagel (unseen test organs)		**81.18**	80.43	N/A	81.04	75.83	**83.27**	80.05	80.60	51.54	49.89	56.01	**57.13**
average (all test organs)		**79.39**	76.23	N/A	79.32	75.93	**82.67**	78.63	81.88	49.39	50.83	55.98	**56.87**

From Table 1, it is evident that for all 14 cases the second stage of the algorithm improves the ability of the model to separate touching nuclei (as evidenced by improved F1-score and AJI) compared to the stand-alone U-Net, while it does not have a significant effect on the overall semantic segmentation performance (expressed by the average Dice score).

Compared to the other approaches, on average our algorithm is shown to be superior in terms of overall AJI while being roughly equivalent in terms of average Dice score and F1-score. Moreover, the overall generalisation ability of the proposed method for images from previously unseen organs is better compared to the other methods in terms of AJI, while interestingly better results are obtained on images from unseen organs compared to (unseen) images from organs that formed the training dataset.

By running additional experiments to investigate the effect of ground truth modification on the segmentation U-Net results, we noted a significant improvement of the overall AJI from 44.41% to 49.39% (due to space restrictions, we only report these improved results in Table 1) which confirms the importance of this step. It is worth noting that the kernel size of the Gaussian filter in the second stage of our algorithm is determined by the results of the first stage U-Net and hence we aimed to have acceptable instance segmentation performance even in the first stage. Estimating nucleus size can be further improved by calculating it from the final instance segmentation results instead of the first stage U-Net results in an iterative manner which can be addressed in future work.

Figure 4 shows example results of the single raw U-Net model as well as the results from our proposed method for some of the selected test images and confirms that our obtained segmentations are close to the defined ground truth and that the proposed method performs significantly better than a single segmentation U-Net.

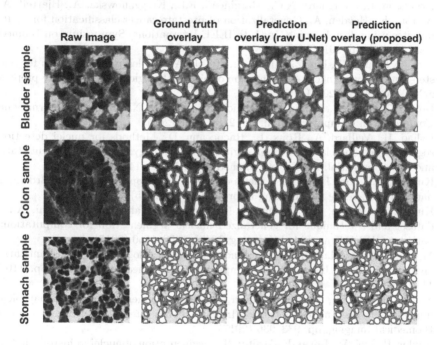

Fig. 4. Examples of segmentation results.

We also entered our approach in the MICCAI 2018 Multi-Organ Nuclei Segmentation Challenge[2] which used the same 30 H&E-stained images mentioned above as training data while evaluating competing algorithms on a further 14 test images whose type and ground truth were available only to the contest

---

[2] https://monuseg.grand-challenge.org/.

organisers. In total, 36 teams participated in the challenge and achieved average AJI results ranging from 13.01% to 69.07% on the test data. Our proposed method ranked 10-th with a very competitive average AJI of 65.74%.

4   Conclusions

In this paper, we have proposed a fully automatic approach for nuclei segmentation for multi-organ H&E stained microscopic images in two sequential steps based on U-Net models. The obtained segmentation results on a challenging dataset containing images from different organs are shown to be very competitive and outperform several state-of-the-art algorithms.

References

1. Arvidsson, I., Overgaard, N.C., Marginean, F.E., Krzyzanowska, A., Bjartell, A., Åström, K., Heyden, A.: Generalization of prostate cancer classification for multiple sites using deep learning. In: 15th IEEE International Symposium on Biomedical Imaging, pp. 191–194 (2018)
2. Cui, Y., Zhang, G., Liu, Z., Xiong, Z., Hu, J.: A deep learning algorithm for one-step contour aware nuclei segmentation of histopathological images. arXiv preprint arXiv:1803.02786 (2018)
3. He, K., Gkioxari, G., Dollár, P., Girshick, R.: Mask R-CNN. In: IEEE International Conference on Computer Vision, pp. 2980–2988 (2017)
4. Irshad, H., Veillard, A., Roux, L., Racoceanu, D.: Methods for nuclei detection, segmentation, and classification in digital histopathology: a review - current status and future potential. IEEE Rev. Biomed. Eng. 7, 97–114 (2014)
5. Kingma, D.P., Ba, J.: Adam: a method for stochastic optimization. In: 3rd International Conference for Learning Representations (2015)
6. Kumar, N., Verma, R., Sharma, S., Bhargava, S., Vahadane, A., Sethi, A.: A dataset and a technique for generalized nuclear segmentation for computational pathology. IEEE Trans. Med. Imaging 36(7), 1550–1560 (2017)
7. Macenko, M., et al.: A method for normalizing histology slides for quantitative analysis. In: IEEE International Symposium on Biomedical Imaging, pp. 1107–1110 (2009)
8. Naylor, P., Laé, M., Reyal, F., Walter, T.: Nuclei segmentation in histopathology images using deep neural networks. In: 14th IEEE International Symposium on Biomedical Imaging, pp. 933–936 (2017)
9. Naylor, P., Laé, M., Reyal, F., Walter, T.: Segmentation of nuclei in histopathology images by deep regression of the distance map. IEEE Trans. Med. Imaging 38, 448–459 (2018)
10. Ronneberger, O., Fischer, P., Brox, T.: U-Net: convolutional networks for biomedical image segmentation. In: Navab, N., Hornegger, J., Wells, W.M., Frangi, A.F. (eds.) MICCAI 2015. LNCS, vol. 9351, pp. 234–241. Springer, Cham (2015). https://doi.org/10.1007/978-3-319-24574-4_28
11. Yang, X., Li, H., Zhou, X.: Nuclei segmentation using marker-controlled watershed, tracking using mean-shift, and Kalman filter in time-lapse microscopy. IEEE Trans. Circuits Syst. I: Regul. Pap. 53(11), 2405–2414 (2006)

Automatic Detection of Tumor Buds in Pan-Cytokeratin Stained Colorectal Cancer Sections by a Hybrid Image Analysis Approach

Matthias Bergler[1]($\boxtimes$), Michaela Benz[1], David Rauber[1], David Hartmann[1], Malte Kötter[2], Markus Eckstein[2], Regine Schneider-Stock[2], Arndt Hartmann[2], Susanne Merkel[3], Volker Bruns[1], Thomas Wittenberg[1], and Carol Geppert[2]

[1] Fraunhofer Institute for Integrated Circuits IIS, Erlangen, Germany
matthias.bergler@iis.fraunhofer.de
[2] Institute of Pathology, University Hospital Erlangen, FAU Erlangen-Nuremberg, Erlangen, Germany
[3] Department of Surgery, University Hospital Erlangen, FAU Erlangen-Nuremberg, Erlangen, Germany

Abstract. This contribution introduces a novel approach to the automatic detection of tumor buds in a digitalized pan-cytokeratin stained colorectal cancer slide. Tumor buds are representing an invasive pattern and are frequently investigated as a new diagnostic factor for measuring the aggressiveness of colorectal cancer. However, counting the number of buds under the microscope in a high power field by eyeballing is a strenuous, lengthy and error-prone task, whereas an automated solution could save time for the pathologists and enhance reproducibility. We propose a new hybrid method that consists of two steps. First possible tumor bud candidates are detected using a chain of classical image processing methods. Afterwards a convolutional deep neural network is applied to filter and reduce the number of false positive candidates detected in the first step. By comparing the automatically detected buds with a gold standard created by manual annotations, we gain a score of 0.977 for precision and 0.934 for sensitivity in our test sets on over 8.000 tumor buds.

Keywords: Convolutional Neural Network (CNN) ·
Medical image analysis · Tumor budding · Deep learning

1 Introduction

In pathology, new markers for assessment of the prognosis in patients with cancer are needed. Frequently specific methods like immunohistochemistry and molecular pathology are used in addition to conventional histopathology. These new methods are crucial for the stratification of cancer patients and the selection of specific therapies. The extent and prognosis of the disease is today estimated

© Springer Nature Switzerland AG 2019
C. C. Reyes-Aldasoro et al. (Eds.): ECDP 2019, LNCS 11435, pp. 83–90, 2019.
https://doi.org/10.1007/978-3-030-23937-4_10

by the TNM-Classification, where "T" stands for the size and depth of invasion of the tumor, "N" for the number of affected lymph nodes and "M" for the presence of distant metastases [14]. In addition, the differentiation of the tumor is given according to tumor morphology and is graded within a range from G1 to G3, where G1 represents a high and G3 a low similarity to healthy tissue [14]. The detection of tumor buds is a new approach which can serve as an independent prognostic factor. Tumor budding is currently investigated in many tumor types and could be an additional marker for tumor differentiation and poor prognosis [8].

1.1   Tumor Budding as an Independent Adverse Prognostic Factor

Tumor buds are defined as single or isolated cells or as a cell cluster with up to four cells located at the invasion front of a tumor. The invasion front describes the area where the tumor cells invade into the surrounding healthy tissue. With the aim of counting the number of buds in the area of highest tumor bud density, the pathologist first searches for the "hotspots". For this method one needs to estimate the tumor buds in ten different high power fields with a size of $0.785\,\text{mm}^2$ along the invasion front, and for further analysis, the field of view with the estimated highest count of tumor buds per mm is used for a precise counting. The selected field of view is now classified as "low", "intermediate" or "high" budding. It is recommended to state the exact number of tumor buds to avoid the loss of crucial information [8]. The fewer tumor buds are present, the better is the survival rate for the patient. The exact criteria and scoring methodology for a tumor budding in colorectal cancer have been agreed upon during the International Tumor Budding Consensus Conference (ITBCC) 2016 [8]. Additionally a German guideline has been published this year for colorectal cancer treatment [11]. The criteria for counting the cell cluster as a tumor bud are as follows:

- the cluster is composed of one up to four cells
- optionally, cells in the cluster are allowed to touch each other
- cells are not allowed to touch the main mass of the tumor
- cells are not counted, if the tissue in the slide is fractured or overlapping

Manual counting of tumor buds in multiple fields is time-consuming and is prone to errors. In the clinical routine, a pathologist would examine the H&E stained biopsy and count the tumor buds in the hotspots as suggested in [8].

1.2   State of the Art

Nowadays computer systems have sufficient power to support pathologists for routine tasks, especially in repetitive tasks that involve counting cells. Specifically for quantifying tumor budding a computer assisted solution is presented by Jepsen et al. in [6]. Jepsen first eliminates the background and objects at a 5x magnification that would be too large to be tumor buds and defines a new region of interest (ROI) for further processing. In the second step the previously calculated ROI in a 20x magnification is evaluated in order to segment possible tumor buds. They are then matched against a series of conditions in order to filter out non-buds: (1) the bud candidate must have a suitable size, (2) it must contain nuclei, (3) it must not be located in debris, (4) it must not contain white pixel clusters and finally (5) it must have sufficiently sharp cell borders [6]. In a third step they process the detected tumor buds further by calculating a heat map to locate the hotspot in a whole slide. In contrast to Jepsen et al. [6] we use a two-step hybrid approach by first detecting possible objects with a similar chain of image processing steps and then distinguishing true from false buds by classifying them with a convolutional neural network (CNN). The CNN can be regarded as a last filter step, which reduces the problem with the high count of false positives significantly as seen in [6]. Deep learning has been shown to be a generically applicable solution for medical image analysis tasks as seen in [4] for example when detecting cerebral micro bleeds [3] or for classification of nuclei in histopathological images [12]. Therefore, we have chosen this approach here as well to reduce the number of false tumor buds and create an automatic solution for the tumor bud and later the hotspot detection. Another difference is that Jepsen et al. detect tumor buds solely at the invasion front of the tumor. We instead detect also intra-tumoral buds located in the malignant tissue.

2   Material

Pan-cytokeratin stained colon sections have been prepared by pathologists of the Institute of Pathology at the University Hospital Erlangen, FAU Erlangen-Nuremberg. The slides were scanned with the two 3DHISTECH scanners, Pan-noramic P250 and Pannoramic Scan, with a 40x Plan-Achromat objective by Zeiss and the VCC-FC60FR19CL CIS camera. The resolution of the digitized slides is $0.194 \times 0.194\,\mu m^2$ per pixel. Tumor buds have been annotated manually in 87 slides (Fig. 1). Additionally, so called unsure objects have been annotated which could not be clearly classified as tumor buds and thus have been discarded in the development and evaluation of the approach. Finally, the slides were split up into disjoint databases for training (51 slides, 27980 tumor buds), validation (18 slides, 4362 tumor buds) and testing (18 slides, 8169 tumor buds) of the approach. The test database was never seen by the CNN during the training process.

3   Methods

Our approach consists of two steps, the detection of possible tumor bud candidates and the reduction of false positives. We applied our method in user selected field of views on the whole slides which covered almost all areas containing expert annotations (Fig. 2) to reduce processing time. Therefore, the number of field of views varies from 3 to 36 depending on the expert annotations. Within these field of views, possible tumor bud candidates are detected by the classical image

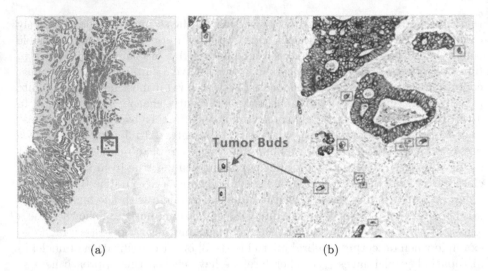

Fig. 1. Expert annotated pan-cytokeratin slide, with a size of $0.194 \times 0.194\,\mu m^2$ per pixel, containing the tumor area and the invasive margin. Figure (a) shows the whole slide and (b) a zoomed in region, marked by the red box, showing annotated tumor buds. (Color figure online)

processing steps described in Subsect. 3.1. Afterwards, detected candidates are compared to the expert annotations and are accordingly labeled as true positive tumor buds or false positive ones. Moreover, the number of missed tumor bud annotations (false positive) is counted. In the next step a convolutional neural network was trained with the true positive and false positive candidates in order to learn how to tell true from false tumor buds. The applied network and training procedure is described in Subsect. 3.2.

3.1 Detection of Candidates for Tumor Budding

For the detection of candidates classical methods like thresholding, filtering and morphological operations are applied. As a result of the pan-cytokeratin staining, the cell membrane of tumor cells is brown and the cores are blue (because of a counter staining with hematoxylin). Therefore, the depicted color of the stains plays an important role for the detection of the tumor buds. We tested different color spaces such as RGB, Lab and HLS to derive a grey value image with the best contrast between cell core and membrane and found the blue channel of the RGB color space to be the best choice. Afterwards, a Median-filter is applied to smoothen the image by reducing noise. The image is then binarized with the Otsu thresholding algorithm [9]. A crucial criterion for being a tumor bud is the number of connected tumor cells. A tumor bud consists of four or less tumor cells [8]. However, tumor cell clusters and tumor buds are three-dimensional objects and only a thin section is prepared on the glass slides. Therefore the decision whether two objects (tumor cells or tumor cell clusters) are connected or not is

Fig. 2. The blue boxes show manually set field of views based on expert annotations. This reduces processing time on whole-slide-images on a 40x magnification, because we dont need to iterate over the whole slide and detect tumor buds just in the selected regions. Automatic detection on complete WSIs is also possible. (Color figure online)

not trivial and in fact cannot be answered with absolute certainty due to the fact that only a two-dimensional slice is available. So we regard two cells or cell clusters as connected, if the distance between them is smaller than the mean diameter of a tumor cell. This knowledge-driven approach has been implemented by morphological operations. First, a binary erosion removes small artifacts, such as small staining leftovers. A binary dilation afterwards increases the size of the remaining objects to their original size plus an additional distance threshold. Thus, small gaps between unconnected cells that are probably located in the same cluster are filled. The second erosion reduces the tumor buds to their original size and cells in the same cluster stay connected. The morphological approach is based on two parameters, the size of the first erosion mask defining the minimal size of a single tumor bud and the dilation defining the distances between tumor buds. The size of the second erosion's filter mask is given by the difference of the first erosion and the dilation corresponding to the distance threshold that determines whether two cells are connected. The output generates possible candidates containing a lot of false positive candidates due to staining artifacts or larger groups of cell clusters. This results in a high sensitivity, but poor precision as seen in (Table 1). Thus, two simple filter steps are implemented to check the color and size of the detected objects.

3.2   Reduction of False Positives

In order to distinguish between "true positive" and "false positive" tumor bud candidates a convolutional neural network was trained and applied. We chose the AlexNet architecture [7] as it has already been successfully applied for the similar task of colonic polyp classification [10] and for the detection of malaria infected cells [2]. We retrained the weights on all convolutional and fully connected layers and used as initialization the pre-trained weights of the ImageNet dataset [1]. We trained the network on our testdataset as stated in Subsect. 2 with a pixelsize of 227×227 and a batchsize of 100 images per batch. As an input for the network we use the detected possible candidates from the first step and resize them to the input dimensions of 227×227 for the network. The labeling of the candidates as true positive or false positive was based on the manual expert annotations. When comparing the results from the ground truth with the algorithm based annotation (Fig. 3), the manual and automatic rectangular annotations were counted as a match, when the centers of their binarized masks are spaced no more than five pixels apart. This step is important for the comparison, because our algorithm produces the annotations based on the binary mask of the cells and therefore doesnt align with the expert annotations.

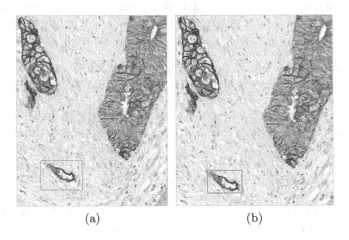

(a)   (b)

Fig. 3. Figure (a) shows the expert annotation and Fig. (b) our algorithm-detected candidate. It is seen that the two annotations do not align because the algorithm produces an annotation based on the pixel border of the binary mask. Therefore a additional step for the comparison is needed.

4   Results and Discussion

We evaluated the proposed hybrid approach for tumor bud detection separately for each step on a test dataset disjoint to the training and validation set in comparison to the manual expert annotation. Table 1 shows the result of the

Table 1. Detection results of possible tumor buds before applying a neuronal network listed as false negatives (FN), false positives (FP), true positives (TP) and the calculated precision and sensitivity based on the comparison with the annotated ground truth.

Data	FN	FP	TP	Precision	Sensitivity
Validation	144	58131	4218	0.068	0.967
Test	363	87304	7806	0.082	0.956

Table 2. Detection results on the test data set of tumor buds after applying a selection step using AlexNet.

Data	FN	FP	TP	Precision	Sensitivity
Validation	279	107	4083	0.974	0.936
Test	537	181	7632	0.977	0.934

first step and Table 2 the result after applying AlexNet. Therefore we need to compare the detected possible tumor buds with the annotated datasets in the 18 validation and test slides as seen in Table 2. It was shown that similar results were scored for the training and test dataset. In comparison to the results in Table 1 applying AlexNet yields a significantly improved precision while diminishing the sensitivity only very slightly. Potentially, more advanced neural networks such as Inception V3 by Google may improve the results further [13] and will be tested. We reduced the number of false positives from 87304 to 181 in the test dataset, with only a small decrease in the sensitivity. A direct comparison with [6] is not possible yet, because of different evaluation approaches. While Jepsen et al. evaluates their system based on the detected hotspots, we compare the detected tumor buds with the ground truth. In future experiments we want to reduce the number of missed tumor buds. As seen in Table 2 the number is still quite high (~7%). After finishing our experiments we will use the detected tumor buds on the slides to detect the hotspots in a automated approach and make a direct comparison with [6] based on the hotspots. We also want to test different neural networks for classification as well as an end to end approach based on so called Mask R-CNNs [5]. We are steadily increasing our databases and want to test our approach on the new datasets. Meanwhile, our database counts over 92.000 annotated tumor buds on 114 slides. Additionally, we want to alternate our algorithm to correspond with the newly published guideline in Germany [11].

References

1. Deng, J., Dong, W., Socher, R., Li, L.J., Li, K., Fei-Fei, L.: ImageNet: a large-scale hierarchical image database. In: 2009 IEEE Conference on Computer Vision and Pattern Recognition, CVPR 2009, pp. 248–255. IEEE (2009)

2. Dong, Y., et al.: Evaluations of deep convolutional neural networks for automatic identification of malaria infected cells. In: 2017 IEEE EMBS International Conference on Biomedical and Health Informatics (BHI), pp. 101–104. IEEE (2017)
3. Dou, Q., et al.: Automatic detection of cerebral microbleeds from mr images via 3D convolutional neural networks. IEEE Trans. Med. Imaging **35**(5), 1182–1195 (2016)
4. Greenspan, H., Van Ginneken, B., Summers, R.M.: Guest editorial deep learning in medical imaging: overview and future promise of an exciting new technique. IEEE Trans. Med. Imaging **35**(5), 1153–1159 (2016)
5. He, K., Gkioxari, G., Dollár, P., Girshick, R.B.: Mask R-CNN. CoRR abs/1703.06870 (2017). http://arxiv.org/abs/1703.06870
6. Jepsen, R.K., et al.: Digital image analysis of pan-cytokeratin stained tumor slides for evaluation of tumor budding in pT1/pT2 colorectal cancer: results of a feasibility study. Pathol. Res. Pract. **214**(9), 1273–1281 (2018). https://doi.org/10.1016/j.prp.2018.07.002. http://www.sciencedirect.com/science/article/pii/S0344033818304230
7. Krizhevsky, A., Sutskever, I., Hinton, G.E.: ImageNet classification with deep convolutional neural networks. In: Advances in Neural Information Processing Systems, pp. 1097–1105 (2012)
8. Lugli, A., et al.: Recommendations for reporting tumor budding in colorectal cancer based on the International Tumor Budding Consensus Conference (ITBCC) 2016. Mod. Pathol. **30**(9), 1299–1311 (2017). https://doi.org/10.1038/modpathol.2017.46
9. Otsu, N.: A threshold selection method from gray-level histograms. IEEE Trans. Syst. Man Cybern. **9**(1), 62–66 (1979). https://doi.org/10.1109/tsmc.1979.4310076
10. Ribeiro, E., Uhl, A., Wimmer, G., Häfner, M.: Exploring deep learning and transfer learning for colonic polyp classification. Comput. Math. Methods Med. **2016** (2016)
11. Schmiegel, W., Pox, C.P., et al.: S3-Leitlinie Kolorektales Karzinom. Arbeitsgemeinschaft der Wissenschaftlichen Medizinischen Fachgesellschaften e.V. (2019)
12. Sirinukunwattana, K., Raza, S.E.A., Tsang, Y.W., Snead, D.R., Cree, I.A., Rajpoot, N.M.: Locality sensitive deep learning for detection and classification of nuclei in routine colon cancer histology images. IEEE Trans. Med. Imaging **35**(5), 1196–1206 (2016)
13. Szegedy, C., Vanhoucke, V., Ioffe, S., Shlens, J., Wojna, Z.: Rethinking the inception architecture for computer vision. In: 2016 IEEE Conference on Computer Vision and Pattern Recognition (CVPR), June 2016. https://doi.org/10.1109/cvpr.2016.308
14. Wittekind, C.: TNM: Klassifikation maligner Tumoren, vol. 8. Wiley, New York (2017)

Improving Prostate Cancer Detection with Breast Histopathology Images

Umair Akhtar Hasan Khan[1], Carolin Stürenberg[2], Oguzhan Gencoglu[1]([✉]),
Kevin Sandeman[3], Timo Heikkinen[1], Antti Rannikko[4], and Tuomas Mirtti[2]

[1] Top Data Science Ltd., Helsinki, Finland
oguzhan.gencoglu@topdatascience.com
[2] Faculty of Medicine, Department of Pathology and Research Program
in Systemic Oncology, University of Helsinki, Helsinki, Finland
[3] Department of Laboratory Medicine, Department of Pathology,
Skåne University Hospital, Malmö, Sweden
[4] Helsinki University Hospital, Faculty of Medicine, Department of Urology
and Research Program in Systemic Oncology, University of Helsinki, Helsinki, Finland

Abstract. Deep neural networks have introduced significant advancements in the field of machine learning-based analysis of digital pathology images including prostate tissue images. With the help of transfer learning, classification and segmentation performance of neural network models have been further increased. However, due to the absence of large, extensively annotated, publicly available prostate histopathology datasets, several previous studies employ datasets from well-studied computer vision tasks such as ImageNet dataset. In this work, we propose a transfer learning scheme from breast histopathology images to improve prostate cancer detection performance. We validate our approach on annotated prostate whole slide images by using a publicly available breast histopathology dataset as pre-training. We show that the proposed cross-cancer approach outperforms transfer learning from ImageNet dataset.

Keywords: Prostate cancer · Convolutional neural networks · Computer aided diagnosis · Breast cancer · Transfer learning

1 Introduction

Prostate cancer (PCa) is the second most common solid malignant disease among males in Western world and it derives from the glands within the prostate [23]. The incidence of PCa is especially high in Northern America, Europe and most parts of Africa, and it is the second common cause of cancer-related deaths in western countries [4]. PCa is commonly found in older men over the age of 65 years, with a chance of 1 in 8 men diagnosed with the disease during their lifetime [23].

C. C. Reyes-Aldasoro et al. (Eds.): ECDP 2019, LNCS 11435, pp. 91–99, 2019.
https://doi.org/10.1007/978-3-030-23937-4_11

Histological examination of the surgical tissue and detection of cancer by a pathologist is still the gold standard in cancer diagnostics. PCa diagnostics is heavily time-consuming. Furthermore, it is based on subjective grading, i.e., there is considerable inter-pathologist variability in assessing the diagnosis. For instance, the study by Ozkan et al. reports that two pathologists disagreed on the presence of cancer in 31 out of 407 biopsy cores and the overall concordance of the assessed Gleason scores was only 51.7%, depicting the challenges in diagnosing PCa consistently [19]. Therefore, development of computer-aided decision support tools is crucial for saving time, increasing precision and enhancing standardisation in diagnostics for pathologists.

There has been substantial interest in developing digital image processing and machine learning-based methods for automatic analysis of pathology images in order to perform tissue classification and disease grading, as well as predicting disease outcome and enhancing precision medicine [15]. Specifically, recent advancements in machine learning research involving deep neural networks, i.e., deep learning, have successfully increased the performance of such analyses [9]. However, proposed deep learning models often require significant amount of annotated data in order to be successfully trained. As cohort sizes can be small and the annotation of histopathology images is very time consuming, a concept called *transfer learning*, i.e., training a neural network with an external dataset and then fine-tuning the model with the dataset at hand, may prove beneficial. Such an approach of fine-tuning a pre-trained model has been shown to outperform training the same neural network architecture from scratch in studies involving analysis of digital pathology images [13,16,17]. Transfer learning may also be beneficial for adapting to domains in which images are obtained with different microscopes or staining procedures.

In this work, we propose a cross-domain transfer learning approach, specifically from breast histopathology images to prostate histopathology images, in order to train a deep convolutional neural network (CNN) for the detection of cancerous regions in PCa whole slide images (WSIs). From the pathological point of view, breast cancer (BrCa) and PCa are both adenocarcinomas (glandular origin) and the most common cancers among the respective genders. The rationale for this approach is that the cellular composition of BrCa and PCa have more visual similarity than the images in conventional pre-training materials, such as ImageNet dataset [6], applied in earlier studies. Based on this hypothesis, we propose a cross-domain transfer learning scheme between the images of two types of cancers. We show that pre-training a neural network model on BrCa histopathology images and fine-tuning it with PCa histopathology images increases the performance compared to training the model from scratch. In addition, we show that this approach outperforms models pre-trained on ImageNet dataset which has been the standard dataset for transfer learning models in deep learning-based digital pathology analysis. The main focus of this work has not been to maximize detection performance through rigorous data augmentation, neural architecture search, hard negative mining, hyper-parameter optimization or model ensembling but rather to propose a cross-cancer transfer learning alternative to ImageNet dataset. To the best of our knowledge, this study is the first study to propose a cross-domain (breast tissue to prostate tissue) transfer learning scheme for deep learning based PCa diagnosis.

2   Related Work

There have been several studies utilising transfer learning, especially with CNNs, to detect, classify, segment cancerous regions or to predict the Gleason grade in PCa histopathology images [1,2,5,11,12,18,21]. A typical approach recurring in previous studies is to divide the image into smaller tiles/patches (overlapping or non-overlapping) and to perform binary or multi-class classification of the tiles. Reconstruction of tile-level or pixel-level probability map of a given class for the original image is similarly performed in a sliding window fashion using the inference results of the tiles. Tile dimensions (in pixels) as well as the dimensions that are fed into a CNN vary between studies, e.g., 250×250 [11], 400×400 downscaled to 224×224 [1], 512×512 downscaled to 256×256 and further cropped to 224×224 [21], 750×750 downscaled to 250×250 [2], 911×911 [18].

One common transfer learning approach is to use an architecture that has performed well in other tasks (e.g. object detection in natural images) and to train it from scratch. Such an approach has been utilized by different works [11, 18]. For Gleason grading, Nagpal et al. [18] employed an architecture that has been shown to reach significant performance on well-known ImageNet dataset [6], i.e., InceptionV3 [25] and the study by Isaksson et al. [11] proposes a U-net [20] based semantic segmentation of prostate tissue.

Another transfer learning method is to use a pre-trained model as a feature extractor and perform further classification with a separate classifier. This is achieved by extracting the representations out of the intermediate layers of a pre-trained network. This approach has been used to predict Gleason score by extracting features from different layers of the 22-layer OverFeat architecture [22] (pre-trained on ImageNet) and feeding the features into random forest and support vector machine classifiers [12].

Finally, the most prevalent way to perform transfer learning is to employ a pre-trained model and to fine-tune it with the data at hand. Several fine-tuning approaches can be utilised such as fine-tuning all the layers, freezing the initial neural network layers (usually the convolutional layers) and fine-tuning only the last few layers or sequential layer-wise fine-tuning [1,2,5,21]. Used architectures for this purpose include either original implementations or implementations with small modifications of the following: AlexNet [14] in [5], VGG [24] in [2,5], ResNet [7] in [1,2,5,21], InceptionV3 [25] in [2], MobileNet [8] in [2] and DenseNet [10] in [2].

Even though the domains are considered both visually and in nature very different (natural images vs. prostate tissue images), most of the transfer learning schemes use architectures or models trained on ImageNet dataset. This is due to the absence of publicly available, large-scale, extensively annotated PCa histopathology datasets. In addition, the high number of images (over 1.2 million images with 1000 classes) and availability of several CNN models pre-trained on it, renders ImageNet a prominent dataset for the basis of transfer learning.

The performance of the deep neural network models in the abovementioned studies varies depending on the overall task at hand, dataset used, evaluation setup (sampling, cross-validation, training/validation/test splitting etc.), whether data augmentation was used or not and whether an ensemble of several classifiers was used or not. Therefore, fair comparison between studies is a non-trivial task. Most frequently used performance metric for reporting tile-level classification is *area under the receiver operating characteristic curve* (AUC) [5].

3   Methods

3.1   Data

Here, we aim to utilize a well known image dataset ImageNet and a previously annotated BrCa dataset, Cancer Metastases in Lymph Nodes Challenge 2016 (CAMELYON16)[1], to improve cancer detection with CNNs in our PCa database. The dataset of 28 macro (2 in. × 3 in.) histological surgical specimen WSIs was prepared from 28 patients with clinically relevant PCa (Gleason score ≥ 6) who had undergone prostatectomy during the years 2014 or 2015 in the Helsinki University Hospital, Helsinki, Finland. The slides were stained with H&E staining in a clinical-grade laboratory (HUSLAB Laboratory Services) at the Helsinki University Hospital. The scanning of the WSIs was performed by Zeiss Axio Scan.Z1 at a resolution of $0.220\,\mu m \times 0.220\,\mu m$ per pixel. Cancerous loci were annotated with polygons using the open source Automated Slide Analysis Platform[2] (ASAP) software at $750\,\mu m$ magnification. Annotation of a single slide took 0.5 to 6 h depending on the slide, resulting in an average of 3 h per slide. An example WSI and corresponding annotations are shown in Fig. 1. Minimum, mean and maximum cancerous area percentages with respect to the image size are 0.7%, 7.4% and 29.1%, respectively. Minimum and maximum number of polygon annotations (corresponding to the cancerous area/region in an image) are 4 and 208, respectively.

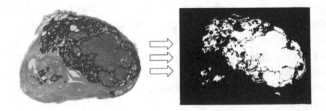

Fig. 1. An example of WSI with its annotations and corresponding binary mask.

---

[1] https://camelyon16.grand-challenge.org/.

[2] https://github.com/computationalpathologygroup/ASAP.

For pre-training, publicly available CAMELYON16 dataset was employed with 110 WSIs with nodal metastases verified by H&E staining [3]. In this dataset, WSIs have been acquired by 2 different scanners, i.e., Panoramic 250 Flash II - 3DHISTECH and NanoZoomer-XR Digital slide scanner C12000-01 - Hamamatsu Photonics with resolutions of 0.243 μm × 0.243 μm and 0.226 μm × 0.226 μm per pixel, respectively [3].

3.2 Classification and Transfer Learning

We divided 28 WSIs of PCa, each corresponding to a single patient, into training and held-out test sets with 22 and 6 images, respectively. Each image is then divided into non-overlapping tiles of 256 × 256 pixels to be fed into CNNs. From the training set, we randomly sampled 300,000 cancerous tiles and 300,000 non-cancerous tiles (white background is not sampled) in order to ensure a 50%–50% class balance for binary classification (in total 600,000 tiles). Randomness in the explained procedure is fixed for every experiment in order to ensure the exact same sampling and data splits.

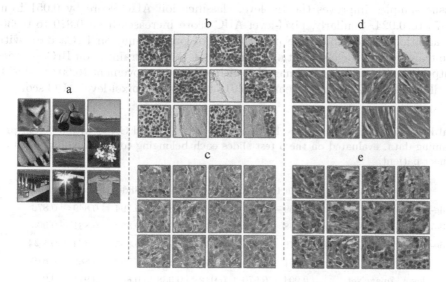

Fig. 2. Examples of data from a. ImageNet b. benign breast tissue c. cancerous breast tissue d. benign prostate tissue e. cancerous prostate tissue.

For classification, we used an InceptionV3 architecture [25], i.e., the convolutional backbone of the well-known architecture followed by 2 fully-connected layers with 512 and 128 units, respectively and a single unit output layer. Dense layers employed *ReLU* activation functions and a dropout rate of 0.8. Output layer employed a *sigmoid* activation. Loss function is chosen to be *binary crossentropy* and the optimizer is chosen to be *Adam* with a learning rate of 10^{-4}. Three different models were trained with the same architecture and same training data:

training from scratch (random weight initialization), fine-tuning on ImageNet pre-trained model, fine-tuning on BrCa pre-trained model. Only the convolutional layer weights were used from pre-trained models (fully-connected layers are still randomly initialized). Example data used during the training of the models can be seen in Fig. 2. For BrCa pre-training, 110 WSIs (no held-out test set) from CAME-LYON16 dataset were used with a total of 500,000 randomly sampled tiles (again 50%–50% target distribution). For all PCa and BrCa models, a random split of 80%–20% was employed for training and validation data, respectively. Each training was run for 50 epochs and the model weights reaching lowest validation error in that particular training were saved. Finally, models were evaluated on the 6 held-out test PCa WSIs and tile-level as well as pixel-level AUC scores were calculated.

4   Results and Discussion

Results of the experiments can be examined from Table 1. We show that pre-training the model on breast tissue samples and fine-tuning it with prostate tissue samples improves the tile-level classification AUC score by 0.051 from 0.873 to 0.924. Similarly, pixel-level AUC score increases from 0.879 to 0.936. In addition, we compare the performance of pre-training on BrCa data with pre-training on ImageNet data. We show that the pre-training on BrCa images outperform pre-training of ImageNet with a 2.3% improvement (0.903 to 0.924) in tile-level and 2.2% improvement (0.916 to 0.936) in pixel-level AUC score.

Table 1. Tile-level and pixel-level AUC scores of the trained CNNs with different pre-training data, evaluated on the 6 test slides each belonging to an individual prostate cancer patient.

	Pre-training	Slide 1	Slide 2	Slide 3	Slide 4	Slide 5	Slide 6	Overall
Tile-level	None	0.859	0.964	0.902	0.831	0.794	0.849	0.873
Tile-level	ImageNet	0.898	0.952	0.933	0.932	0.854	0.881	0.903
Tile-level	CAMELYON16	0.916	0.971	0.946	0.953	0.885	0.874	**0.924**
Pixel-level	None	0.861	0.973	0.911	0.835	0.792	0.882	0.879
Pixel-level	ImageNet	0.904	0.970	0.942	0.938	0.859	0.915	0.916
Pixel-level	CAMELYON16	0.920	0.979	0.955	0.958	0.890	0.912	**0.936**

Contributions of this work lie in the transfer learning paradigm which has been shown to be beneficial to the model performance in several studies involving digital pathology analysis with deep neural networks [13,16,17]. Due to the absence of a large, publicly available, extensively annotated prostate histology image dataset, transfer learning inside the same domain has not been possible so far. This led to frequent use of ImageNet dataset for this purpose [1,2,5,21]. Our results bolster the intuition behind this practice, i.e., first-layer representations learned by deep neural networks are not specific to a particular dataset but applicable to many even though the tasks are visually different. However, our study proposes an alternative to ImageNet pre-training by utilising a large dataset of breast WSIs. Our experiment results show evidence of enhanced knowledge transfer due to visual similarities of the two cancer domains which is lacking in natural images of objects, i.e., ImageNet. In addition, such cross-domain transfer learning may also improve the generalization ability of the models to different scanners, image resolutions and stainings.

As our methodology can be generalized to other cancer domains, future work includes extensive analysis of cross-domain pre-training from different cancer pathology images, with varying neural network architectures and training schemes. In addition, double pre-training scheme will be examined in which a model can be first trained on ImageNet (or on a large dataset of similar nature), followed by a fine-tuning with breast histopathology images and then finally further fine-tuned with the data at hand.

5 Conclusion

In this work we propose a cross-domain, deep convolutional neural network-based transfer learning scheme, specifically from breast to prostate histopathology images, to enhance prostate cancer detection performance. In addition, we compare the proposed breast histopathology pre-training with the well-known ImageNet dataset pre-training. Our results show that the model pre-trained on breast cancer images, further fine-tuned with prostate cancer images performs better than the model that is trained from scratch or pre-trained on ImageNet dataset. We believe our study serves as an advancement in the field of machine learning-based analysis of prostate cancer histopathology images by providing evidence for a transfer learning scheme between different cancer domains.

References

1. Arvaniti, E., Claassen, M.: Coupling weak and strong supervision for classification of prostate cancer histopathology images. arXiv preprint arXiv:1811.07013 (2018)
2. Arvaniti, E., et al.: Automated gleason grading of prostate cancer tissue microarrays via deep learning. bioRxiv p. 280024 (2018)
3. Bejnordi, B.E., et al.: Diagnostic assessment of deep learning algorithms for detection of lymph node metastases in women with breast cancer. JAMA 318(22), 2199–2210 (2017)
4. Bray, F., Ferlay, J., Soerjomataram, I., Siegel, R.L., Torre, L.A., Jemal, A.: Global cancer statistics 2018: GLOBOCAN estimates of incidence and mortality worldwide for 36 cancers in 185 countries. CA: A Cancer J. Clin. 68(6), 394–424 (2018)
5. Campanella, G., Silva, V.W.K., Fuchs, T.J.: Terabyte-scale deep multiple instance learning for classification and localization in pathology. arXiv preprint arXiv:1805.06983 (2018)
6. Deng, J., Dong, W., Socher, R., Li, L.J., Li, K., Fei-Fei, L.: ImageNet: a large-scale hierarchical image database. In: IEEE Conference on 2009 Computer Vision and Pattern Recognition, CVPR 2009, pp. 248–255. IEEE (2009)

7. He, K., Zhang, X., Ren, S., Sun, J.: Deep residual learning for image recognition. corr, vol. abs/1512.03385 (2015)
8. Howard, A.G., et al.: MobileNets: efficient convolutional neural networks for mobile vision applications. arXiv preprint arXiv:1704.04861 (2017)
9. Hu, Z., Tang, J., Wang, Z., Zhang, K., Zhang, L., Sun, Q.: Deep learning forimage-based cancer detection and diagnosis-a survey. Pattern Recogn. **83**, 134–149 (2018)
10. Huang, G., Liu, Z., Van Der Maaten, L., Weinberger, K.Q.: Densely connected convolutional networks. In: 2017 IEEE Conference on Computer Vision and Pattern Recognition (CVPR), pp. 2261–2269. IEEE (2017)
11. Isaksson, J., Arvidsson, I., Åaström, K., Heyden, A.: Semantic segmentation of microscopic images of H&E stained prostatic tissue using CNN. In: 2017 International Joint Conference on Neural Networks (IJCNN), pp. 1252–1256. IEEE (2017)
12. Källén, H., Molin, J., Heyden, A., Lundström, C., Åström, K.: Towards grading gleason score using generically trained deep convolutional neural networks. In: 2016 IEEE 13th International Symposium on Biomedical Imaging (ISBI), pp. 1163–1167. IEEE (2016)
13. Kieffer, B., Babaie, M., Kalra, S., Tizhoosh, H.R.: Convolutional neural networks for histopathology image classification: training vs. using pre-trained networks. In: 2017 Seventh International Conference on Image Processing Theory, Tools and Applications (IPTA), pp. 1–6. IEEE (2017)
14. Krizhevsky, A., Sutskever, I., Hinton, G.E.: ImageNet classification with deep convolutional neural networks. In: Advances in Neural Information Processing Systems, pp. 1097–1105 (2012)
15. Madabhushi, A., Lee, G.: Image analysis and machine learning in digital pathology: challenges and opportunities (2016)
16. Mehra, R., et al.: Breast cancer histology images classification: training from scratch or transfer learning? ICT Express **4**(4), 247–254 (2018)
17. Mormont, R., Geurts, P., Marée, R.: Comparison of deep transfer learning strategies for digital pathology. In: Proceedings of the IEEE Conference on Computer Vision and Pattern Recognition Workshops, pp. 2262–2271 (2018)
18. Nagpal, K., et al.: Development and validation of a deep learning algorithm for improving gleason scoring of prostate cancer. arXiv preprint arXiv:1811.06497 (2018)
19. Ozkan, T.A., Eruyar, A.T., Cebeci, O.O., Memik, O., Ozcan, L., Kuskonmaz, I.: Interobserver variability in gleason histological grading of prostate cancer. Scand. J. Urol. **50**(6), 420–424 (2016)
20. Ronneberger, O., Fischer, P., Brox, T.: U-Net: convolutional networks for biomedical image segmentation. In: Navab, N., Hornegger, J., Wells, W.M., Frangi, A.F. (eds.) MICCAI 2015. LNCS, vol. 9351, pp. 234–241. Springer, Cham (2015). https://doi.org/10.1007/978-3-319-24574-4_28
21. Schaumberg, A.J., Rubin, M.A., Fuchs, T.J.: H&E-stained whole slide image deep learning predicts SPOP mutation state in prostate cancer. BioRxiv p. 064279 (2018)
22. Sermanet, P., Eigen, D., Zhang, X., Mathieu, M., Fergus, R., LeCun, Y.: Overfeat: integrated recognition, localization and detection using convolutional networks. arXiv preprint arXiv:1312.6229 (2013)

23. Siegel, R.L., Miller, K.D., Jemal, A.: Cancer statistics, 2017. CA: A Cancer J. Clin. **67**(1), 7–30 (2017)
24. Simonyan, K., Zisserman, A.: Very deep convolutional networks for large-scale image recognition. arXiv preprint arXiv:1409.1556 (2014)
25. Szegedy, C., Vanhoucke, V., Ioffe, S., Shlens, J., Wojna, Z.: Rethinking the inception architecture for computer vision. In: Proceedings of the IEEE Conference on Computer Vision and Pattern Recognition, pp. 2818–2826 (2016)

Multi-tissue Partitioning for Whole Slide Images of Colorectal Cancer Histopathology Images with Deeptissue Net

Jun Xu[1], Chengfei Cai[1], Yangshu Zhou[2], Bo Yao[3], Geyang Xu[4],
Xiangxue Wang[5], Ke Zhao[3], Anant Madabhushi[5], Zaiyi Liu[3(✉)],
and Li Liang[2(✉)]

[1] Nanjing University of Information Science and Technology, Nanjing 210044, China
xujung@gmail.com
[2] Southern Medical University, Guanzhou 510515, China
[3] Guangdong Provincial People's Hospital, Guangzhou 510080, China
[4] Nanjing Foreign Language School, Xianlin Campus, Nanjing 210046, China
[5] Case Western Reserve University, Cleveland, OH 44106-7207, USA

Abstract. Tissue composition plays an essential role in diagnosis and prognosis of colorectal cancer (CRC). Studies have shown that the relative proportion of tissue composition on colorectal specimens is potentially prognostic of outcome in CRC patients. Some of the important tissue partitions include blood vessel, tumor epithelium, adipose tissue, mucosal glands, mucus, muscle, stroma, necrosis, immune cell, and background/other tissues. A challenge in accurately determining quantitative measurements of tissue composition however is in the need for automated tissue partitioning image analysis tools. Towards this goal, we present a Deeptissue Net, a deep learning strategy which involves integrating DenseNet with Focal Loss. In order to show the effectiveness of Deeptissue Net, the model was trained with 40 WSIs from one site and tested on 620 WSIs from two sites. 10 distinct tissue partitions are blood vessel, tumor epithelium, adipose tissue, mucosal glands, mucus, muscle, stroma, necrosis, immune cell, and background/other tissues. The ground truth for training and evaluating Deeptissue Net involved careful annotation of the different tissue compartments by expert pathologists. The Deeptissue net was trained with the tissue partitions delineated for the 10 classes on the 40 WSIs and subsequently evaluated on the remaining $N = 620$ datasets. By measuring with confusion matrices, the Deeptissue Net achieves the accuracy of 0.72, 0.84, and 0.88 in classifying mucus, stroma, and necrosis on the 2nd batch of Dataset 1; 0.85 and 0.96 in classifying mucus and muscle on Dataset 2, respectively, which significantly outperformed DenseNet and ResNet.

J. Xu, C. Cai, Y. Zhou and B. Yao—are the joint first authors.

© Springer Nature Switzerland AG 2019
C. C. Reyes-Aldasoro et al. (Eds.): ECDP 2019, LNCS 11435, pp. 100–108, 2019.
https://doi.org/10.1007/978-3-030-23937-4_12

1   Introduction

Colorectal cancer (CRC) is the third most commonly diagnosed and fourth major killer among all cancers for both sexes [3]. CRC accounts for 6.1% and 9.2% for cancer incidence and mortality, respectively [3]. Recently, there is growing evidence that the relative composition of different tissue partitions in histopatology specimens might be correlated with cancer prognosis and outcome. For instance the recent revision of the Gleason grading scheme [15] for prostate cancer involved explicitly accounting for the presence of cribiform patterns, presence of which has been associated with worse outcome in prostate cancer. In the context of CRC, as well, there is interest in exploring the association of tissue partitions and relative composition with disease outcome [17]. However, a critical prerequisite to evaluating the association between relative tissue composition ratios and outcome is the need for accurate estimation of the different tissue partitions on the histopathology images. Broadly speaking, previous approaches for achieving this goal have either comprised deep learning or hand-crafted feature based approaches. In [12], texture features were used for discriminating epithelium and stromal tissue compartments in tissue microarray (TMA) images. In [2], image features based on visual perception was leveraged for discriminating epithelium and stroma in colorectal cancer. [1] presented a cascade-learning approach to the segmentation of tumour epithelium in colorectal cancer on immunohistochemistry images. In [9], 8 different tissues of CRC were classified with texture and morphological features. In [8,18], deep convolutional neural network (CNN) based models were developed for epithelial and stromal tissues' classification. In [10], a deep VGG19 CNN was used to identify 9 different tissues and then stromal compartment was found to be an important prognostic factor for survival prediction on CRC patients. In [4,5] a CNN based model was presented for detecting presence of invasive tumor on whole slide images. In [14], CNN based model was used to predict cardiac outcome from endomyocardial biopsy.

ResNets [6] is one of most popular and efficient CNN model in object detection and image classification problem [16]. ResNets improved traditional CNNs by adding a skip-connection that bypasses the non-linear transformations with an identity function. The DenseNet further improved the information flow by introducing direct connections from any layer to all subsequent layers. The concatenate operation can utilize the features more effectively, thus enhancing feature propagation. It also reduces the parameters of the model and effectively solves the gradient disappearance problem of the deep network. In order to further improve the nonlinear transformation associated with ResNet and DenseNet. A new loss function called focal loss was presented in [11] to deal with class imbalance as part of the object detection problem. The new loss function adds a factor $(1 - p_t)^\gamma$ to the standard cross entropy criterion that has been used in conjunction with a number of CNN [6].

This paper presents a Deeptissue Net which integrates DenseNet Network with Focal Loss for 10 tissues classification from WSIs of CRC. These 10 types of tissue regions are blood vessel, epithelium, adipose tissue, mucosal glands, mucus, muscle, stroma, necrosis, immune cell, and background. The major contribution of the paper is to integrates DenseNet and Focal Loss for multiple tissue identification. The Focal Loss functions aim to enable DenseNet to converge easily and deal with the class imbalance problem during the model training.

2   Methodological Description

The Deeptissue Net presented in this paper integrates DenseNet [7] with Focal Loss [11]. The architecture of Deeptissue Net is shown in Fig. 1(b). The Net mainly comprises of 4 dense blocks and 3 transition layers, and uses Focal Loss as the output loss to optimize the Deeptissue Net. Equation (1) is DenseNet's nonlinear transformation formula [7].

$$x_l = H_l([x_0, x_1, ..., x_{l-1}]) \tag{1}$$

where l represents the l-th layer, x_{l-1} represents the output of l-th layer, and $H_l(\cdot)$ represents a nonlinear transformation of the l-th layer. The $[x_0, x_1, ..., x_{l-1}]$ indicates that the output feature map of the 0 to $(l-1)$-th layer is concatenate. The DenseNet used the traditional cross entropy loss at output layer which can be written as

$$\mathbf{CE}(p, y) = \mathbf{CE}(p_t) = -\log(p_t) \tag{2}$$

where $y \in \{\pm 1\}$ specifies the ground-truth class and $p \in [0, 1]$ is the model's estimated probability for the class with label $y = 1$

$$p_t = \begin{cases} -\log(p), & \text{if } y = 1 \\ -\log(1-p), & \text{otherwise} \end{cases} \tag{3}$$

The α-balanced variant of focal loss is defined as

$$\mathbf{FL}(p_t) = -\alpha_t (1 - p_t)^\gamma \log(p_t) \tag{4}$$

where $\alpha \in [0, 1]$ is a weighting factor for class 1 and $1 - \alpha$ for class -1. $\gamma \geq 0$ is tunable focusing parameter. The Focal loss function can resolve both sample class imbalances and similarities problem. As the new Deeptissue Net integrates DenseNet and Focal Loss, it can greatly improve the performance of original DenseNet for multi-tissue composition classification.

3   Experimental Design

3.1   Datasets Description

A total of 660 digitalized colorectal cancer specimens of WSI were gathered from two sites as illustrated in Table 2. The slides from Site #1 (S_1) were scanned with a NanoZoomer S210 and Site #2 (S_2) slides with an Aperio AT2, respectively. The first batch (B_1) of 100 slides from S_1 were digitalized at $20X$ ($0.5\,\mu$ per pixel) and the second batch (B_2) from S_1 and all slides from S_2 were digitalized at $40X$ ($0.25\,\mu$ per pixel). In this work, $20X$ magnification of all WSIs were used for training and validation. Color normalization were applied to reconcile the site-specific variation by different institutions and scanners [13].

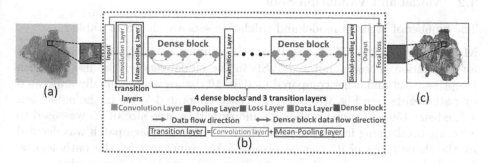

Fig. 1. The diagram illustrating the architecture of Deeptissue Net (b) and the flowchart for classifying each input 150×150 patch from a WSI (a) into one of 10 tissues maps in (c)

Table 1. The number of patches in the model and validation sets for B_1, B_2, S_2

Site		Model Set ♯	Validation Set♯	Total ♯	Scanner	Magnification
S_1	B_1	40	60	384	NanoZoomer Scanner S210	20X
	B_2	0	284			40X
S_2		0	276	276	Leica Aperio AT2	40X

Table 2. The illustration of overall datasets used in the paper

Tissues	Model Set (B_1)		Validation Set (B_1, B_2, S_2)		
	Training (B_1)	Validation (B_1)	B_1	B_2	S_2
Background	73992	10570	34828	16174	14726
Blood vessel	71203	10172	6250	7575	184
Tumor epithelium	70867	11206	27485	31089	1246
Adipose tissue	70867	10123	32178	23064	3018
Mucosal glands	75807	10829	3468	3519	198
Mucus	79197	11313	344	343	359
Muscle	83631	11947	12800	14853	4241
Stroma	78180	11168	10903	11138	403
Necrosis	73621	10517	4695	5874	293
Immune cell conglomers	70673	10096	1551	1372	179
All	755613	106941	134502	115001	24847

3.2   Model and Validation Sets

The number of WSIs in model and validation sets are shown in Table 2.

Model Set (B_1). 40 WSIs were randomly chosen from B_1 as the model sets for annotation. These annotated WSIs in the model sets will be used to train Deeptissue Net and other compared models. 10 tissues were manually annotated by pathologists (see Fig. 3(a, b, f)). For each annotated WSIs in the model set, a fixed-size 150 × 150 pixels sliding window with a step size of 75 was used to generate overlapping image patches. The label of each image patch was decided by the tissue types of its central pixel $(75, 75)$ annotated by the pathologists. Table 1 shows the number of image patches in the model set for training.

Validation Sets (B_1, B_2, and B_2). 10 WSIs were randomly chosen for annotation from the validation sets of B_1, B_2, and S_2, respectively. Each WSIs were sub-divided into non-overlapping 150 × 150 square window images using a sliding window. The procedure of generating sub-images for WSIs from validation sets is shown in Figs. 2(g, h).

The number of image patches in the validation sets of B_1, B_2, and S_2 are shown in Table 1.

3.3   Training, Validation and Performance Measures

The training and validation procedures of Deeptissue Net are shown in Fig. 2. During training, different data argument approaches such as data argumentation approaches such as centre cropping, rotations, affine transform, mirroring, color variation, and PCA Jattering were used. After training, each patch in the validation set was then classified by DeepTissue Net into one of more than 10 tissue categories (see Fig. 2(i–j)). We employed confusion matrix of classification accuracy on 10 different tissues to evaluate the performance of Deeptissue Net and compared models (see Fig. 2(j–k))

3.4   Experimental Results and Discussion

Experiment 1: Deeptissue Net vs. DenseNet: Our first experiment was to compare the performance between Deeptissue Net and DenseNet. The goal of this experiment was to show the contribution of focal loss to DenseNet. The DenseNet implementation was based on the codes provided in the paper [7]. The qualitative results of Deeptisse Net and compared models are shown in Fig. 3(c–e), respectively. The quantitative performance for 10 tissues' segmentation and classification for 10 WSIs on B_1, B_2, and S_2 are shown in Fig. 4, where the confusion matrices were employed to show the classification accuracy of each type of tissue and the error rate of the tissue being classified into others. Overall, the Deeptissue Net yields near perfect results in terms of segmentation accuracy of 10 tissues.

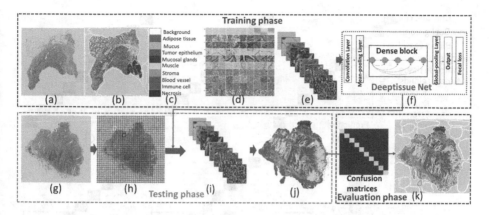

Fig. 2. The illustration of Deeptissue Net (f) for tissues classification on WSI (g). It includes training (a–f), testing (g–j), and evaluation (k) phases. 10 tissues (b–c) were annotated on WSI (a) and training image patches were generated from (b) for training Deeptissue Net (f). The original WSI (g) is sub-divided into non-overlapping patches and are then classified by trained Deeptissue net into 10 tissues (i–j). The performance is evaluated via confusion matrices by comparing with manual annotations (k)

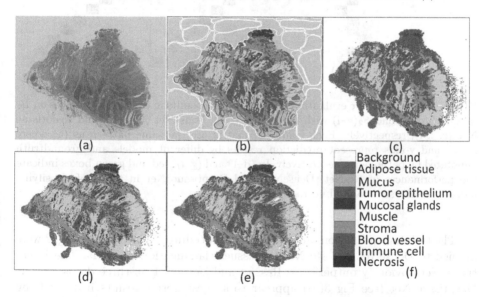

Fig. 3. The illustration of the qualitative segmentation results on 10 tissues from a WSI (a) in B_2 by DenseNet (c), ResNet 50 (d), and Deeptissue Net (e). (b) and (f) are pathologist's annotation and corresponding color maps of 10 tissues, respectively

Experiment 2: Deeptissue Net vs. ResNet: The second experiment was to compare the performance between Deeptissue Net and ResNet. The ResNet implementation was based on the codes provided in the paper [6].

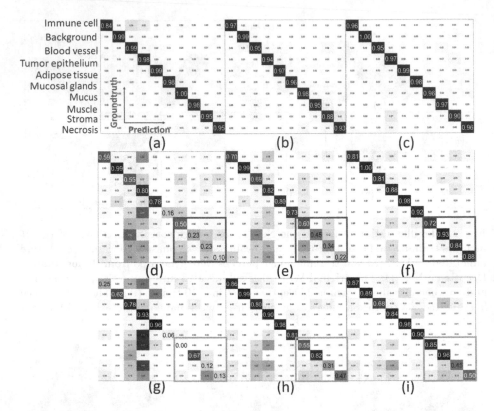

Fig. 4. The quantitative evaluation of segmentation results in confusion matrices on B_1 (a–c), B_2(d–f), and S_2(g–i) with ResNet (a, d, g), DenseNet (b, e, h), and Deeptissue Net (c, f, i), respectively. Each confusion matrix use the same pattern as (a) where x-axis and y-axis represent prediction results by different models and groundtruth annotated by pathologist, respectively. In (d–f) and (g–i), red and green boxes indicate the performances of ResNet, DenseNet, and Deeptissue Net in terms of classifying mucus, muscle, stroma, and necrosis, respectively

The training, validation, and evaluation procedures illustrated in Fig. 2 were applied to DenseNet and ResNet for tissues classification of WSIs. The Deeptissue Net obviously outperforms ResNet and DenseNet on three datasets. The Deeptissue Net (see Fig. 3(e)) apprear to suggest better results in identifying 10 tissue compartments as compared to DenseNet (see Fig. 3(c)) and ResNet (see Fig. 3(d)). DenseNet and ResNet appeared more unordered results. However, the mucus regions were not identified very well for three models, in turn leading to misclassification of many glands and cancerous regions. In addition, there are also many mucus in the gland, which will lead to partially wrong classification. For the WSIs in S_2, most blood vessels, muscle, and necrotic areas were wrongly classified across all three models. As compared with Deeptissue Net, ResNet achieves similar classification accuracy on B_1, but the immune cells is not as good as Deeptissue Net. ResNet achieves 84% for immune cells while

Deeptissue Net was 96%. However, ResNet gets poor performance on B_2 and S_2 as comparing with Deeptissue Net. By introducing focal loss, Deeptissue Net can better solve the problem of sample inhomogeneity and similarity as compared to DenseNet. In the ResNet deep network, the add operation is performed on the obtained feature map, and some features are not effectively utilized. Deeptissue Net shows better performance in terms of classifying mucus, muscle, stroma, and necrosis on three datasets. Finally, the performances of three models on S_2 were not as good as on S_1 since the training samples were chosen from a batch B_1 of S_1. The results also appear to suggest that different institutions and scanners can effect the performance of classification models.

4   Conclusion

In this paper we presented a new Deeptissue Net for automated partitioning of a total 10 different tissue compartments from colorectal slides from two different sites and scanners. We compared the Deeptissue Net with ResNet and DenseNet in identify 10 tissues. Deeptissue Net yielded the best performance across three datasets from two sites. Future work will entail survival prediction based off relative composition of the tissue compartments.

References

1. Abdelsamea, M.M., et al.: A cascade-learning approach for automated segmentation of tumour epithelium in colorectal cancer. ESA **118**, 539–552 (2019)
2. Bianconi, F., et al.: Discrimination between tumour epithelium and stroma via perception-based features. Neurocomputing **154**, 119–126 (2015)
3. Bray, F., et al.: Global cancer statistics 2018: GLOBOCAN estimates of incidence and mortality worldwide for 36 cancers in 185 countries. CA: Cancer J. Clin. **68**(6), 394–424 (2018)
4. Cruz-Roa, A., et al.: Accurate and reproducible invasive breast cancer detection in whole-slide images: a deep learning approach for quantifying tumor extent. NSR **7**, 46450 (2017)
5. Cruz-Roa, A., et al.: High-throughput adaptive sampling for whole-slide histopathology image analysis (HASHI) via convolutional neural networks: application to invasive breast cancer detection. PLOS One **13**(5), e0196828 (2018)
6. He, K., et al.: Deep residual learning for image recognition. In: CVPR (2016)
7. Huang, G., et al.: Densely connected convolutional networks. In: CVPR (2017)
8. Janowczyk, A., Madabhushi, A.: Deep learning for digital pathology image analysis: a comprehensive tutorial with selected use cases. JPI **7**(1), 29–29 (2016)
9. Kather, J.N., et al.: Multi-class texture analysis in colorectal cancer histology. NSR **6**, 27988 (2016)
10. Kather, J.N., et al.: Predicting survival from colorectal cancer histology slides using deep learning: a retrospective multicenter study. PLOS Med. **16**(1), e1002730 (2019)
11. Lin, T.Y., et al.: Focal loss for dense object detection. TPAMI (2018)
12. Linder, N., et al.: Identification of tumor epithelium and stroma in tissue microarrays using texture analysis. Diagn. Pathol. **7**(1), 22 (2012)

13. Magee, D., et al.: Colour normalisation in digital histopathology images (2009)
14. Nirschl, J.J., et al.: A deep-learning classifier identifies patients with clinical heart failure using whole-slide images of H&E tissue. PLOS One **13**(4), e0192726 (2018)
15. Pierorazio, P.M., Walsh, P.C., Partin, A.W., Epstein, J.I.: Prognostic Gleason grade grouping: data based on the modified Gleason scoring system. BJU Int. (2019)
16. Russakovsky, O., et al.: Imagenet large scale visual recognition challenge. IJCV **115**(3), 211–252 (2015)
17. Sirinukunwattana, K., et al.: Novel digital signatures of tissue phenotypes for predicting distant metastasis in colorectal cancer. NSR **8**(1), 13692 (2018). Sep
18. Xu, J., et al.: A deep convolutional neural network for segmenting and classifying epithelial and stromal regions in histopathological images. Neurocomputing **191**, 214–223 (2016)

Rota-Net: Rotation Equivariant Network for Simultaneous Gland and Lumen Segmentation in Colon Histology Images

Simon Graham[1,2]([✉]), David Epstein[3], and Nasir Rajpoot[2]

[1] Mathematics for Real-World Systems Centre for Doctoral Training,
University of Warwick, Coventry, UK
s.graham.1@warwick.ac.uk
[2] Department of Computer Science, University of Warwick, Coventry, UK
[3] Mathematics Institute, University of Warwick, Coventry, UK

Abstract. Analysis of the shape of glands and their lumen in digitised images of Haematoxylin & Eosin stained colon histology slides can provide insight into the degree of malignancy. Segmenting each glandular component is an essential prerequisite step for subsequent automatic morphological analysis. Current automated segmentation approaches typically do not take into account the inherent rotational symmetry within histology images. We incorporate this rotational symmetry into an encoder-decoder based network by utilising group equivariant convolutions, specifically using the symmetry group of rotations by multiples of 90°. Our rotation equivariant network splits into two separate branches after the final up-sampling operation, where the output of a given branch achieves either gland or lumen segmentation. In addition, at the output of the gland branch, we use a multi-class strategy to assist with the separation of touching instances. We show that our proposed approach achieves the state-of-the-art performance on the GlaS challenge dataset.

Keywords: Computational pathology · Gland segmentation · Rotation equivariant · Deep learning

1 Introduction

Almost 95% of all colorectal cancers are adenocarcinomas formed from glands in the epithelial tissue. An intestinal gland is made up of a single sheet of columnar epithelium, forming a tubular structure that extends from the inner surface of the colon into the underlying connective tissue. Therefore, a histological cross-section of colon tissue will result in glands displaying an elliptical appearance, with the lumen positioned at the centre. However, as glands become malignant, this typical glandular appearance is lost and therefore the morphology of the gland and the lumen can provide insight into the degree of malignancy [11]. As can be observed in Fig. 1, as the grade of cancer increases, typical glandular appearance is less evident.

© Springer Nature Switzerland AG 2019
C. C. Reyes-Aldasoro et al. (Eds.): ECDP 2019, LNCS 11435, pp. 109–116, 2019.
https://doi.org/10.1007/978-3-030-23937-4_13

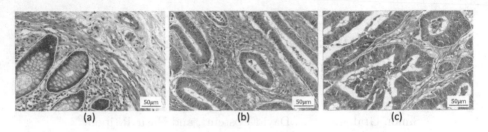

Fig. 1. Example image tiles. Yellow and green boundaries show the pathologist annotation of gland lumen respectively. (a), (b) and (c) show images with benign, moderately differentiated and poorly differentiated glands respectively. (Color figure online)

Assessment of glands is typically done via histological examination, most commonly with the Haematoxylin & Eosin (H&E) stain. However, manual examination of each tissue specimen is a time consuming and subjective procedure, due to the complex nature of the task. Instead, there has been a surge of interest in computational pathology, where techniques are developed to automatically and objectively analyse large-scale histopathology slides, that have been digitised via a scanning device. Within computational pathology, to understand how various components within a tissue sample contribute to disease, segmentation must be carried out as an initial step. In particular, gland and lumen segmentation enable subsequent morphological analysis, which can consequently assist the pathologist with diagnostic decision making.

Since achieving remarkable results in image recognition, deep learning has been widely used in the field of computational pathology and has notably been successfully applied to automated gland segmentation. For example, U-Net [8] achieved excellent performance by using an encoder-decoder network architecture and skip connections to incorporate low-level features at the output. A deep contour-aware network [1] was proposed by Chen *et al.* that incorporated the gland contour to assist the separation of instances and achieved the best performance in the gland segmentation (GlaS) challenge [9] at the MICCAI 2015 conference. Micro-Net, by Raza *et al.* [7], considers the input at multiple resolutions and generates the output using multi-resolution deconvolution filters. Xu *et al.* [13] implemented a multi-channel approach, that combines bounding box, contour and object predictions for a superior performance. Graham *et al.* proposed MILD-Net [4] that minimises the loss of information from max pooling by incorporating two additional custom residual units. Despite all recent methods achieving excellent performance, they fail to leverage the inherent rotational symmetry[1] within histology images.

Data augmentation is a well known technique for improving the performance of a network. For example, multiple rotated versions of an image can be introduced to

---

[1] Rigidly rotating a histopathology image neither increases nor decreases its information content. It is the information content, not the geometry, that is symmetric under rotation.

boost the network's ability to be invariant to these transformations. However, this requires the network to relearn essentially the same filter at various orientations and therefore leads to redundancy in the learned weights. Also, invariant features have no knowledge of the relative spatial configuration of the image components. Instead, it is desirable for a network to be *equivariant* to certain transformations, where changes in the input image will lead to a predictable transformation of the filter responses. There have been various methods that have recently been developed to achieve rotation equivariance [3,12], yet we choose to focus on the group equivariant convolutional neural networks (CNNs) [2], that have recently been applied to digital pathology images [10] for classification. In this work, we propose a dual-branch rotation equivariant fully convolutional neural network (FCN) that simultaneously segments the lumen and the gland within colon histology images. For the gland branch, we segment the gland and the gland contour to help determine where touching glands should be split.

2   Methods

2.1   Rotation Equivariance

Histopathology images are symmetric under rotation, yet typically CNNs do not leverage this prior knowledge and need to learn weights at different orientations. Furthermore, the filter responses of current CNNs do not transform in a predictable manner with the rotation of the input image, which does not allow us to recognise the relative spatial configuration of the image components deeper within the network. Instead, to fully exploit the rotation symmetry, we employ a framework based on the G-CNN [2] to make the network equivariant to additional symmetry groups, other than translations. Specifically, we incorporate the $p4$ group, that consists of all compositions of translations and rotations by 90° about any center of rotation in a square grid. To enable a given layer to exploit rotation symmetry, all preceding layers must preserve this symmetry. Therefore, it is necessary for the entire network to be rotation equivariant if we wish for deeper layers to be rotation equivariant. To ensure full equivariance, we use the G-convolution, as proposed in [2], and a rotation equivariant batch normalization, where we aggregate moments per group rather than spatial feature map. Other operations, including the rectified linear unit, spatial pooling and bilinear interpolation are all naturally equivariant under rotation.

Note, a conventional CNN will require significantly more kernels to represent the same *irregular* shape appearing in many different orientations than a rotation equivariant CNN. Therefore, it is expected that a rotation equivariant CNN will be particularly advantageous when segmenting malignant glands, where there is more variability in the different orientations.

2.2 G-Convolution

Within our framework, we use the G-convolution [2] on the $p4$ symmetry group, which contains translations and rotations by multiples of 90°. A G-convolution

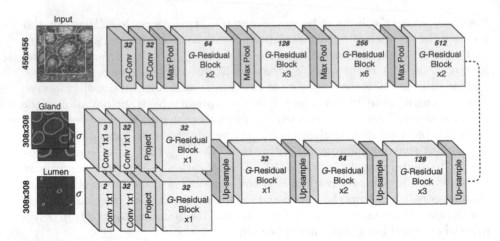

Fig. 2. Network architecture. The yellow box within the input denotes the part of the image considered at the output. The number at the top of each operation denotes the number of feature maps produced. Note, for group operations, this is the number per orientation of the kernel (4 orientations in the $p4$ group). σ is the softmax operation. (Color figure online)

is an extension of the standard convolution, but additionally rotates the kernel as it translates over the feature map. This action leads to a predictable transformation in the filter responses and enables the symmetry to be fully exploited throughout the network. In particular, a rotation of the input image results in a rotation and channel permutation at the output of the G-convolution. A further advantage of utilising the G-convolution is that weights do not need to be learned at different orientations, which allows the model to learn more discriminative features. Formally, in the first layer we define the $(\mathbb{Z}^2 \to G)$-convolution on image $f : \mathbb{Z}^2 \to \mathbb{R}^K$ as:

$$[f \star w](g) = \sum_{y \in \mathbb{Z}^2} \sum_{k=1}^{K} f_k(y) w_k(g^{-1}y) \tag{1}$$

where w_k denotes kernel k, with corresponding input channel f_k and g is a roto-translation. We can see from above that the operation is a function on the plane $\mathbb{Z}^2$, i.e the original RGB image, whereas the output is a function on the group G. Because of this, there are 4 feature maps generated per kernel, corresponding to the respective number of orientations in the $p4$ group. Similarly, we define the $(G \to G)$-convolution on feature maps $f : \mathbb{G} \to \mathbb{R}^K$ as:

$$[f \star w](g) = \sum_{h \in \mathbb{G}} \sum_{k=1}^{K} f_k(h) w_k(g^{-1}h) \tag{2}$$

We observe that the $(G \to G)$-convolution is computed across all orientation channels of the group G. As a consequence of a given feature map f_k being a function on the group G, its respective kernel w_k must also be a function on this group.

2.3   Rota-Net for Accurate Gland and Lumen Segmentation

The overall network architecture, as shown in Fig. 2, is based on the fully convolutional network [6] architecture, with residual blocks [5] for efficient gradient propagation. Because the sum of two rotation equivariant feature maps is also rotation equivariant, residual blocks are well suited within this network design. Within our framework, a G-residual block consists of multiple G-residual units, where each unit consists of two 3×3 G-convolutions and a shortcut connection. Similar to U-Net [8], we utilise skip connections with addition to incorporate low level features at the output of the network. In the same vein as the residual unit, this addition is rotation equivariant. All G-convolutions are followed by rotation equivariant batch normalisation, where moments are aggregated per group, and a ReLU. During feature extraction, we utilise max-pooling to decrease the spatial size of the feature maps by a factor of 16, which in turn increases the size of the receptive field. After feature extraction, we up-sample features using bilinear interpolation. The network splits after the final up-sampling operation, where each branch is subsequently devoted to either gland or lumen segmentation. Because feature maps within the network are functions on the $p4$ group, features need to be projected from $G \rightarrow \mathbb{Z}^2$ at the output of the network. We achieve this by defining the *projection layer* that takes the average over the 4 orientations. This operation is followed by two consecutive planar 1×1 convolution operations to obtain the final output.

3   Experimental Results

3.1   Dataset and Pre-processing

For our experiments, we used the Gland Segmentation (GlaS) challenge dataset[2], used as part of MICCAI 2015. Data was extracted from 16 H&E stained histological WSIs, scanned with a Zeiss MIRAX MIDI Slide Scanner with a pixel resolution of 0.465 μm/pixel.

After scanning, the WSIs were rescaled to 0.620 μm/pixel (equivalent to 20× objective magnification) and then a total of 165 image tiles were extracted. These 165 images consist of 85 training (37 benign and 48 malignant) and 80 test images (37 benign and 43 malignant). The test images are split into two test sets: Test A and Test B. Test A was released to the participants of the GlaS challenge one month before the submission deadline, whereas Test B was released on the final day of the challenge. Images are mostly of size 775×522 pixels and all training images have associated instance-level segmentation ground truth that precisely highlight the gland boundaries. In addition, two expert pathologists provide accurate lumen annotations for all glands within the GlaS dataset. The lumen

---

[2] https://warwick.ac.uk/fac/sci/dcs/research/tia/glascontest.

Table 1. Comparative results for gland segmentation.

Method	F_1 score		Object dice		Object hausdorff		Weighted
	Test A	Test B	Test A	Test B	Test A	Test B	Rank
Rota-Net	**0.920**	0.824	**0.919**	**0.849**	**40.99**	**95.72**	**3.5**
MILD-Net [4]	0.914	**0.844**	0.913	0.836	41.54	105.89	5.75
Xu et al. [13]	0.893	0.843	0.908	0.833	44.13	116.82	10.25
Micro-Net [7]	0.913	0.724	0.906	0.785	49.15	133.98	12.25
CUMedVision2 [1]	0.912	0.716	0.897	0.781	45.418	160.347	14
Freidburg2 [8]	0.870	0.695	0.876	0.786	57.09	148.47	17.25

annotations have been further refined since they were initially used in [4]. We set 20% of the training set aside for evaluating the performance of our model during training.

During training, we use an input patch size of 456×456 with an output size of 308×308. This difference is due to valid convolution applied during up-sampling. For each gland annotation, we perform a series of morphological operations to convert the gland label to a 3 class target that consists of: inner gland; gland contour and background. We perform flip, rotation, scaling, Gaussian blur, elastic deformation and colour augmentation to the input patches during training.

3.2 Comparative Results

To assess the performance of our algorithm, we used the same evaluation metrics that were used in the GlaS challenge [9], consisting of F_1 score, object-level dice and object-level Hausdorff distance.

In Table 1 we compare the gland segmentation performance of our proposed approach with recent top performing methods, using a weighted rank score, that was first proposed by Xu *et al.* [13]. This score weighs the ranks of each metric according to the number of images in each dataset. Therefore, the rank of Test A is multiplied by 0.75 and the rank of Test B is multiplied by 0.25. Therefore, it makes sense to pay greater attention to Test A. We note that the proposed approach achieves the state-of-the-art performance, given by the best weighted rank score. Figure 3 displays some visual results of the proposed method compared to the ground truth. We also display some areas of interest, shown by the black boxes in Fig. 3(b) and (c), where the algorithm successfully segments lumen, but is missed by the pathologist. It is important to note that the proposed approach makes one prediction per pixel and no patch overlap is used during processing, whereas other approaches may make multiple predictions per pixel. For example, MILD-Net merges overlapping predictions and also uses a test-time augmentation strategy.

Table 2 shows comparative results for simultaneous gland and lumen segmentation. For effective evaluation, we compare with a modified U-Net and FCN where, in a similar fashion to Rota-Net, the branches split after the final

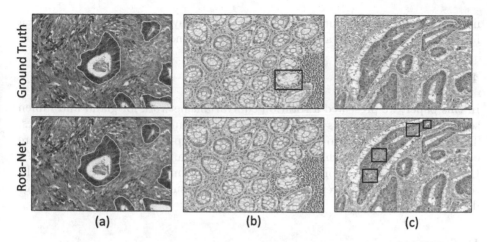

Fig. 3. Visual results of gland and lumen segmentation using our proposed method. Yellow and green boundaries denote gland and lumen boundaries respectively. Black boxes show areas of interest. (Color figure online)

Table 2. Comparative results for simultaneous gland and lumen segmentation. All networks are converted to a dual-branch architecture, where the network splits after the final up-sampling operation. Note, for conciseness we only evaluate on test set A.

Method	F_1 score		Object dice		Object hausdorff	
	Gland	Lumen	Gland	Lumen	Gland	Lumen
Rota-Net	**0.920**	**0.831**	**0.919**	**0.824**	**40.99**	**49.17**
U-Net [8]	0.857	0.643	0.846	0.725	86.63	70.59
FCN-8 [6]	0.800	0.735	0.820	0.762	99.98	68.80

Table 3. Ablation study. RE denotes rotation equivariant network. RE$^+$ denotes rotation equivariant network, utilising a multi-class strategy at the gland output.

Method	F_1 Score		Obj. dice		Obj. hausdorff		Parameters
	Gland	Lumen	Gland	Lumen	Gland	Lumen	
Baseline	0.905	0.715	0.899	0.739	50.29	73.36	70.6M
RE	0.916	0.789	0.913	0.807	46.00	57.49	71.3M
RE$^+$	**0.920**	**0.831**	**0.919**	**0.824**	**40.99**	**49.17**	71.3M

up-sampling operation. We observe that our proposed approach is able to simultaneously segment both glands and lumen with high accuracy.

Finally, in Table 3 we perform an ablation study to show the effect of the various network components. It is clear that the rotation equivariant approach leads to a significantly better performance, which is improved further when the contours are considered for effective gland separation. Compared to the baseline network, we reduce the number of kernels in each layer of the RE network by a factor of two to maintain a similar number of parameters.

4 Conclusion

In this paper, we presented a rotation equivariant network for gland and lumen segmentation that exploits the rotation symmetry inherent in histology images. The network splits into two branches after the final up-sampling operation, where each branch separately achieves the tasks of gland and lumen segmentation. At the output of the gland branch, we incorporate a multi-class strategy to split touching instances. We report state-of-the art results on the GlaS challenge dataset.

References

1. Chen, H., Qi, X., Yu, L., Dou, Q., Qin, J., Heng, P.A.: Dcan: deep contour-aware networks for object instance segmentation from histology images. Med. Image Anal. **36**, 135–146 (2017)
2. Cohen, T., Welling, M.: Group equivariant convolutional networks. In: International Conference on Machine Learning, pp. 2990–2999 (2016)
3. Cohen, T.S., Welling, M.: Steerable CNNs. arXiv preprint arXiv:1612.08498 (2016)
4. Graham, S., et al.: MILD-Net: minimal information loss dilated network for gland instance segmentation in colon histology images. Med. Image Anal. **52**, 199–211 (2018)
5. He, K., Zhang, X., Ren, S., Sun, J.: Deep residual learning for image recognition. In: Proceedings of the IEEE Conference on Computer Vision and Pattern Recognition, pp. 770–778 (2016)
6. Long, J., Shelhamer, E., Darrell, T.: Fully convolutional networks for semantic segmentation. In: Proceedings of the IEEE Conference on Computer Vision and Pattern Recognition, pp. 3431–3440 (2015)
7. Raza, S.E.A., et al.: Micro-Net: a unified model for segmentation of various objects in microscopy images. Med. Image Anal. **52**, 160–173 (2019)
8. Ronneberger, O., Fischer, P., Brox, T.: U-Net: convolutional networks for biomedical image segmentation. In: Navab, N., Hornegger, J., Wells, W.M., Frangi, A.F. (eds.) MICCAI 2015. LNCS, vol. 9351, pp. 234–241. Springer, Cham (2015). https://doi.org/10.1007/978-3-319-24574-4_28
9. Sirinukunwattana, K., et al.: Gland segmentation in colon histology images: the glas challenge contest. Medi. Image Anal. **35**, 489–502 (2017)
10. Veeling, B.S., Linmans, J., Winkens, J., Cohen, T., Welling, M.: Rotation equivariant CNNs for digital pathology. arXiv preprint arXiv:1806.03962 (2018)
11. Washington, M.K., et al.: Protocol for the examination of specimens from patients with primary carcinoma of the colon and rectum. Arch. Pathol. Lab. Med. **133**(10), 1539–1551 (2009)
12. Worrall, D.E., Garbin, S.J., Turmukhambetov, D., Brostow, G.J.: Harmonic networks: deep translation and rotation equivariance. In: 2017 IEEE Conference on Computer Vision and Pattern Recognition (CVPR), pp. 7168–7177. IEEE (2017)
13. Xu, Y., et al.: Gland instance segmentation using deep multichannel neural networks. IEEE Trans. Biomed. Eng. **64**(12), 2901–2912 (2017)

Histopathological Image Analysis on Mouse Testes for Automated Staging of Mouse Seminiferous Tubule

Jun Xu[1], Haoda Lu[1], Haixin Li[2], Xiangxue Wang[3], Anant Madabhushi[3], and Yujun Xu[2(✉)]

[1] Nanjing University of Information Science and Technology, Nanjing 210044, China
xujung@gmail.com
[2] Nanjing Medical University, Nanjing 211166, China
xuyujun@njmu.edu.cn
[3] Case Western Reserve University, Cleveland, OH 44106-7207, USA

Abstract. Whole slide image (WSI) of mouse testicular cross-section contains hundreds of seminiferous tubules. Meanwhile, each seminiferous tubule also contains different types of germ cells among different histological regions. These factors make it a challenge to segment distinct germ cells and regions on mouse testicular cross-section. Automated segmentation of different germ cells and regions is the first step to develop a computerized spermatogenesis staging system. In this paper, a set of 28 H&E stained WSIs of mouse testicular cross-section and 209 Stage VI-VIII tubules images were studied to develop an automated multi-task segmentation model. A deep residual network (ResNet) is first presented for seminiferous tubule segmentation from mouse testicular cross-section. According to the types and distribution of germ cells in the tubules, we then present the other deep ResNet for multi-cell (spermatid, spermatocyte, and spermatogonia) segmentation and a fully convolutional network (FCN) for multi-region (elongated spermatid, round spermatid, and spermatogonial & spermatocyte regions) segmentation. To our knowledge, this is the first time to develop a computerized model for analyzing histopathological image of mouse testis. Three segmentation models presented in this paper show good segmentation performance and obtain the pixel accuracy of 94.40%, 91.26%, 93.47% for three segmentation tasks, respectively, which lays a solid foundation for the establishment of mouse spermatogenesis staging system.

Keywords: Mouse testis histology · Seminiferous tubules · Whole slide image · Germ cell segmentation · Deep learning

1 Introduction

The testes are reproductive organs of male mammals, which is capable of producing germ cells, developing spermatogenesis, secreting androgen, and maintaining

---

J. Xu, H. Lu and H. Li—are the joint first authors.

© Springer Nature Switzerland AG 2019
C. C. Reyes-Aldasoro et al. (Eds.): ECDP 2019, LNCS 11435, pp. 117–124, 2019.
https://doi.org/10.1007/978-3-030-23937-4_14

male sexual characteristics [1,2]. Due to the similarity of mammalian testicular pathology, early studies of human reproduction are usually modeled on mouse testes. During spermatogenesis, specific combinations of germ cells at different developmental periods is called cellular associations or "stages" and "phases" of spermatogenesis. The accurate spermatogenic phase division makes the dynamic spermatogenesis process become stable, which can more accurately describe the histopathological changes of germ cells. However, seminiferous tubule contains diverse germ cells with complex structures and consecutive phases have little difference, which both leads to difficult manual discrimination. By observing the periodic morphological changes of spermatogenic phases, mouse spermatogenesis is divided into I-XII stages [3]. Especially, stages VI-VIII tubules are the most difficult consecutive phases to be distinguished by pathologists. In recent years, with the rapid development of whole slide digital scanners, tissue slides can be digitized and stored in digital image form [4]. It makes computerized quantitative analysis of histopathological images become possible. The development of a computerized staging system can help pathologists in making more accurate staging decisions. Segmentation of different germ cells and regions in WSI is the basis for building an automated spermatogenic staging system.

High-resolution histopathological images of a mouse testicular cross-section (see Fig. 1(b)) are very large in size and there are many different germ cells and histological regions in each tubule (see Fig. 1(c–g)). In general, there are (1) three types of germ cells: spermatid (see Fig. 1(d)), spermatocyte (see Fig. 1(e)), and spermatogonia round spermatids (see Fig. 1(f)), and (2) four histological regions: round spermatids (see purple region in Fig. 1(c)), spermatogonia and spermatocyte region (see red region in Fig. 1(c)), the lumen and elongated spermatid (see green region in Fig. 1(c)), and background (see white region in Fig. 1(c)) regions. Therefore, automated segmentation of different germ cells and histological regions in WSI is a challenged problem. Figure 1 shows the challenges to segment various germ cells and histological regions in the mouse seminiferous tubules.

In recent years, deep convolution neural network (CNN) has achieved great success in the field of image classification and segmentation. The most famous models are AlexNet [5], VGG Net [6], and ResNet [7], which all make outstanding performance in the ImageNet Classification Competition. The structure of histopathological images is complex. It is difficult to process histopathological images by traditional image analysis methods. Fortunately, the emergence of CNN in recent years is very suitable for dealing with such complex problems. Deep learning methods can discover morphological and texture patterns from histological images in a data-driven manner, and thus perform well in various applications such as classification, segmentation and quantitative description [8]. Comparing with the classification problem, the segmentation task in pixel-wise fashion is more challenging. Most of pixel-wise segmentation models were based on patch-wise sliding window and the pixel-wise segmentation results were determined by the prediction results of its central pixel [9]. Recently, fully convolutional network (FCN) has attracted considerable attention [10]. It can capture

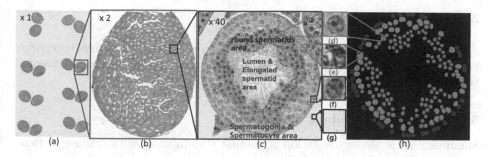

Fig. 1. Histopathological images of a mouse testicle slide at different resolutions and a tubule with different germ cells and histological regions at 40X magnification. (a) a digitalized WSI of mouse testicles at $1X$ magnification, (b) a testicular region at $2X$ magnification, (c) a tubule region from (b) in Stage VII at $40X$ magnification where different germ cells: round spermatid (d), spermatocyte (e), and spermatogonia (f) are congested in three regions in (c): round spermatids region (purple), spermatogonia and spermatocyte region (red). In the middle and outside of a tubule region (c) are the lumen and elongated spermatid in green and background regions (g) in white, respectively. (h) shows the manually annotated mask of three types germ cells in (c). (Color figure online)

and utilize global context information on semantic segmentation tasks, which is fitted to with our task of region segmentation according to the histological distribution of different regions shown in Fig. 1(c).

Inspired by these works, we aimed at three segmentation tasks in mouse testicular cross-section, including seminiferous tubule segmentation, multi-cell (spermatid, spermatocyte, and spermatogonia) segmentation and multi-region (elongated spermatid, round spermatid, and Spermatogonial & Spermatocyte regions) segmentation. To our knowledge, this is the first time to develop computerized model to analyze histopathological image of mouse testis. The rest of the paper is organized as follows. The datasets used in the paper are introduced in Sect. 2. Segmentation methods for three tasks are presented in Sect. 3. The results are shown in Sect. 4. Finally, the discussion and concluding remarks are given in Sect. 5.

2   Datasets

A set of 28 cross-sectioned testis slides were obtained from a institution as Dataset 1 (D_1). All of the slides were prepared in H&E staining and diagnosed by experts. The size of each WSI is around 21000×23000 pixels and the compressed storage space is approximate 1.5 GB. From these WSIs, 209 cross-sectioned seminiferous tubules of Stage VI-VIII were selected by expert pathologists and served as Dataset 2 (D_2) for this study.

3 Methodology

Automated image analysis on mouse testicular cross-section comprises two parts:
(1) seminiferous tubule segmentation; (2) multi-cell and multi-region segmentation.

3.1 Seminiferous Tubule Segmentation

Seminiferous tubule segmentation is the first step to analyze the mouse testicular cross-section. The goal is to identify each seminiferous tubule from a cross-sectioned testes. The flowchart of seminiferous tubule segmentation is shown in Fig. 2. For each mouse testicular cross-section from WSI (see Fig. 2(f)), the image was downsampled to $2X$ magnification (see Fig. 2(g)) and the seminiferous tubule segmentation procedure worked under this magnification which was based on the best resolution to visualize the tubule regions. Then the pixel-wise segmentation model (see Fig. 2(a–e)) was developed to tubule regions' segmentation. The flowchart of seminiferous tubule segmentation framework comprises training (see Fig. 2(a–e)) and seminiferous tubule segmentation phases (see Fig. 2(f–l)). We used ResNet-18 model [7] whose network structure is shown in Fig. 2(e). The network ends with a global average pooling layer and a 2-way fully-connected layer with softmax. A detailed description of them can be referenced in [7].

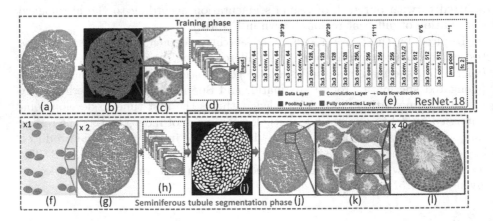

Fig. 2. The flowchart of seminiferous tubule segmentation. It comprises training (a–e) and seminiferous tubule segmentation (f–l) phases.

Method for Generating Training Samples. Figue 2(a–d) shows how training samples were built. The training set includes two types of image patches: tubule and non-tubule, whose sizes are 39×39 pixels. Each image patch is a context patch which accommodates the local spatial dependencies among central pixel and its neighborhoods. As Fig. 2(b) shows, the boundaries of tubules, tubule regions, and background were labeled in green, red, and black, respectively. As Fig. 2(c) shows, the randomly selected red patches whose central pixels are in the tubule region in Fig. 2(b) are tubule patches while green and black patches whose central pixels are on the boundary and background are non-tubule patches. These tubule and non-tubule patches build the training set (see Fig. 2(d)).

Pixel-Wise + Sliding Window Scheme for Seminiferous Tubule Segmentation. In the training phase (see Fig. 2(a–e)), the ResNet 18 model was trained with the training samples built in the previous section. In the tubule segmentation phase (see Fig. 2(f–l)), the trained ResNet and a sliding window scheme was leveraged to choose the context image patches from Fig. 2(g). The window slides across the entire image row by row from upper left corner to the lower right with a step size of 1 pixel. Border padding is employed to address issues of boundary artifacts. The pixel-wise segmentation is achieved (see Fig. 2(i)) by predicting the class probabilities of the central pixel of each context patch chosen by sliding window scheme. The segmentation results were then upsampled back into the original image size via bilinear interpolation (see Fig. 2(j–l)).

3.2   Multi-cell and Multi-region Segmentation on Stage VI-III

ResNet for Multi-cell Segmentation. The flowchart of multi-cell segmentation framework comprises training (see Fig. 3(a–g)) and multi-cell segmentation phases (see Fig. 3(h, k–n)). Different from seminiferous tubule segmentation, as can be seen in Fig. 3, we focus on round spermatid (see Fig. 3(c)), spermatocyte (see Fig. 3(d)), and spermatogonia (see Fig. 3(e)) in a cross-sectioned seminiferous tubule. This is no longer a two-class problem, but a multi-class problem. As shown in Fig. 3(g), the network ends with a global average pooling layer and a 4-way fully-connected layer with softmax. The construction of training set here is similar with what we have stated in Sect. 3.1. The difference is turnning two categories into four categories. The corresponding data set generation method is shown in Fig. 3(a–f).

FCN for Multi-region Segmentation. The flowchart of multi-region segmentation framework comprises training (see Fig. 3(o–q)) and multi-region segmentation phases (see Fig. 3(h, q, i)). According to the distribution of nuclei in Fig. 3(o), we use FCN to semantically segment three regions. The FCN we used in this paper is AlexNet-FCN. The traditional CNN can be transformed into a FCN with some simple modifications. In this paper, we treated each neuron in the fully connected layer of the convolutional neural network as the convolution kernel by keeping the same dimension as its input [10]. The training set of FCN model was built by manually annotating region masks of three regions as showed in Fig. 3(p). The region mask has the same size as the original image.

The values of the pixel points in different areas on the label map can be represented by category information. For example, the elongated spermatids region is labeled as the first category, and the values of this region in all the label maps are marked as 1. As can be seen in Fig. 3(p), there are 4 categories of the entire label map, including the elongated spermatids region (light blue) labeled 1, the round spermatid region (yellow) labeled 2, the Spermatogonial&Spermatocyte region (brown) labeled 3, and the background (dark blue) labeled 4.

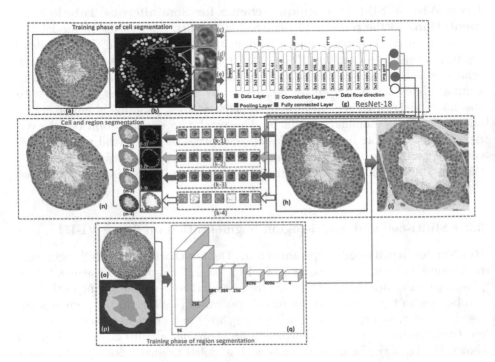

Fig. 3. The flowchart of multi-cell and multi-region segmentation. (Color figure online)

4 Results

4.1 Seminiferous Tubule Segmentation

The number of training set shows in Table 1. In order to reflect the effectiveness of proposed method, two other methods: gLoG [11], CoNNACaeF [12] were compared in terms of segmentation accuracy. Four quantitative measurements: Pixel accuracy, mean accuracy, mean IU, frequency weight IU [10] were used. The qualitative and quantitative segmentation results of proposed model and compared models are shown in Fig. 4 and Table 2, respectively. The results suggests that proposed model outperformed two compared models. The pixel accuracy of our model is 94.40%, which suggests best performance in spermatogenic tubule segmentation.

Table 1. The illustration of datasets studied in the paper and corresponding quantitative evaluation results for three segmentation tasks with proposed segmentation models.

Segmentation	Datasets	Total	Patches	Model	Training Set				Testing Set	
					# of images	model set	validation set	Classification accuracy	# of images	Pixel accuracy
Tubule	D1	28	Tubule	ResNet-18	7	98449	16402	97.93%	21	94.40%
			Background			90745	16947			
Multi-cell	D2	209	round spermatid	ResNet-18	120	85157	37950	99.13%	89	91.26%
			spermatocyte			83068	33948			
			spermatogonia			81774	36384			
			Background			134810	36136			
Multi-region	D2	1254	-	AlexNet-FCN	720	720	-	-	534	93.47%

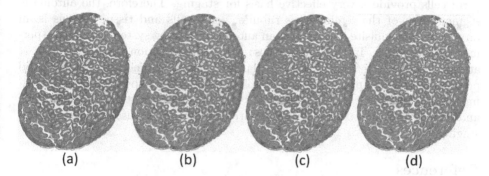

Fig. 4. The illustration of the tubule region segmentation on a mouse testicular cross-section (a) by gLoG (b), CoNNACaeF (c), and model presented in this paper (d).

Table 2. Quantitative results of proposed and compared models in tubule segmentation on D_1. The accuracy showed in the table reflects the average values across all the testing samples.

	Proposed	gLoG [11]	CoNNACaeF [12]
Pixel accuracy	94.40%	58.77%	86.33%
Mean accuracy	92.73%	45.94%	84.87%
Mean IU	88.32%	33.74%	74.28%
Frequency weight IU	89.30%	43.17%	76.11%

4.2 Multi-nuclei and Muti-region Segmentation on Stage VI-VIII

The number of training set shows in Table 1. In nuclei segmentation part, Fig. 3(a–g, h, k–n) shows the flowchart of nuclei segmentation using pixel-wise method. The ResNet model achieves an classification accuracy of 99.13% (see Table 1) on the validation set. The accuracy of the pixels on the test set is 91.26% (see Table 1). Because our data for FCN training is relatively small. In region segmentation part, we roll the image horizontally, vertically, and rotate it every 90 degrees, expanding D_2 to six times. Meanwhile, we adopt transfer learning methods using the model parameters which have already been trained in [10] as initialization parameters of our FCN model. Figure 3(h, q, i) is the flowchart of region segmentation using semantic segmentation method. The pixel accuracy of the FCN model on the test set is 93.47% (see Table 1).

5   Discussion and Concluding Remarks

The establishment of automated staging system for mouse seminiferous tublues can not only assist pathologists in staging, but also combine with mouse gene data in future research to explore new comprehensive staging criteria. As the active center of spermatogenesis process, the distribution and morphology of germ cells provide a very effective basis for staging. Therefore, the automatic segmentation of the seminiferous tubules, germ cells and tissue regions is an important prerequisite to construct an automatic staging system for mouse spermatogenic tubules. In this paper, these three segmentation tasks are our first attempts to analyze the mouse tesiticular pathology. Our models achieved good performance, which provides a good basis for establishing spermatogenesis staging system. In the future, we will extract the histological features of the nucleus and region, and then train the appropriate classifier for mouse spermatogenesis staging.

References

1. Russell, L.D., Ettlin, R.A., Hikim, A.P.S., Clegg, E.D.: Histological and histopathological evaluation of the testis. Int. J. Androl. 16(1), 83–83 (1993)
2. Clermont, Y.: Kinetics of spermatogenesis in mammals: seminiferous epithelium cycle and spermatogonial renewal. Physiol. Rev. 52(1), 198–236 (1972)
3. Oakberg, E.F.: Duration of spermatogenesis in the mouse and timing of stages of the cycle of the seminiferous epithelium. Am. J. Anat. 99(3), 507–516 (1956)
4. Gurcan, M.N., Boucheron, L., Can, A., Madabhushi, A., Rajpoot, N., Yener, B.: Histopathological image analysis: a review. IEEE Rev. Biomed. Eng. 2, 147–171 (2009)
5. Krizhevsky, A., Sutskever, I., Hinton, G.E.: ImageNet classification with deep convolutional neural networks. In: NIPS, pp. 1097–1105 (2012)
6. Simonyan, K., Zisserman, A.: Very deep convolutional networks for large-scale image recognition. Comput. Sci. (2014)
7. He, K., et al.: Deep residual learning for image recognition. In: CVPR (2016)
8. Shen, D., Wu, G., Suk, H.I.: Deep learning in medical image analysis. Ann. Rev. Biomed. Eng. 19(1), 221–248 (2017)
9. Ciresan, D.C., Giusti, A., Gambardella, L.M., Schmidhuber, J.: Mitosis detection in breast cancer histology images with deep neural networks. Med. Image Comput. Comput. Assist. Interv. 16(Pt 2), 411–418 (2013)
10. Long, J., Shelhamer, E., Darrell, T.: Fully convolutional networks for semantic segmentation. In: CVPR (2015)
11. Xu, H., Lu, C., Berendt, R., Jha, N., Mandal, M.: Automatic nuclei detection based on generalized laplacian of gaussian filters. IEEE J. Biomed. Health Inform. 21(3), 826–837 (2016)
12. Xu, J., et al.: Convolutional neural network initialized active contour model with adaptive ellipse fitting for nuclear segmentation on breast histopathological images. J. Med. Imaging 6, 017501 (2019)

Deep Features for Tissue-Fold Detection in Histopathology Images

Morteza Babaie[1] and Hamid R. Tizhoosh[1,2(✉)]

[1] Kimia Lab, University of Waterloo, Waterloo, Canada
tizhoosh@uwaterloo.ca
[2] Vector Institute, Toronto, Canada
http://kimia.uwaterloo.ca

Abstract. Whole slide imaging (WSI) refers to the digitization of a tissue specimen which enables pathologists to explore high-resolution images on a monitor rather than through a microscope. The formation of tissue folds occur during tissue processing. Their presence may not only cause out-of-focus digitization but can also negatively affect the diagnosis in some cases. In this paper, we have compared five pre-trained convolutional neural networks (CNNs) of different depths as feature extractors to characterize tissue folds. We have also explored common classifiers to discriminate folded tissue against the normal tissue in hematoxylin and eosin (H&E) stained biopsy samples. In our experiments, we manually select the folded area in roughly 2.5 mm × 2.5 mm patches at 20x magnification level as the training data. The "DenseNet" with 201 layers alongside an SVM classifier outperformed all other configurations. Based on the leave-one-out validation strategy, we achieved 96.3% accuracy, whereas with augmentation the accuracy increased to 97.2%. We have tested the generalization of our method with five unseen WSIs from the NIH (National Cancer Institute) dataset. The accuracy for patch-wise detection was 81%. One folded patch within an image suffices to flag the entire specimen for visual inspection.

Keywords: Digital pathology · Tissue folds · Deep features · SVM

1 Introduction

For most types of cancer, biopsy is a dominant procedure for diagnosis. During the biopsy, a small part of suspicious tissue is cut out. After tissue preparation, a tiny section of tissue is mounted on a glass slide. Pathologists visually inspect these glass slides under a microscope and write a report to justify a primary diagnosis [24].

The rapid progress of image acquisition technologies over the past decade has led to a dramatic change in the pathology field by developing digital pathology. Most whole slide scanners can produce a high-resolution digital image of histology glass slides in a few minutes [1]. These WSIs can be analyzed on

© Springer Nature Switzerland AG 2019
C. C. Reyes-Aldasoro et al. (Eds.): ECDP 2019, LNCS 11435, pp. 125–132, 2019.
https://doi.org/10.1007/978-3-030-23937-4_15

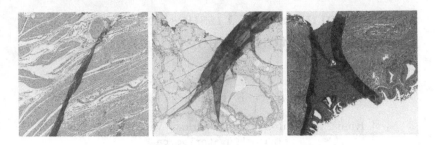

Fig. 1. Sample folded tissues from our dataset.

a display rather than through the microscope. In addition, sharing scans for teleconsultation purposes are much more convenient in digital version compared to shipping the glass slides to other laboratories to solicit a second opinion [20].

Regardless whether we use digitization or microscopy, the presence of artifacts such as folded tissue might negatively affect the diagnosis [4]. When digital technology is used other artifacts like blur may also reduce the quality of computerized algorithms [10]. Tissue fold can occur in the sectioning part of tissue processing when a thin tissue slice is folded [11]. Figure 1 shows three samples of folded tissue.

The difference in tissue thickness changes the precise lens focus when one or more focus points are localized on the folded parts. Most WSI scanners start with a lower resolution pre-scan phase which selects focus points in the some areas with possibility of manual adjustment. Tissue-fold detection can avoid placing focus points on the folded areas. In addition, different tissue cuts are available in the laboratories. Selecting a suitable glass slide by a rapid pre-scan quality control system could save valuable scanning time and improve the workflow.

2   Related Works

The research on tissue-fold detection is relatively young. Pinky et al. [2] proposed a technique to use colour information to detect tissue folds. The fact that the saturation of the folded area is different from other parts justifies the development of a colour shifting method to magnify the colour metric difference in folded and non-folded areas [3]. Other authors have suggested adding the intensity level to the saturation criteria to develop a fold segmentation method. In such algorithms, if saturation minus intensity is higher than a certain threshold, this area is segmented as a folded tissue [10]. More recently, statistical approaches such as the rank-sum method have been applied to find image features (e.g., colour and connectivity descriptors) that are discriminated from the same set of WSIs with and without folds [11].

Generally, there is an inevitable drawback associated with the use of colour information as a feature for tissue-fold distinction. Colour-based approaches might easily fail due to the colour fluctuations which occur in digital pathology relatively often. These changes might happen mainly because of "differences in manufacturing techniques of stains, laboratories' staining protocols, and colour responses of digital scanners" [21]. Convolutional neural networks (CNNs), on the other hand, have been widely used recently in almost every field of machine vision due to their unique ability to capture accurate data-driven features [7]. As result of augmentation techniques in their training process, these networks are fairly robust to a variety of changes including colour changes [13]. As a matter of fact most CNNs are trained through diverse augmentation techniques, among others variations of color. In the deep learning literature, the importance of labeled data is undeniable. Deep networks need more and more labeled training data to train each layer's parameters when the networks become deeper and deeper [18]. On the other hand, providing a large number of labeled data in the medical domain by the expert physicians is expensive. In contrast, transfer learning is considered to be an applicable solution to fine-tune a pre-trained deep network with a much smaller training set compared to training from scratch. The idea behind transfer learning is that if the network is trained with a large dataset such as ImageNet [5], it learns useful (general) information that can be applied in completely different domains. In general, for any given pre-trained network, the first layers will be held unchanged (i.e., *frozen*), while the weights of the last few layers will be adjusted by re-training with the data of the new domain [12,14]. Moreover, using deep pooling or the weights of fully connected layers have been reported to be excellent sources for feature extraction [8,22].

In this work, we have compared five well-known pre-trained CNNs as feature extractors for classifying folded tissue against normal tissue. VGG16, GoogleNet, Inception V3, ResNet 101 and DenseNet 201 are the networks that have compared in our experiments. We also examined the discrimination power of decision trees, SVM and k-NNs with respect to the classification of different deep features.

3   Materials and Methods

3.1   Folded-Tissue Dataset

In our experiments, we created a training dataset of folded tissue images. We had access to 79 *rejected* WSIs from Huron Digital Pathology[1]. These scans had been rejected due to presence of different artifacts. Since there was a large number of folded-tissue cases in these slides, we created a folded-tissue training dataset and did not consider other types of artifacts. The folded regions are selected on fairly large windows at 20x magnification (about 5000 × 5000 pixels) which is roughly equivalent to 250 × 250 pixels at 1x magnification. In practice, low magnification images could be easily obtained in the fast pre-scan mode.

We have manually selected 112 folded-tissue patches as the training set through visual inspection. Since we needed to classify them against the normal (unfolded) tissue, we selected 315 images from the area around the folded regions as negative samples (i.e., unfolded tissue). We augmented each image to

---

[1] http://www.hurondigitalpathology.com/.

12 images by rotating ($0°$ and $90°$), flipping (flipped/no-flipped) and changing the illumination (original, suppressed, amplified). As a result, we established a dataset of 1,344 folded patches and 3,780 fold-free patches. Change in illumination was done by converting each image to the CIELAB colour space (LAB), amplifying and suppressing the L channel by a factor of 1.25 and 0.75, respectively. Finally, we converted them back to RGB colour space. At the end, all patches were re-sized to input size of each pre-trained network required size (e.g. 255×255 for DenseNet).

To evaluate the generalization and the practical performance, we also selected five WSIs from the NIH dataset[2]. We selected WSIs from three different organs (kidney,lung and colon). Figure 3 shows two sample WSIs alongside the boundary boxes of our classifier.

3.2 Pre-trained CNNs

CNNs are a class of deep networks designed to learn a large bank of filters. These filters are convolved with the input image in a hierarchical fashion. The major advantage of CNNs is their independence from prior knowledge and handcrafted feature design. There are several deep networks that have been trained with available public images and can be employed for classification in different domains. VGG16 [16], GoogleNet [18], Inception-V3 [19], ResNet [6] and DenseNet-201 are major examples for pre-trained networks.

DenseNet-201 is a CNN that is designed to overcome the *gradient vanishing* problem by adding dense blocks and transition layers. The vanishing gradient prevents a network from growing. As a result of DenseNet extensions, the network learns rich feature representations for a wide range of images due to its extremely deep architecture. We used the last fully connected layer of the network with 1024 elements as the feature vector.

4   Experiments and Results

We experimented with several learning methods to classify the dense features including SVM [17], decision trees [15] and k-NNs [23] to find the optimal classifier for tissue fold detection. As listed in Table 2, the ability of the quadratic SVM to classify the folded and non-folded tissue was the highest with 96.3% accuracy. However, median Gaussian SVM and fine k-NN also achieved acceptable results with accuracy values of 94.8% and 94.1%, respectively. Table 2 compares the performance of different classifiers when DenseNet features were used.

Augmentation and leave-one-out schemes were selected to compensate for the small size of training data. Since the size of the training data was relatively small, we applied augmentation techniques to increase the number of observations. As well, the leave-one-out strategy [9] to evaluate the accuracy was used to perform as many experiments as possible.

---

[2] https://gdc.cancer.gov.

Table 1. The accuracy of five pre-trained networks.

	Network	Depth	Sensitivity	Recall	Accuracy
1	VGG-16	16	87.55%	90.8%	91.8%
2	Google Net	22	90.8%	92.6%	93.7%
3	inceptionv3	48	90.5%	92.85%	93.7%
4	resnet101	101	93.2%	92.95%	94.6%
5	densenet201	201	**94.6%**	**96.85%**	**96.7%**

Table 2. The accuracy of different classifiers.

	Classifier	Sub-type	Accuracy
1	Tree	Fine	81.5%
2	Tree	Coarse	82.9%
3	SVM	Quadratic	**96.3%**
4	SVM	Med Gaussian	94.8%
5	k-NN	Fine	94.1%
6	k-NN	Cosine	87.1%

Figure 2 shows the confusion matrices of leave-one-out quadratic SVM with augmentation on the right side versus no augmentation on the left side. By applying the augmentation method, not only did the total accuracy increase slightly to 97.2% but also the false negative (folded patch, but classified as normal patch) also decreased from 2.6% to 2.1%. However, the false positive (normal patch, but classified as a folded patch) remained unchanged. In general, any type of error is not desirable, nevertheless, in our case, false positive might be preferred over false negative.

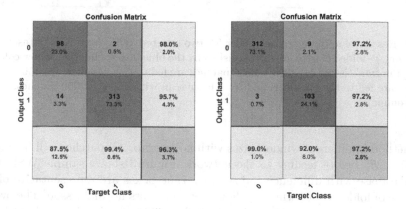

Fig. 2. Confusion matrices of folded tissue classification. The left matrix depicts the classification without augmentation while the right matrix shows the values after augmentation.

Table 1 shows the performance of the networks when their features were classified by SVM. As it can be seen from the table, the performance of deep features increase in our application when the depth of network increased.

Classifiers, which are trained on small datasets predominantly fail to generalize on new classification categories. In our experiments, we selected five new WSIs with a noticeable amount of folded tissue from the NIH dataset to evaluate the ability of deep features and SVM to generalize to unseen cases. We applied

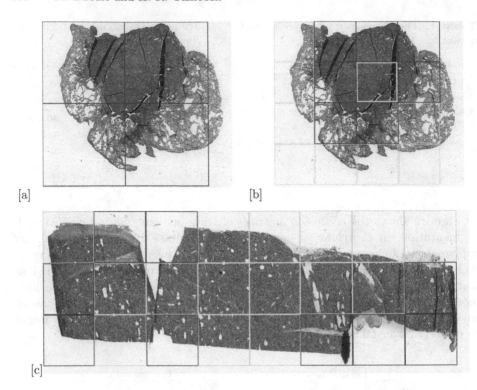

Fig. 3. Results of applying our classifier for two selected WSIs from NIH dataset (lung and kidney) - folded classes are distinguished by the blue boxes while the yellow colour is used for normal tissue: (a) 3000 × 3000 patches are fed to the classifier, (b) 1500 × 1500 patches are fed to the classifier, and (c) a large scan with 4000 × 4000 patches. (Color figure online)

our method in different window sizes with no overlap. All patches will be resized to 255 × 255 before feeding to the network. Figure 3 shows sample WSIs from NIH database with different window sizes. Blue boxes are representative of the presence of folded tissue while a yellow box represents normal tissue. The overall accuracy in generalization test set with 4000 × 4000 pixel size dropped to 81%. A possible explanation for this result may be the lack of adequate fold pattern samples in the training set. Besides the difference in an organ type, scanner brand should also be considered. However, as we trained and tested the classifiers for patch-wise tissue detection, one has to bear in mind that the detection of one tissue fold is sufficient to flag a scan for visual inspection.

It can be seen in Fig. 3(b) that there is a folded patch which has not been detected. There might be some justifications for this false negative -yellow window in Fig. 3(b)-. The first one is that our training dataset enclosed the entire folded tissue within each patch (i.e., no folded tissue was split between two patches). In this false negative example, however, the patch does not contain all of the folded tissue, and parts of the folded tissue are contained within the neighbouring patches. The same error has occurred in Fig. 3(c). The second justification is that the training patch sizes were about 5000 by 5000 pixels, while the experiment window size was 1500 by 1500, therefore training with bigger size patches (patch in lower magnification) might have been the reason for false negatives.

5   Conclusions

Quality control for artifact detection in histopathology slides could be used in order to reject defective slides. This procedure may save time in clinical practice. Not only can folded tissue, as one of the most common artifacts in histopathology slides, lead to rejection of slides in clinical practice, but it may also negatively affect the diagnosis. In this paper, a procedure based on deep features has been proposed to detect folded tissues in large scan regions. We trained an SVM classifier based on the features of augmented training patches to classify folded and normal tissues. The accuracy in the presented dataset was quite high, whereas the model's generalization on new WSIs was acceptable.

Several topics can be anticipated for the future works. A larger dataset, with a known source of organ could boost up the generalization. And different patch size selection for dataset also could help to boost the accuracy.

References

1. Al-Janabi, S., Huisman, A., Van Diest, P.J.: Digital pathology: current status and future perspectives. Histopathology **61**(1), 1–9 (2012)
2. Bautista, P.A., Yagi, Y.: Detection of tissue folds in whole slide images. In: Annual International Conference of the IEEE Engineering in Medicine and Biology Society, EMBC 2009, pp. 3669–3672. IEEE (2009)
3. Bautista, P.A., Yagi, Y.: Improving the visualization and detection of tissue folds in whole slide images through color enhancement. J. Pathol. Inform. **1**, (2010)
4. Bindhu, P., Krishnapillai, R., Thomas, P., Jayanthi, P.: Facts in artifacts. J. Oral Maxillofac. Pathol.: JOMFP **17**(3), 397 (2013)
5. Deng, J., Dong, W., Socher, R., Li, L.J., Li, K., Fei-Fei, L.: ImageNet: a large-scale hierarchical image database. In: IEEE Conference on Computer Vision and Pattern Recognition, CVPR 2009, pp. 248–255. IEEE (2009)
6. He, K., Zhang, X., Ren, S., Sun, J.: Deep residual learning for image recognition. In: Proceedings of the IEEE Conference on Computer Vision and Pattern Recognition, pp. 770–778 (2016)
7. Khatami, A., Babaie, M., Khosravi, A., Tizhoosh, H.R., Nahavandi, S.: Parallel deep solutions for image retrieval from imbalanced medical imaging archives. Appl. Soft Comput. **63**, 197–205 (2018)
8. Kieffer, B., Babaie, M., Kalra, S., Tizhoosh, H.R.: Convolutional neural networks for histopathology image classification: training vs. using pre-trained networks. In: 2017 Seventh International Conference on Image Processing Theory, Tools and Applications (IPTA), pp. 1–6. IEEE (2017)
9. Kohavi, R., et al.: A study of cross-validation and bootstrap for accuracy estimation and model selection. In: Ijcai, Montreal, Canada, vol. 14, pp. 1137–1145 (1995)

10. Kothari, S., Phan, J.H., Osunkoya, A.O., Wang, M.D.: Biological interpretation of morphological patterns in histopathological whole-slide images. In: Proceedings of the ACM Conference on Bioinformatics, Computational Biology and Biomedicine, pp. 218–225. ACM (2012)
11. Kothari, S., Phan, J.H., Wang, M.D.: Eliminating tissue-fold artifacts in histopathological whole-slide images for improved image-based prediction of cancer grade. J. Pathol. Inform. **4** (2013)
12. Kumar, M.D., Babaie, M., Tizhoosh, H.: Deep barcodes for fast retrieval of histopathology scans. arXiv preprint arXiv:1805.08833 (2018)
13. Lafarge, M.W., Pluim, J.P.W., Eppenhof, K.A.J., Moeskops, P., Veta, M.: Domain-adversarial neural networks to address the appearance variability of histopathology images. In: Cardoso, M.J., et al. (eds.) DLMIA/ML-CDS -2017. LNCS, vol. 10553, pp. 83–91. Springer, Cham (2017). https://doi.org/10.1007/978-3-319-67558-9_10
14. Pan, S.J., Yang, Q., et al.: A survey on transfer learning. IEEE Trans. Knowl. Data Eng. **22**(10), 1345–1359 (2010)
15. Safavian, S.R., Landgrebe, D.: A survey of decision tree classifier methodology. IEEE Trans. Syst. Man Cybern. **21**(3), 660–674 (1991)
16. Simonyan, K., Zisserman, A.: Very deep convolutional networks for large-scale image recognition. arXiv preprint arXiv:1409.1556 (2014)
17. Suykens, J.A., Vandewalle, J.: Least squares support vector machine classifiers. Neural Process. Lett. **9**(3), 293–300 (1999)
18. Szegedy, C., et al.: Going deeper with convolutions. In: Proceedings of the IEEE Conference on Computer Vision and Pattern Recognition, pp. 1–9 (2015)
19. Szegedy, C., Vanhoucke, V., Ioffe, S., Shlens, J., Wojna, Z.: Rethinking the inception architecture for computer vision. In: Proceedings of the IEEE Conference on Computer Vision and Pattern Recognition, pp. 2818–2826 (2016)
20. Tizhoosh, H.R., Pantanowitz, L., et al.: Artificial intelligence and digital pathology: Challenges and opportunities. J. Pathol. Inform. **9**(1), 38 (2018)
21. Vahadane, A., et al.: Structure-preserving color normalization and sparse stain separation for histological images. IEEE Trans. Med. Imaging **35**(8), 1962–1971 (2016)
22. Van Ginneken, B., Setio, A.A., Jacobs, C., Ciompi, F.: Off-the-shelf convolutional neural network features for pulmonary nodule detection in computed tomography scans. In: 2015 IEEE 12th International Symposium on Biomedical Imaging (ISBI), pp. 286–289. IEEE (2015)
23. Xu, Y., Zhu, Q., Fan, Z., Qiu, M., Chen, Y., Liu, H.: Coarse to fine k nearest neighbor classifier. Pattern Recogn. Lett. **34**(9), 980–986 (2013)
24. Zerbino, D.: Biopsy: its history, current and future outlook. Likars' ka sprava **14**(3–4), 1–9 (1994)

Computer-Assisted Diagnosis and Prognosis

A Fast Pyramidal Bayesian Model
for Mitosis Detection
in Whole-Slide Images

Santiago López-Tapia[1](✉), José Aneiros-Fernández[2](✉),
and Nicolás Pérez de la Blanca[1](✉)

[1] Computer Science and Artificial Intelligence Department,
University of Granada, Granada, Spain
sltapia@decsai.ugr.es, nicolas@ugr.es
[2] Intercenter Unit of Pathological Anatomy,
San Cecilio University Hospital, Granada, Spain
janeirosf@hotmail.com

Abstract. Mitosis detection in Hematoxylin and Eosin images and its
quantification for mm^2 is currently one of the most valuable prognostic
indicators for some types of cancer and specifically for the breast cancer.
In whole-slide images the main goal is to detect its presence on the full
image. This paper makes several contributions to the mitosis detection
task in whole-slide in order to improve the current state of the art and
efficiency. A new coarse to fine pyramidal model to detect mitosis is
proposed. On each pyramid level a Bayesian convolutional neural network
is trained to compute class prediction and uncertainty on each pixel. This
information is propagated top-down on the pyramid as a constraining
mechanism from the above layers. To cope with local tissue and cell
shape deformations geometric invariance is also introduced as a part
of the model. The model achieves an F1-score of 82.6% on the MITOS
ICPR-2012 test dataset when trained with samples from skin tissue. This
is competitive with the current state of the art. In average a whole-slide
is analyzed in less than 20 s. A new dataset of 8236 mitoses from skin
tissue has been created to train our models.

Keywords: Mitosis detection · Pyramid · Bayesian model ·
Multiscale processing

1 Introduction

The quantification of mitotic cells in Hematoxylin and Eosin (H&E) images and
more specifically its density per square millimeter is one of the current most
stronger markers in cancer prognosis.

This paper has been supported by the Spanish Ministry of Economy and Competitiveness and the European Regional Development Fund (FEDER) under the grant
DPI2016-77869-C2-2-R.

© Springer Nature Switzerland AG 2019
C. C. Reyes-Aldasoro et al. (Eds.): ECDP 2019, LNCS 11435, pp. 135–143, 2019.
https://doi.org/10.1007/978-3-030-23937-4_16

The advent of the high-resolution scanner technology to the computational pathology field has allowed to obtain digital whole-slides images (WSI). Nevertheless, the huge size of the images and the computing time of the current detection algorithms impose in practice a partial rather than a fully image detection and counting.

Several difficulties can be identified as responsible of the current low detection rate on H&E stained images. On one hand, the variability in RGB color map due to different stain intensities and scanners technology [9,12]. On the other hand, the presence of very hard false positives due to Hematoxylin staining of non-cells tissue also makes harder the detection process. In addition, the mitosis undergoes four different stages with different shapes and appearances. This geometric variability and the low number of mitosis pixels per WSI also represent a new source of false positive. These difficulties all together make the design of an efficient and accurate mitosis detection algorithms a challenge task [16].

Different Challenges such as TUPAC-2016 [10], MITOS-ATYPIA [5] and MITOS ICPR-2012 [13] have been organized in the last years to foster the detection algorithms. But the contributed datasets from them all are too small and only from breast cancer tissue. Currently, there are no other larger open access mitosis datasets. We have created a mitosis dataset from skin cancer images to train our model. In this type of cancer mitosis detection is also a very relevant prognostic indicator [14]. In order to compare our model with other results in the literature we have tested with MITOS ICPR-2012.

2   Related Works

Many contributions to the use of CNN model for mitosis detection have been proposed since the ICPR-2012 challenge MITOS ICPR-2012 [13] was available [2,3,17]. The best result from all these approaches is an F1 score of 78.8%. In [8] an adaptation to the general object detection framework from CNN, Faster R-CNN, is proposed. They focus on the use of very deep architectures for mitosis detection achieving an F1-score of 83.2% in MITOS ICPR-2012. More recently in [15] a new way of approaching the detection task is proposed. They stain twice each slide using Phospho-histone H3 (PHH3) and H&E and leverage on the complementary properties of these stains to improve the detection. They succeed in removing many of the false positives but at the cost of a very complex processing. Our method addresses a similar goal but from a pyramidal approach. All mentioned approaches exploit the depth increment in the architectures as the main mechanism to generate good features. In [19] an approach inspired in Wide Residual networks (WRN) [18] focus on the wide of the layer, instead of the number of layers. This fact simplifies the architecture making it more efficient at test time and easier of training. They reached an F1 score of 64.8% in the challenge TUPAC-2016 [10], which is a result competitive with the state of the art for this dataset. Our architectures are inspired by this network.

The feature extraction stage of all above approaches either use the 40x scale or use a fine to coarse feature pyramid starting in 40x. In both cases the highest resolution scale is the input information. In contrast, here we propose a coarse to fine approach in a top-down pass through a pyramid representing three scales of the image. We find benefits in both efficiency and accuracy. The standard CNN models lack uncertainty measurements about the predictions as well as specific layers to obtain invariance to geometric deformations. The use of a Bayesian approach to CNN allows us to compute uncertainty in a natural way. On each internal pyramid level, prediction and uncertainty from the above levels are used as input to improve the final model prediction. We find that information from lower resolutions allow us to constraint the optimization process at the highest resolution. In addition, and to cope with both the cell shape variability induced by the phases of the mitosis and the tissue local deformations, our model incorporate specific layers to compute geometric invariant features [6].

In summary our contributions are: (a) A new and fast pyramidal mitosis detection algorithm for WSI achieving a F1-score competitive with the state of the art on MITOS ICPR-2012 dataset; (b) A new information propagation mechanism between scales from a cascade of Bayesian CNN model; (c) The use of uncertainty and geometric invariance to improve the detection score; (d) A model able of learning knowledge transfer between tissues; (e) Mitosis detection time on WSI faster than ever before.

The rest of the paper is as follows. Section 3 we describes the model. Section 4 describes the training and test stages. Section 5 shows the experiment and Sect. 6 show the discussion and conclusions.

3   Model Description

Our model is defined as a forward cascade of classifiers applied on a course-to-fine image pyramid build from a WSI at three magnification scales 10x, 20x and 40x. We assume 40x represents the sample image and the lowest pyramid level. Figure 1 shows a diagram of the architecture. On each pyramid level a Bayesian CNN classifier inspired in the design of a Wide Residual Network [18] is trained. The three classifiers in the cascade output a mask of detected mitosis, a feature map, and the uncertainty per feature in terms of standard deviation as shown in Fig. 1.

These feature maps are used by the next detectors, top-down, as soft constraints to focus the training on the most difficult negative samples (see Fig. 1). We call this model PB-CNN. Furthermore, to make the model resistant to local and shape deformations, appearing by both the process of collecting and staining tissue and cells shape deformation, a Spatial Transforming Layer [6] is applied before the residual blocks 4th and 7th in scale x40 (see Fig. 2). We call this model PB-CNN-STP. On the output of last classifier, we put to zero the predictions of those pixels which uncertainty is higher than a threshold fixed in training. The experiments show that these higher values are usually associated to WSI artifacts of low frequency in the training dataset. Finally, a non-maximum suppression step is carried out to keep, in cluster of overlapping regions, only the one with the highest probability. Our final output is a list of coordinates joint

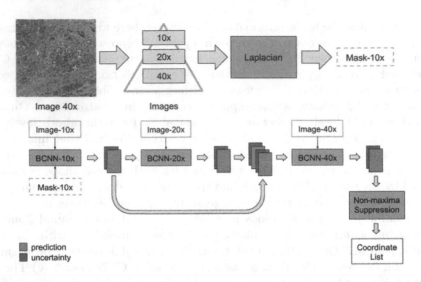

Fig. 1. Diagram showing the pyramidal model and the cascade of classifier to process the pyramid. The top of the figure shows, in this order, the input image, the pyramid building and the computation of the initial mask at 10x. The bottom shows how the first two pyramid levels provide input information to the third pyramid level. The result is the output of a non-maxima suppression process. See details in the text.

to their corresponding probability and standard deviation. As it can be seen in Fig. 2, we use a late fusion criteria incorporating feature maps and uncertainty, of the above levels, at the end of network. We have found in our experiments that this late fusion of features provides better results that doing it earlier.

The architecture of our detector is shown in Fig. 2. The architecture is a Wide Residual Network [18] that uses three Wide Residual Units (WRU) (see right block). To reduce the spatial size of processed patch, we use a stride of 2 at certain layers (indicated by "/2" in the figure), in the case of the WRU block, the stride is applied at the first convolutional layer. The same architecture is used for PB-CNN-SPT adding a Spatial Transforming Layer [6] at the scale 40x as indicated previously.

4   Training and Test

4.1   Dataset

The dataset is created from 22 WSI of melanoma skin cancer. The images were acquired using a scanner Philips with a resolution of $0.25\,\mu$ per pixel. A senior pathologist of the Unit of Computational Pathology of the University Hospital San Cecilio in Granada labeled the WSI at 40x by indicating the center of the mitosis. 8236 were annotated mitosis.

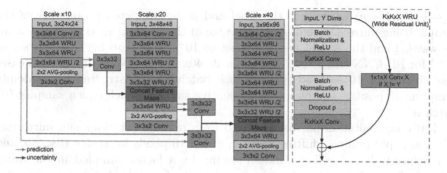

Fig. 2. Network architecture used for PB-CNN (see left figure). $K \times K \times N$ Conv indicates a convolution layer with $K \times K$ kernel and N filters. /2 idicates that the convolutution layer uses a stride of 2. 2×2 AVG-pooling indicates an average pooling layer of kernel 2×2.

4.2 Input Mask at 10x

To detect initial relevant regions at 10x we apply a Laplacian of the Gaussian (LoG) filter with $\sigma = 9$ over the Hematoxylin band obtained by color deconvolution [9]. Then a thresholding for negative values that are less than -0.28 is applied. We select the windows centered at each connected component as possible candidates to contain a mitosis. A window of size 24×24 pixels is used.

4.3 Learning and Testing

Let's denote by GTL the pyramid ground-truth labeling defined by the coordinates of mitosis centers in all scales. A strong labeling pyramid (MGTL) is generated, by labeling as 1 those windows inside circles of fixed radius centered at the GTL's mitosis centers. Radius of 96, 48 and 24 pixels are used for 40x, 20x and 10x scale respectively. The windows of label 0 on each level are computed in runtime as the difference between the MGTL mask and the mask obtained by thresholding and extrapolating the predicted probabilities from the above pyramid level, let denote it as PR. The used threshold is fixed in training time in order to keep all GTL windows within the class 1. The label 0 at each level represents hard false positive, since not being mitosis were predicted as such with high probability by the above level. In the case of the first level (10x), the mask computed in Sect. 4.2 is used as PR. At each pyramid level the negative training samples are obtained by sampling of the mask of class 0. The positive samples are patches centered at the coordinates indicated in GTL. The patch size used is 24×24, 48×48 and 96×96 for scales 10x, 20x and 40x, respectively. Before extracting the patches for training, we use the stain normalization algorithm proposed in [12] to reduce the variation in the training dataset. This normalization is also used during testing before the WSI is processed.

Each classifier in the pyramid is trained for 90 epochs with the Adam optimizer [7] to minimized the binary cross-entropy loss: $\mathrm{BCE}(y, p) = y \log(p) +$

$(1 - y) \log(1 - p)$ where y is the label and p the predicted probability of the sample being mitosis. The probability value of the dropout used in all the models was 0.4 and the weight decay was set to 10^{-4}. The learning rate was set to 10^{-3} for PB-CNN and $5 \cdot 10^{-4}$ for the scale 40x of PB-CNN-STP; in both cases was divided by 10 each 30 epochs. Each batch was constructed by randomly sampling 32 positive samples and 32 negative samples. Each epoch samples 10^6 batches.

Data augmentation has been applied from random rotations and mirroring. We also apply random shifting up to 4, 8 and 16 pixels for scales 10x, 20x and 40x respectively, as well as random scaling by a factor sampled in the range [0.75, 1.25]. Additive Gaussian noise with 0.05 of standard deviation was also added to the input. Finally, in order to introduce robustness to color variation, we use the stain augmentation process proposed in [8] with α and β parameters sampled in the ranges [0.995, 1.05] and [−0.05, 0.05] respectively.

We implement the Bayesian approach according to [4]. For it, we sample the dropout units from a Bernoulli distribution with probability $p = 0.4$. Once trained, the prediction and uncertainty of the network per each input image are computed as the average of the values of 10 new samples of the dropout units after weight adaptation by the forward pass.

Finally, we have found necessary to apply a high Dropout rate to the feature maps of previous levels at the beginning of the training process. This was done in order to force not to rely too much in previous predictions and extract useful information from the current scale. We set this dropout rate to 0.8 and linearly decrease it to 0 at epoch 40.

5   Experiments

To demonstrate the benefits of our proposed PB-CNN, we first test it on our dataset conformed by 22 WSIs. We separate the WSIs in training and test sets by randomly selecting 5 WSIs as the test set and leaving the remaining 17 ones for training. We have 7133 mitoses for training and 1103 for testing.

Table 1. Two first rows show a comparison with state of the art methods on ICPR-2012 MITOSIS test set [13]. Last three rows show a comparison on our test dataset of 5 WSI. Evolution of the F1-score and processing time are shown by scales. Results for the times were calculated applying sliding window on each pixel and using a Nvidia Titan X.

Method	PBCNN-STP	DeepDet [8]	RR [11]	CasNN [1]	
F1 score	82.6%	83.2%	82.3%	78.8%	
Method	PBCNN10x	PBCNN20x	PBCNN	PBCNN-STP	WRCNN40x
F1-score	62.8%	72.5%	78.1%	81.3%	71.2%
Ave.Time WSI	27 ± 11	28 ± 10	29 ± 11	31 ± 11	56 ± 23

At the second row of Table 1 we show the F1-score and time increase of adding each level of the pyramid, as well as using the Spatial Transforming Layer [6]. All models were tested using the same framework and the same computer with a Nvidia Titan X with 12 GB of RAM. As the table shows, each level comes with a significant increase in performance at the cost of a small increase in computational time. Adding the Spatial Transforming Layer [6] we get an increase of 3.2% in F1-score at the cost of a slightly impact on the processing time. For the sake of comparison, we train a Bayesian Wide Residual Network identical to the one used on the 40x scale only, we call it WR-CNN-40x. The training process was the same as described for our PB-CNN in Sect. 4.3, although we change the dropout probability to 0.3 since we find it gives better results. The results of this WR-CNN-40x are show in the two first rows of the Table 1. The propose PB-CNN is almost two times faster and gets a significant better F1-score than this WR-CNN-40x, showing that the increase obtained is due to the pyramid architecture.

In order to compare our models with other in the literature, we train our best performing model PB-CNN-STP with our 22 WSI and test it on MITOS-ICPR2012 test set containing images produced by the Aperio XT scanner. Then, we extract the features provide by each scale before the last classification layer and train a Random Forest classifier on the training dataset of the Aperio XT scanner. Table 1 shows the results in comparison with other state of the art methods. We can see that the best of our proposed method get a competitive result against current state of the art in F1-score, despite being trained on WSI of a different tissue.

6   Discussion and Conclusions

A new coarse to fine cascade of CNN Bayesian models for mitosis detection has been proposed. The new mechanism of information propagation from top to bottom, using the uncertainty of the prediction, allow to get results competitive with the state of the art on MITOS ICPR-2012 dataset. To the best of our knowledge, this is the first time that a coarse to fine approach combined with uncertainty is used in mitosis detection. In our experiments, the Bayesian pyramid approach reduces the computation time by a factor of two and increases by 7% the F1-score with respect to the same CNN architecture applied only over the 40x scale. We have also shown the benefits of using Spatial Transforming Layers to deal with local geometric deformations. On our dataset this invariance increases the F1-score score by a 3.2%. It is also remarkable that our architecture is trained with samples from a different tissue than breast cancer. This shows that our model is able of learning useful mitosis features for the transfer of learning between tissues. Regarding efficiency, the times measured on whole WSI make our method a good candidate for daily clinic. More experiments on harder databases have to be carried out in order to assess the good properties pointed out for the model. The addition of new input information from inmunohistochemistry stains is also other relevant issue for future work.

References

1. Chen, H., Dou, Q., Wang, X., Qin, J., Heng, P.A.: Mitosis detection in breast cancer histology images via deep cascaded networks. In: Proceedings of the Thirtieth AAAI Conference on Artificial Intelligence (AAAI-16), pp. 1160–1166 (2016)
2. Chen, H., Wang, X., Heng, P.A.: Automated mitosis detection with deep regression networks. In: IEEE International Symposium on Biomedical Imaging, pp. 1204–1207 (2016)
3. Cireşan, D.C., Giusti, A., Gambardella, L.M., Schmidhuber, J.: Mitosis detection in breast cancer histology images with deep neural networks. In: Mori, K., Sakuma, I., Sato, Y., Barillot, C., Navab, N. (eds.) MICCAI 2013. LNCS, vol. 8150, pp. 411–418. Springer, Heidelberg (2013). https://doi.org/10.1007/978-3-642-40763-5_51
4. Gal, Y., Ghahramani, Z.: Dropout as a Bayesian approximation: representing model uncertainty in deep learning. In: Proceedings of the 33rd International Conference on Machine Learning (ICML-16) (2016)
5. ICPR (2014). https://mitos-atypia-14.grand-challenge.org/
6. Jaderberg, M., Simonyan, K., Zisserman, A., Kavukcuoglu, K.: Spatial transformer networks. In: Advances in Neural Information Processing Systems, vol. 28. pp. 2017–2025 (2015)
7. Kingma, D.P., Ba, J.: Adam: a method for stochastic optimization. CoRR abs/1412.6980 (2014). http://arxiv.org/abs/1412.6980
8. Li, C., Wanga, X., Liua, W., Latecki, L.J.: DeepMitosis: mitosis detection via deep detection, verification and segmentation networks. Med. Image Anal. **45**, 121–133 (2018)
9. Macenko, M., et al.: A method for normalizing histology slides for quantitative analysis. In: IEEE International Symposium on Biomedical Imaging: From Nano to Macro, pp. 1107–1110 (2009)
10. MICCAI (2016). http://tupac.tue-image.nl/
11. Paul, A., Dey, A., Mukherjee, D.P., Sivaswamy, J., Tourani, V.: Regenerative random forest with automatic feature selection to detect mitosis in histopathological breast cancer images. In: Navab, N., Hornegger, J., Wells, W.M., Frangi, A.F. (eds.) MICCAI 2015. LNCS, vol. 9350, pp. 94–102. Springer, Cham (2015). https://doi.org/10.1007/978-3-319-24571-3_12
12. Reinhard, E., Ashikhmin, M., Gooch, B., Shirley, P.: Color transfer between images. IEEE Comput. Graph. Appl. **21**(5), 34–41 (2001)
13. Roux, L., et al.: Mitosis detection in breast cancer histological images an ICPR 2012 contest. J. Pathol. Inform. (2013)
14. Tejera-Vaquerizo, A., et al.: Is mitotic rate still useful in the management of patients with thin melanoma? J. Eur. Acad. Dermatol. Venereol. **31**(12), 2025–2029 (2017)
15. Tellez, D., et al.: Whole-slide mitosis detection in "H&E" breast histology using PHH3 as a reference to train distilled stain-invariant convolutional networks. IEEE Trans. Med. Imaging **37**(9), 2126–2136 (2018)
16. Veta, M., et al.: Assessment of algorithms for mitosis detection in breast cancer histopathology images. Med. Image Anal. **20**(1), 237–248 (2015)
17. Wang, H., et al.: Mitosis detection in breast cancer pathology images by combining handcrafted and convolutional neural network features. J. Med. Imaging **1**, 034003 (2014)

18. Zagoruyko, S., Komodakis, N.: Wide residual networks. In: Proceedings of the British Machine Vision Conference (BMVC), pp. 87.1–87.12, September 2016
19. Zerhouni, E., Lányi, D., Viana, M., Gabrani, M.: Wide residual networks for mitosis detection. In: IEEE 14th International Symposium on Biomedical Imaging (ISBI), pp. 924–928 (2017)

Improvement of Mitosis Detection Through the Combination of PHH3 and HE Features

Santiago López-Tapia[1](✉), Cristobal Olivencia[1](✉),
José Aneiros-Fernández[2](✉), and Nicolás Pérez de la Blanca[1](✉)

[1] Computer Science and Artificial Intelligence Department, University of Granada, Granada, Spain
sltapia@decsai.ugr.es, cristoly94@gmail.com, nicolas@ugr.es
[2] Intercenter Unit of Pathological Anatomy, San Cecilio University Hospital, Granada, Spain
janeirosf@hotmail.com

Abstract. Mitosis detection in hematoxylin and eosin (H&E) images is prone to error due to the unspecificity of the stain for this purpose. Alternatively, the inmunohistochemistry phospho-histone H3 (PHH3) stain has improved the task with a significant reduction of the false negatives. These facts point out on the interest in combining features from both stains to improve mitosis detection. Here we propose an algorithm that, taking as input a pair of whole-slides images (WSI) scanned from the same slide and stained with H&E and PHH3 respectively, find the matching between the stains of the same object. This allows to use both stains in the detection stage. Linear filtering in combination with local search based on a kd-tree structure is used to find potential matches between objects. A Siamese convolutional neural network (SCNN) is trained to detect the correct matches and a CNN model is trained for mitosis detection from matches. At the best of our knowledge, this is the first time that mitosis detection in WSI is assessed combining two stains. The experiments show a strong improvement of the detection F1-score when H&E and PHH3 are used jointly compared to the single stain F1-scores.

Keywords: Mitosis detection · WSI · PHH3 and HE · Siamese CNN

1   Introduction

The quantification of mitosis in histopathological tissues and specifically its ratio per square millimeter is one of the most relevant factors in the prognosis of cancer. Unfortunately, the process of mitosis detection on images stained with standard hematoxylin and eosin (H&E) is difficult and prone to errors due to

This paper has been supported by the Spanish Ministry of Economy and Competitiveness and the European Regional Development Fund (FEDER) under the grant DPI2016-77869-C2-2-R.

C. C. Reyes-Aldasoro et al. (Eds.): ECDP 2019, LNCS 11435, pp. 144–152, 2019.
https://doi.org/10.1007/978-3-030-23937-4_17

multiple factors consequence of its unspecificity [16]. H&E staining only helps indirectly to mitosis identification, being the hyperchromaticity induced on the mitotic cell nucleus one of the its most salient features. Unfortunately, many others tissue parts are stained with a similar color too.

Phospho-histone H3 (PHH3) is a well-known immunomarker, specific for cells undergoing mitoses [14]. This fact causes PHH3 to improve the inter-observer variability of the mitosis count by a decrease in false negatives, but at the same time is prone to false positives as for instance in inter-phase tumor cells with phosphorylated core protein H3. The staining with PHH3 has meant an important improvement in mitosis detection for many type of cancers [4,12].

The technology for the whole scanning of tissue slides (WSI) is able of digitizing a slide at resolutions of $0.25 - 0.16\,\mu$ per pixel, which means image sizes of 10^{10} pixels. In this setting, the task of mitosis detection can only be addressed using accurate and efficient algorithms. The convolutional neuronal network (CNN) models have demonstrated, in recent years, a clear superiority over traditional approaches in this task. [6,10]. Here we focus on these kind of models.

An issue that remains to be explored in some detail is the relevance of the combination of stains in the mitosis detection process. Recently, in [15] an interesting approach taking advantage of the properties of both stains, H&E and PHH3, to build a mitosis detector on H&E has been proposed. This approach uses the PHH3 information to locate ground-truth mitosis on WSI but the goal is a classifier on H&E. Although the approach means an important step in the detection of mitosis in WSI, several issues still remain open. First, to design a simple training model taking advantage of both stains simultaneously. Second, the labeling process should take into account both stains. Figure 1 shows some cases of mitosis where the labeling from a single stain is misleading. Finally, assessing the contribution of trained detectors with both stains is a relevant issue to improve routine in daily practice.

In contrast to the above discussed approach, here we propose the simultaneous use of both stains in the labeling and detection stages. To do that we stain twice each slide taking advantage of the property of the antigenic recovering of the immunochemistry for destaining the H&E. This strategy reports important benefits: (i) better labeling, (ii) training dataset with both stains, (iii) improvement in detection score. The two most important challenges in our approach are a fast search for potential correct matches and an assessment model for matches.

Our main contributions in this paper are: (i) a fast and efficient technique to generate matching between both stains of the same object, (ii) the proposal of a SCNN model to validate the matches; (iii) we show that training from both stains means a clear improvement in detection score compared to use of only one. Finally, we emphasize that our searching algorithm makes very easy the labeling of pairs.

The rest of the paper is as follows. Section 2 defines the problem. Section 3 discuss the proposed approach. Section 4 shows the experimental results, and in Sect. 5 the discussion and conclusions are presented.

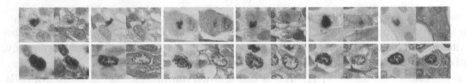

Fig. 1. This figure shows by rows examples of two difficult scenarios regarding mitosis detection in H&E or PHH3. The first row shows examples where the mitoses are very difficult to detect in H&E but can be easily detected on PHH3. The second row shows examples where the PHH3 stain indicates positive mitosis but the H&E stain shows that it is not.

2   Problem Definition

To begin with we focus on the automatic object matching between stains of the same histological tissue. The relevance of this task is due to the lack of consensus between pathologists when they are asked to label a set of cells as mitosis or no-mitosis in H&E images. In the MYTHOS-ATYPIA challenge [5], for instance, multi-labels had to be considered. Daily practice has shown that many ambiguities can be solve when both stains are observed together. Figure 1 shows some examples. This has motivated the interest to know how much a detector can improve when training with both stains. The automatic identification of correct matches between stains it is not a straightforward task. The manipulation of the slide in the double staining process, that is, staining with H&E and scanning, destaining, and restaining again with PHH3 and new scanning, introduce small local deformations on the tissue that makes impossible automatic matching of the images using geometrical registering. In addition, the different response of the tissue to each one of the stains also introduce strong differences in the shape and color of the surfaces of the cells as shows Fig. 1. To overcome all these deformations, we propose a search strategy to extract possible matches and a similarity distance to find correct matches. For this latter task, we propose a Siamese CNN (SCNN) [3,8] since the CNN models have shown to be very efficient in extracting similar features from images, that being visually different, are similar in a some semantic context. At one last step, the correct matches are assessed, for mitosis presence, by a CNN classifier.

3   Methodology

3.1   Matches Extraction

Let's denote by p-WSI $= (I_{PHH3}, I_{HE})$ the two WSI images of the same slide with different stain. We extract the objects present in each image applying standard cell detection functions, [1], and eliminating all those objects with a size greater than a preset threshold. For this, we use the hematoxiline and DAB bands of the H&E and PHH3 images respectively. The center of mass of the remaining connected components (CC) is computed. A kd-tree data structure (KdT) [2]

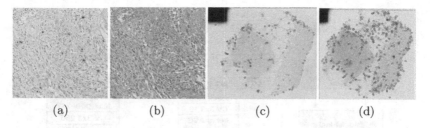

Fig. 2. Images (a) and (b) show, inside circles, objects detected on PHH3 and H&E respectively. Images (c) and (d) show, in circles of color, SURF points detected in PHH3 and H&E respectively. (Best see it at higher magnification)

is fed with the coordinates of the centers of the H&E image. The centers of the PHH3 image are saved as a list of points, L_{DAB}. In order to reduce the number of pair to analyze we take advantage of the specificity of the PHH3 stain to identify the potential mitosis presents in the image. To this end, each vector of coordinates in the DAB list is used as query to the KdT to retrieve matching candidates from the H&E image. Figure 2(a, b)) shows an example of how unbalanced is the number of detections in both stains. In order to make easier the searching process we register the bounding boxes of the tissue area in both images through an affine transformation, $\mathcal{A} : I_{PHH3} \rightarrow I_{HE}$, estimate from SURF points [2] detected from grey levels after sub-sampling the image by a factor of ten. For each point $x \in L_{DAB}$, its coordinates are projected onto the axes of H&E by the affine transformation, $y = \mathcal{A}x$, and all points $z \in \mathrm{KdT}$ such that $distance(y, z) < thr$ are extracted, where thr is a prefixed threshold. Let's denote by p-center the pair formed by the coordinates of the query-point, x, and the coordinates of anyone of its matches. For each p-center, image-patches of size 80×80 pixels centered on them are extracted from the images. Let's denote them as p-patch. These p-patch are assessed by the SCNN that output a similarity distance in terms of a probability. For each x the p-patch with maximun probability is considered the true match. Let's denote a correct p-patch as p-match. In summary, our matching algorithms is as follows:

ALGORITHM: $MS(H\&E, PHH3, T, \mathcal{P}_{HE}, \mathcal{P}_{PHH3})$
Input:
- $(H\&E, PHH3)$: WSI of the same slide
- T: distance-threshold for searching
- $\mathcal{P}_{HE}$: list of coordinates of the object centers detected in H&E
- $\mathcal{P}_{PHH3}$: list of coordinates of the object centers detected in PHH3
Preprocessing:
- Build a KdT from $\mathcal{P}_{HE}$.
- Compute SURF points: $SURF_{HE}$, $SURF_{PHH3}$
- Compute Global affine transformation: $\mathcal{A} : SURF_{PHH3} \rightarrow SURF_{HE}$. .
Correspondences:
For each item $p \in \mathcal{P}_{PHH3}$

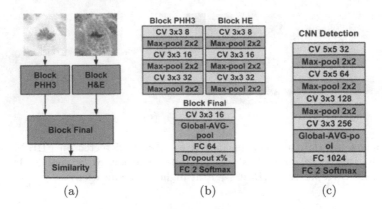

Fig. 3. Siamese architecture: (a) shows the global network design composed of two parallel branches to process each one of the images. After the feature extraction a function of the feature vectors compute the similarity between the images. In (b) we show the three main blocks that compose the model. CV correspond to Convolution and ReLU activation and FC to full connected layer followed by ReLU. We use batch normalization before each ReLU. In (c) the architecture of the CNN model used for mitosis detection is shown.

1.- Compute $\hat{p} = \mathcal{A}p$
2.- Compute $\mathcal{P}_{\mathrm{KdT}}(p) = \{q | q \in \mathrm{KdT}, \mathrm{distance}(\hat{p}, q) < T\}$
3.- Extract patches $\{o_q\}$ centered in $q \in \mathcal{P}_{\mathrm{KdT}}(p)$
4.- Compute $\hat{q} = argmax_{q \in \mathcal{P}_{\mathrm{KdT}}(p)} Similarity_{SCCN}(o_p, o_q)$
5.- Output $(o_{\hat{q}}, o_p)$
where $Similarity_{SCCN}$ denote the probability computed by the Siamese network.

3.2   Dataset and Labeling

Two datasets of p-match have been created. The first dataset, DS1, is defined by 57k (1k = 1000) p-match extracted after staining and scanning 48 slides, 30 of skin cancer (melanoma) and 18 of breast cancer. The second dataset, DS2, is defined by 11k p-match of mitosis and 75k p-patch no mitosis extracted from 17 slides of melanoma. The slides were scanned with a Philips Ultra-Fast Scanner at a spatial resolution of $0.25\,\mu$ per pixel. All p-patch were labeled by a senior pathologist of the Saint Cecilio Universitary Hospital in Granada, who annotated a percentage of the correct matches on each p-WSI. An interactive software which iterates showing p-patches and their surrounding areas was used for this task. A p-patch is tagged with a maximum of two clicks: one click to decide correspondence vs. no correspondence and another click to decide mitosis vs. non-mitosis. This is a very simple routine that allows to label many pairs in a short period of time.

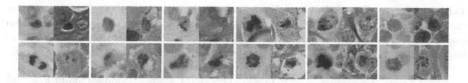

Fig. 4. This Fig. show some examples of the errors of the algorithm-MS. The first row shows examples of false negative p-match. The second row shows examples of false positives p-match. See the pair as (PHH3, HE)

3.3   Training

Our specific SCNN model is shown in Fig. 3(a–b). It can be observed that Block-PHH3 y Block-H&E share the same architecture based on a standard Lenet model of CNN [9]. Block-Final processes the features from the input blocks to learn the similarities. The network is trained during 100 epochs using a batch size of 128 with Adam [7] optimizer and initial learning rate of 0.0002. We reduce the learning rate by a factor of 10 each 10 epochs if the training loss has not been reduced. The training stops if the loss keeps without reducing after another 20 epochs. The networks outputs the probability of a p-patch, {he, phh3}, of being a p-match. We train the network to minimize the binary cross entropy loss $\mathcal{L}(\cdot,\cdot)$, defined for each sample as,

$$\mathcal{L}(\mathrm{he, phh3}) = -y(\log(f_\theta(\mathrm{he, phh3}) + (1-y)\log(1 - f_\theta(\mathrm{he, phh3}))$$

where $y \in \{+1, -1\}$ represents the image-pair's label and f_θ represents the function computed by our SCNN. To regularize the model, we use L2-weight decay of strength 1.0 on the parameters of the network and Dropout [13] with probability of 0.3 before the last full connected layer. The CNN used for mitosis detection from p-match is shown in Fig. 3(c). We minimize the binary cross-entropy loss function using the Adam [7] optimizer with learning rate set to 0.001 during the first 50 epochs, then reduced to 0.0001 for 25 epochs and finally set to 0.00001 for another 25 epochs. We set the weight decay parameter to 0.0001 and use Dropout of 0.5 before each non-linearity except before the Softmax layer. Also, we use data augmentation on the p-match by rotating the input patches by 90°, 180° and 270° and performing horizontal and vertical flips. We also add Gaussian noise with $\sigma = 0.0001$ to the input.

4   Experimental Results

We assess the performance of our algorithm-MS by cross-validation. To do this, we define five folds from the set of 48 p-WSI. On each fold 43 p-WSI are used for training and 5 for testing. In total we use 25 different p-WSI in testing. On each fold the set of p-match, extracted from each image, is used according to the role of the image in that fold. Table 1 shows the number of p-match used in training and testing for each fold. The items for the negative class are

Table 1. Top:results of the correspondence experiment. 1k = 1000. The second row shows the number of corresponding pairs used, in each fold, in training and validation respectively. The third row shows the validation accuracy in each fold for patches of 80 × 80 pixels. Bottom: detection F1-score using the different stains

	Fold-1	Fold-2	Fold-3	Fold-4	Fold-5
Train matches	56.6k	52.5k	47k	54k	45.6k
Valid. matches	721	4.8k	10.4k	3.4k	11.7k
Valid. Accuracy (80 × 80)	98.6%	99.9%	100%	99.9%	99.6%

Patches	H& E	PHH3	H& E+PHH3		
Detection F1-score	73.5%	77.8%	80.6%		

generated by random combinations of the p-match items. We generate as many negative item as there are p-match. The test with each fold begins by detecting and extracting the coordinates of the centers of the objects in the p-WSI test. We use cell detection routines of the QuPath [1] free software to extract the center of the object on each p-WSI. The kd-tree structure is build using [2]. From them the set of p-patch is estimated. Eventually, the p-patch are assessed by the SCNN. In this experiment what we measure is the accuracy of the p-match test elements (see Table 1(top)). In order to evaluate the effect of the number of p-match in the testing matching error, we design the folds to cover a broad range of values in testing. A value of $thr = 60$ is used as searching distance in the KdT. The average query time per image is about 3s. Third row in Table 1 shows the accuracy achieved on each fold. The estimated accuracy of the algorithm-MS for matches is 99.6%±0.58. Figure 4 shows some examples of p-match errors from SCNN. We assess the H&E+PHH3 improvement versus the single stains, on dataset labeled from both stains, using the detector architecture shown in Fig. 3(c). We select this architecture for two reasons. First, it represents an adaptation of Lenet model which is the most popular CNN used for mitosis detection. Second, our dataset is filtered by the matching algorithm that removes much of the false positives. This makes unnecessary a complex architecture for this task. In a first experiment we train and test our detector using each one of the components, H&E and PHH3, of the p-WSI. In the second experiment we use full p-WSI. In all cases the color of the images was normalized using the algorithm given in [11]. From the dataset, DS2, we constructed 5 partitions of WSIs and used them for cross-validation. Table 1 in the bottom shows the detection F1-score achieved by our detector using patches from H&E, PHH3 and H&E+PHH3 respectively. The result shows that using together both stains greatly improve the F1 score with respect to only using one. To evaluate the impact of the p-match errors in detection we test our CNN with the same image dataset but computing the p-match using the algorithm-MS. In this case an F1 score of 80.1 ± 0.4% is achieved, which means a drop of only 0.6 points.

5   Discussion and Conclusions

The proposed approach shows that both stains H&E and PHH3 when used together make a significant contribution to the detection of mitosis. In addition, our approach contributes with a new technique for the labeling of mitosis using both stains simultaneously. The size of the datasets makes our results preliminary but also reliable. It remains to be done a full evaluation of the matching errors and the influence of the detector. The help of our algorithm-MS in the complete labeling of p-WSI opens the door to create larger and more challenging training data sets to evaluate new algorithms. This will be one goal for future work.

References

1. Bankhead, P., et al.: QuPath: open source software for digital pathology image analysis. Sci. Rep. **7**(1), 16878 (2019). https://doi.org/10.1038/s41598-017-17204-5
2. Bradski, G.: The OpenCV library. Dr. Dobb's J. Softw. Tools (2000)
3. Chopra, S., Hadsell, R., LeCun, Y.: Learning a similarity metric discriminatively with application to face verification. Comput. Vis. Pattern Recogn. **1**, 539–546 (2005)
4. Dessauvagie, B.F., Thomas, C., Robinson, C., Frost, F.A., Harvey, J., Sterrett, G.F.: Validation of mitosis counting by automated phosphohistone H3 (PHH3) digital image analysis in a breast carcinoma tissue microarray. Pathology **47**(4), 329–334 (2015)
5. ICPR (2014). https://mitos-atypia-14.grand-challenge.org/
6. Janowczyk, A., Madabhushi, A.: Deep learning for digital pathology image analysis: a comprehensive tutorial with selected use cases. J. Pathol. Inform. **7**(1), 29–29 (2016). Jan
7. Kingma, D.P., Ba, J.: Adam: a method for stochastic optimization. CoRR abs/1412.6980 (2014). http://arxiv.org/abs/1412.6980
8. Koch, G., Zemel, R., Salakhutdinov, R.: Siamese neural networks for one-shot image recognition. In: ICML workshop on Deep Learning (2015)
9. LeCun, Y., Bengio, Y.: Convolutional networks for images, speech, and time series. Handb. Brain Theory Neural Netw. **3361**(10) (1995)
10. Litjens, G.J.S., et al.: A survey on deep learning in medical image analysis. CoRR abs/1702.05747 (2017). http://arxiv.org/abs/1702.05747
11. Macenko, M., et al.: A method for normalizing histology slides for quantitative analysis. In: IEEE International Symposium on Biomedical Imaging: From Nano to Macro, pp. 1107–1110 (2009)
12. Nielsen, P.S., Riber-Hansen, R., Jensen, T.O., Schmidt, H., Steiniche, T.: Proliferation indices of phosphohistone H3 and Ki67: strong prognostic markers in a consecutive cohort with stage I/II melanoma. Mod. Pathol. **26**, 404 (2012). Nov
13. Srivastava, N., Hinton, G., Krizhevsky, A., Sutskever, I., Salakhutdinov, R.: Dropout: a simple way to prevent neural networks from overfitting. J. Mach. Learn. Res. **15**, 1929–1958 (2014)
14. Tapia, C., Kutzner, H., Mentzel, T., Savic, S., Baumhoer, D., Glatz, K.: Two mitosis-specific antibodies, MPM-2 and phospho-histone H3 (Ser28), allow rapid and precise determination of mitotic activity. Am. J. Surg. Pathol. **30**(1), 83–9 (2006)

15. Tellez, D., et al.: Whole-slide mitosis detection in "H&E" breast histology using PHH3 as a reference to train distilled stain-invariant convolutional networks. IEEE Trans. Med. Imaging **37**(9), 2126–2136 (2018)
16. Veta, M., et al.: Assessment of algorithms for mitosis detection in breast cancer histopathology images. Med. Image Anal. **20**(1), 237–248 (2015)

A New Paradigm of RNA-Signal Quantitation and Contextual Visualization for On-Slide Tissue Analysis

Auranuch Lorsakul[1]([⊠]) and William Day[2]([⊠])

[1] Roche Tissue Diagnostics, Imaging and Algorithms, Digital Pathology,
Santa Clara, CA, USA
auranuch.lorsakul@roche.com
[2] Roche Tissue Diagnostics, Tissue Research and Early Development,
Tucson, AZ, USA
bill.day@roche.com

Abstract. An objective digital pathology solution to quantify the ribonucleic acid (RNA) signal in tissue samples could enable analysis of gene expression changes in individual cancer and dysregulated normal cells (immune cells, etc.). Here, we present a new method that leverages the punctate RNA *In-situ* hybridization (ISH) signal to quantify gene expression, while maintaining tissue context and enabling single cell analysis and workflow. This digital pathology solution detects and quantifies the punctate dot signals generated by one- and two-color RNA ISH technology in formaldehyde fixed-paraffin embedded (FFPE) tissue. The digital pathology solution was implemented to determine the characteristics of individual spots including size, intensity, blurriness and roundness all of which were used to determine individual spot feature characteristics. Significantly, we determined that spots maintain similar characteristics irrespective of the RNA biomarker and/or tissue used. The verification on 31 microscope images shows agreement of $R^2 = 0.99$ and a concordance correlation coefficient (CCC) = 0.99 for the total spot counts identified by the observer (115,154) and the algorithm (112,809). We have leveraged the unique detection features of the RNA ISH technology to develop a new method to quantify RNA signal while maintaining tissue context. It is anticipated that this method will enable analysis of gene expression changes in heterogeneous cancer and normal cells and tissues with single cell resolution.

Keywords: In situ hybridization (ISH) · Digital pathology · RNA · Image analysis · Quantitative analysis · Image processing · Cancer · Histopathology imaging

1 Introduction

In-situ hybridization (ISH) can be used to look for the presence of a genetic abnormality or condition such as amplification of cancer causing genes specifically in cells that, when viewed under a microscope, morphologically appear to be malignant. Unique nucleic acid sequences occupy precise positions in chromosomes, cells and

© Springer Nature Switzerland AG 2019
C. C. Reyes-Aldasoro et al. (Eds.): ECDP 2019, LNCS 11435, pp. 153–162, 2019.
https://doi.org/10.1007/978-3-030-23937-4_18

tissues and ISH allows the presence, absence and/or amplification/expression status of such sequences to be determined without major disruption of the sequences. ISH employs labeled deoxyribonucleic acid (DNA) or ribonucleic acid (RNA) probe molecules that bind to a target gene sequence or transcript to catalyze detection or localization of targeted nucleic acid genes within a cell or tissue sample [1].

Historically, the clinical evaluation of proteins and nucleic acids in tissue has relied upon *in situ* immunoenzymatic detection (staining) methods. For example, detection of B cell clonality is useful for assisting in the diagnosis of B cell lymphomas and such an assessment can be accomplished through the evaluation of KAPPA and LAMBDA light chain expression. As seen in Fig. 1, tonsil tissue stained for KAPPA mRNA may be detected using a black chromogen (silver, Ag) and LAMBDA mRNA may be detected using a purple chromogen (tyramide-sulforhodamine). The presence of the signal of interest appears as tiny spots (e.g. discrete dots) and these spots may accumulate to form larger regions of aggregate signal (hereinafter "signal aggregate blobs" or "blobs") depending on the expression level (copy number) of each targeted mRNA in B cells. By way of example, plasma cells have approximately 100,000 mRNA copies per cell, and therefore signal in those cells may appear as blobs.

Quantitative ISH analysis will likely be useful in clinical evaluation of a variety of RNA biomarkers; however, its utility remains uncertain due to limitations of existing technologies. An automated technique for estimating an amount of isolated dot signal and signal aggregate blob may facilitate enhanced clinical interpretation of stained biological samples, enable samples to be interpreted more quickly and accurately, and empower evaluation of RNA biomarker clinical utility. In this study, we have developed an image-analysis system and method that enables the detection and quantification of the number of nucleic acid signals present in stained samples.

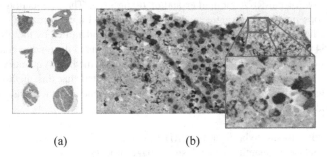

(a)   (b)

Fig. 1. The example of tonsil stained using *in situ* hybridization (ISH) illustrating KAPPA mRNA detected with silver (Ag) in the black color and LAMBDA mRNA detected with tyramide SRB in the purple color: (a) the wholeslide image with six tonsil regions and (b) a field-of-view image at 40X. (Color figure online)

2   Methods

The proposed image-analysis framework for detecting and quantifying the expression of the RNA targets (biomarkers) used in our study is shown in Fig. 2.

In this study, we propose a method of estimating an amount of signal corresponding to at least one biomarker in an image of a biological sample comprising: (1) detecting isolated spots in an image (e.g., an unmixed image channel image corresponding to signals from a biomarker); (2) deriving an optical density value of a representative isolated spot (e.g., based on computed signal features or characteristics from the detected isolated spots); (3) and estimating the number of predictive spots in signal aggregates in each of the sub-regions based on the derived optical density value of the representative isolated spot. The method further includes calculation of a total of number of spots in a sub-region by combining a number of detected isolated spots and the estimated number of predictive spots in signal aggregates in each of the sub-regions. Finally, a total number of detected isolated spots combined (i.e. summed) with the estimated number of predictive spots for each sub-region of signal aggregates for the entire tissue slides can be calculated and stored in a database [1].

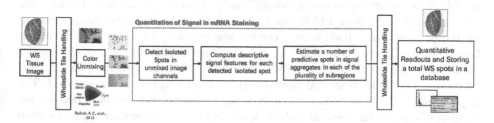

Fig. 2. Image-analysis flowchart illustrating the steps to detect and quantify the expression of RNA targets (biomarkers) in a whole slide image (WS – wholeslide).

2.1   Tissue Staining and Digital Images

Using 2.5-µm formaldehyde fixed-paraffin embedded (FFPE) tissue sections, a total of 189 field-of-view (FOV) microscope images and a total of 31 tissue slides of tonsil, lymphoma, and Calu-3 (xenograft) were included in the algorithm development. Tissue slides were stained with a simplex (one color)- and a duplex (two-color)-ISH protocol using probes targeting GAPDH, KAPPA, MALAT1, and KAPPA/LAMBDA RNA transcripts. The staining process was performed using a VENTANA Benchmark Ultra autostainer. All slides were counterstained with Hematoxylin (HTX) in blue color. The 31 slides were scanned using a VENTANA DP 200 scanner. RGB images were obtained with a resolution of $0.25 \times 0.25 \ \mu m^2$ and a typical size of 3 billion pixels or $20 \times 20 \ mm^2$.

2.2   Pre-processing of Color Unmixing

Preprocessing of a color unmixing is performed using a conventional color-deconvolution method to separate different chromogens e.g., black, purple, and blue. In our study, the approach proposed by Ruifrok *et al.* [2] was selected. The unmixing method can be applied to singleplex stained images with one chromogen and counterstain, or applied to multiplex staining images with more than one chromogen and counterstain, as shown in the examples in Fig. 3.

2.3   Isolated Spot Detection

Following image acquisition and/or unmixing, an image having a single biomarker channel is provided to the spot detection module such that isolated spots within the image may be detected (as opposed to the "blobs" or aggregate dot signals). An unmixed image channel image is used for input for the spot and blob detection module. A morphological operation is performed to detect isolated spots, i.e. dots, within the image.

As seen in Fig. 4, following the detection of each of the isolated spots in the input image, the detected isolated spots are separated from the blobs in the input image, providing an "isolated spots image channel" and a "blob image channel". The detected spots are masked out from a blob image channel. In an isolated spots image channel, small objects or blurred point sources can be detected using a multiscale Difference of Gaussians (DoG) approach. Multiple spot sizes are configured in ascending order (small to large), but the processing is in the order of large to small spots. In each iteration, a DoG filter is created from the given inner and outer filter sizes [3]. The respective detections are collected in a resulting seed/annotation object to become the location of each of the detected isolated spots in the (x, y) coordinates; this location corresponds to the seed center of each detected isolated spot. A seed center can be calculated by determining a centroid or center of mass of each detected isolated spot.

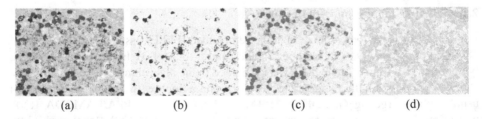

(a)   (b)   (c)   (d)

Fig. 3. (a) A portion of a whole slide image stained using an *in situ* hybridization assay to detect KAPPA mRNA (black color) and LAMBDA mRNA (purple color) with counterstain hematoxylin; (b, c) an example of an image channel image after unmixing, showing only signal corresponding to KAPPA mRNA (black color) and LAMBDA mRNA (purple color), respectively, and (d) an example of an image channel after unmixing, showing the hematoxylin channel (blue). (Color figure online)

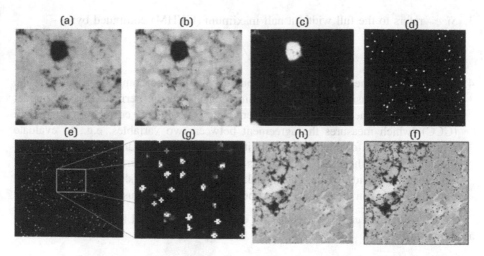

Fig. 4. (a) Provides an example of a portion of a whole slide image stained in an ISH assay, (b) illustrates the result of the unmixing of (a) into a single channel (black channel); (c) illustrates a blob channel image whereby the signals from the detected isolated spots from (d) are masked out; (d) illustrates the result of dot detection (a spot channel image) on the unmixed image channel image of (b); (e, f) illustrates derived (x, y) locations of the detected isolated spots in the spot channel image; and (g) and (h) illustrate an overlay of the detected isolated spots superimposed on the portion of the whole slide image.

2.4   Descriptive Signal Features for Each Detected Isolated Spot

With reference to Fig. 5, the optical density derivation module first computes descriptive signal features for each of the detected isolated spots in the image. The signal feature derivation module implements a Gaussian fitting technique is to analyze and parameterize certain characteristics of the detected isolated spots. The fitting method is performed based on the assumption that the distribution of the optical density and the radius is the normal distribution. A 1D-Gaussian-function fitting method is used to estimate the associated spot parameters within a pre-defined patch size surrounding a detected and isolated spot. The patch size is 7×7 pixels, which was determined to be the most appropriate patch size for any particular application that will facilitate the provisioning of optimal histogram results.

The characteristics derived from the Gaussian fitting technique include the size, intensity, blurriness, and roundness of the detected isolated dots, and each of these characteristics are computed using parameters of the Gaussian function. By solving the linear system $\mathbf{Ax} = \mathbf{b}$, the estimated parameters from the fitting method consist of mean, standard deviation (SD), and full-width-at-half maximum.

By fitting the parameters using the Gaussian model, the computed descriptive signal features of each isolated spot were obtained as following:

1. *Intensity* – is computed using the 98 percentile within the radius of the 5 pixel surrounded the center of the detected spots [no unit].
2. *Blurriness* – refers to the standard deviation (σ) of the Gaussian-function fitting method.

3. *Size* - refers to the full width at half maximum (FWHM) computed by:

$$FWHM = 2\sqrt{2\ln_2}\sigma \approx 2.355\sigma \tag{1}$$

4. *Roundness* – is the characteristic computed based on the comparison between the actual optical density distribution within a patch and the perfect Gaussian model computed from the estimated parameters. The concordance correlation coefficient (CCC) (which measures the agreement between two variables, e.g., to evaluate reproducibility or for inter-rater reliability) was used to compare the relationship (or the agreement), where CCC = 1 shows that the estimated parameters are perfectly agreement to the ideal Gaussian model; whereas, CCC = 0 shows that there is no agreement between the estimated parameters and the ideal Gaussian model [no unit].

Next, histograms can be generated for each computed signal feature characteristic, as shown in Fig. 5.

2.5   Estimation of a Number of Predictive Spots in Signal Aggregates in Each of the Subregions

The generated histograms provide for an understanding of the density of detected isolated cells that have particular values or representative characteristics. The generated histograms therefore provide insight into the characteristics of a representative or typical detected isolated spot. For example, from the intensity histogram (e.g. Fig. 5), it is possible to determine the intensity value of the detected isolated spots that is repeated most often (i.e. the mode of the intensity values). The representative or typical detected isolated spot is then assigned that particular determined intensity value.

The characteristics of the isolated spot representative are used to estimate the number of the spot in the aggregate signals. The estimation assumes a linear relationship between the summation of the optical density for the single spots and the aggregate signals, as following:

$$N = \frac{\sum OD_A}{\sum OD_S}, \tag{2}$$

where N is the number of the spots within an aggregate signal region, OD_A is the optical density of the aggregate signals, and ODS is the optical density of the representative isolated spot signals.

Using the feature histograms of the isolated spots in the previous step, we can apply the individual spot properties in the calculation of their summation of the optical density. The selected properties can be the mode of the intensity (optical density) and the mode of the radius in the feature histograms to calculate the summation of a representative individual spot:

$$\sum OD_S = Area \times \overline{OD_S}, \tag{3}$$

where *Area* refers to a circle (πr^2) or a rectangle (w × h) area assumed to be a shape of a spot, and $(\overline{OD_S})$ refers to the representative optical density of a single dot. This can be the mode of the intensity histogram, the average of the total intensity of the total detected isolated spots, or the weighted intensity, etc.

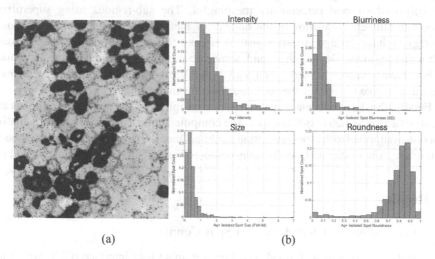

(a)   (b)

Fig. 5. The characteristics of (a) the isolated spots shown in red dots and (b) the feature histograms of intensity, blurriness, size, and roundness, respectively.

2.5.1   Segmentation and Residual Image Generation

Prior to estimating the number of predictive spots in signal aggregates, the input image is segmented into a plurality of sub-regions using segmentation. The generation of sub-regions is used to minimize the computation error due to the fact that the computations are based on a smaller local region rather an entire image. The segmentation also reduces the complexity in computing the spot counting in the aggregate signals and the sub-region concept is useful for the quality control verification by an observer and to reduce the complexity in estimating signal in the aggregate signal blobs.

Fig. 6. (a) Illustrates the result of the unmixed image in a single black channel, (b) illustrates the detected isolated dot image, (c) illustrates the residual image after masking out the black channel image from detected isolated spot image, and (d) the superpixel segmentation method was applied to the residual image (c).

As shown in Fig. 6, the residual signal is computed by masking out the black-channel image with the isolated spot image. On the residual image, irregularly sized sub-regions can be created by a superpixel segmentation method [4]. The sub-regions of the residual channel image are segmented and grouped the clump signals into smaller regions. Using the superpixel segmentation method, it groups the pixels substantially uniform and perceptually meaningful. The sub-regions using superpixels support in efficient estimation of the number of the signals efficiently. Because some sub-regions have little aggregate signal, it is easy to verify the estimated spot count within that segment. On the other hand, some sub-regions segmented by the superpixel method have completely aggregated signals within the segment, so that it creates a consistent approximation of the spot count within that segment.

Finally, the derived intensity parameter is multiplied by the area to give the optical density of a representative isolated spot. The computed optical density of a representative spot is then supplied to the spot estimation module. Once the number of predictive spots in each sub-region is estimated, the data may be stored in a database or other storage module.

3   Results

3.1   Verification of Detected Isolated Spot Counts

The quality control was performed based on a graphic user interface (GUI) which the detected isolated spots overlaid on the original and the observer could correct e.g. add, delete, move the spots. The verification was performed using 31 FOV on the simplex silver microscope images by a trained observer. The agreement plot is shown below with the R^2 of 0.99 and CCC = 0.99. The example of the spot counting results before and after the correction is in Fig. 7. The correspondence of total spot count identified by the observer (115,154) and the algorithm (112,809) is illustrated in the accompanying Table 1.

Table 1. The total spot counts between the algorithm and the observer

Result	Total spot count
Observer	115,154
Algorithm	112,809

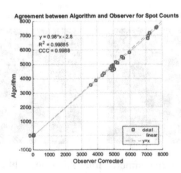

Fig. 7. Illustrates the overall scatter of the spot count correspondence between the expert observer and the algorithm results (R^2 = 0.99, CCC = 0.99) verified on 31 FOVs.

3.2   Individual Spot Feature Characteristics and Number of Predictive Spots in Signal Aggregates

We characterized and compared the dots generated by a single probe (i.e., Kappa 01, Kappa 02, or Kappa 03) versus a cocktail of three probes (e.g., Kappa 01, 02, 03), and no probe control using tonsil tissue. As seen in Fig. 8, the intensity of three probes shows wider range than in the one probe images, whereas, the blurriness, size, and roundness characteristics of the spots generated by one probe are not different to spots generated by three probes. As seen in Fig. 9, the analysis result image overlaid with superpixel outlines (green), the overlaid red dots indicating the isolated spots detected by the algorithm, and a red number indicating the additional spots estimated for the aggregate signal within each superpixel.

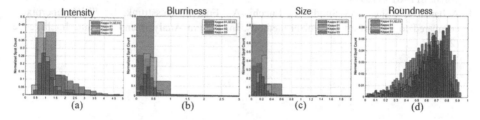

Fig. 8. Illustrates histograms of the spot characteristics of (a) intensity, (b) blurriness, (c) size, and (d) roundness generated by a single probe (i.e., Kappa 01, Kappa 02, or Kappa 03) versus a cocktail of three probes (Kappa 01,02,03).

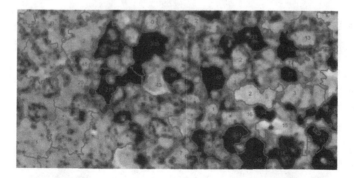

Fig. 9. The analysis result image overplaid with superpixel outlines (green), the overplaid red dots indicating the isolated spots detected by the algorithm, and a red number indicating the additional spots estimated within the aggregate signal with each superpixel. (Color figure online)

4   Conclusions

In this study, we have leveraged the unique detection features of the RNA ISH technology to develop a new method to quantify the RNA signal in FFPE tissue, while maintaining tissue context. It is anticipated that this method will enable analysis of gene expression changes in heterogeneous cancer and normal cells and tissues, with single cell resolution, thereby enabling evaluation of the clinical utility of the plethora of RNA biomarkers encoded in the human genome.

References

1. Wang, F., et al.: RNAscope: a novel in situ RNA analysis platform for formalin-fixed, paraffin-embedded tissues. J. Mol. Dia. **14**(1), 22–29 (2012)
2. Ruifrok, A.C., Johnston, D.A.: Quantification of histochemical staining by color deconvolution. J. Chem. Inf. Model. **53**(9), 1689–1699 (2013)
3. Polakowski, W.E., et al.: Computer-aided breast cancer detection and diagnosis of masses using difference of Gaussians and derivative-based feature saliency. IEEE Tran. Med. Img. **16**(6), 811–819 (1997)
4. Achanta, R., Shaji, A., Smith, K., Lucchi, A., Fua, P., Susstrunk, S.: SLIC superpixels compared to state-of-art superpixel methods. In: Pattern Analysis and Machine Intelligence (2012)

Digital Tumor-Collagen Proximity Signature Predicts Survival in Diffuse Large B-Cell Lymphoma

Talha Qaiser[1], Matthew Pugh[2], Sandra Margielewska[2], Robert Hollows[2], Paul Murray[2,3], and Nasir Rajpoot[1,4,5(✉)]

[1] Department of Computer Science, University of Warwick, Coventry, UK
N.M.Rajpoot@warwick.ac.uk
[2] Institute of Immunology and Immunotherapy, University of Birmingham, Birmingham, UK
[3] Health Research Institute, University of Limerick, Limerick, Ireland
[4] Department of Pathology, University Hospitals Coventry and Warwickshire, Coventry, UK
[5] The Alan Turing Institute, London, UK

Abstract. Diffuse large B-cell lymphoma (DLBCL) is a heterogeneous tumor that originates from normal B-cells. A limited number of studies have investigated the role of acellular stromal microenvironment on outcome in DLBCL. Here, we propose a novel digital proximity signature (DPS) for predicting overall survival (OS) in DLBCL patients. We propose a novel end-to-end multi-task deep learning model for cell detection and classification and investigate the spatial proximity of collagen (type VI) and tumor cells for estimating the DPS. To the best of our knowledge, this is the first study that performs automated analysis of tumor and collagen on DLBCL to identify potential prognostic factors. Experimental results favor our cell classification algorithm over conventional approaches. In addition, our pilot results show that strongly associated tumor-collagen regions are statistically significant ($p = 0.03$) in predicting OS in DLBCL patients.

Keywords: Computational pathology · Deep learning · Survival analysis

1 Introduction

Lymphomas are malignancies derived from lymphocytes, and are broadly categorized in to B-cell and T-cell lymphomas, reflecting the proposed cell of origin. B-cell malignancies are further categorised into low grade and high grade lymphomas. Diffuse large B-cell lymphoma (DLBCL) is the most common high grade

Electronic supplementary material The online version of this chapter (https://doi.org/10.1007/978-3-030-23937-4_19) contains supplementary material, which is available to authorized users.

lymphoma in Western populations. The introduction of modern chemotherapeutic regimens, which include Rituximab, has led to improved survival for DLBCL patients [1]. Despite these advances, approximately 40% of patients will not show a lasting response to therapy and will inevitably die of their disease [2]. This variability in treatment response in part reflects the biological heterogeneity of the disease. In recent years, significant progress has been made in unraveling this heterogeneity. Recent studies have also begun to investigate the role of the tumor microenvironment in DLBCL. Tumor associated macrophages, tumor infiltrating lymphocytes and immune checkpoint gene expression have all been associated with tumor behavior [3]. In contrast, few studies have investigated the role of the acellular stromal microenvironment. Collagen is a component of the acellular stromal microenvironment, and its presence is linked to outcome in urothelial and colorectal carcinomas, warranting further investigation of its role in DLBCL. In previous work we showed that collagen type VI is most closely associated with tumor cells in DLBCL and furthermore that the tumor cells of DLBCL overexpress growth promoting collagen receptors (Margielewska *et al.*, unpublished data).

In this paper, we investigate the spatial arrangement of tumor cells and collagen VI in DLBCL and describe a novel digital proximity signature (DPS), which serves as a marker of regions of the tumor likely to be enriched for active collagen signaling. The core components of the proposed framework involve: *(a)* cell detection and classification, and *(b)* estimation of DPS. In this regard, we propose a novel deep learning framework, Hydra-Net, for simultaneous cell detection and classification, enabling the end-to-end learning on a multi-task problem. During testing, we introduce a multi-stage ensembling predictor that combines cell detection and classification predictions by leveraging information about the local neighborhood of cells. The comparative analysis of cell classification demonstrates the efficacy of Hydra-Net over single-task learning models. The tumor-collagen proximity analysis is then performed by aggregating the tumor cell statistics within the vicinity of collagen VI. We further show that strongly associated tumor-collagen regions are linked with overall survival (OS) in DLBCL patients.

2   Related Work

Computational pathology has paved the way for histology based patient survival analysis. Recently, Zhu *et al.* [4] studied geometry and texture features to detect and segment cells in non-small cell lung cancer (NSCLC). Selected handcrafted features were fed into a supervised principal component regression model to improve predictive performance. Weng *et al.* [5] demonstrated that histology-driven imaging data can better describe the tumor morphology and outperformed conventional biomarkers for predicting survival in NSCLC patients. They employed a deep learning (DL) model for cell sub-type classification and imaging biomarkers were then identified using cellular features. More recently, a survival analysis based on WSISA with whole-slide images (WSIs) of glioma and NSCLC cancer patients was performed [6]. They trained a DL survival predictor to aggregate the patient-level predictions from clustered data. One of the potential shortcomings of prior approaches has been the random selection or uniformly sampled visual fields for survival analysis. In contrast, we computed summary-level statistics from the entire WSI and define a novel tumor-collagen proximity signature. Related work regarding cell detection and classification is discussed in the Supplementary Material Sect. 1.

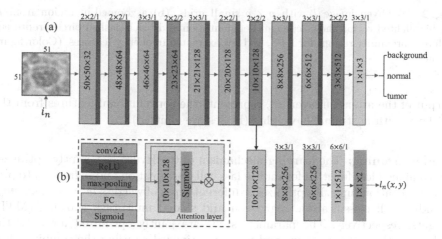

Fig. 1. (a) A schematic illustration of our proposed Hydra-Net and (b) description of different sub-components.

3   Methods

3.1   Hydra-Net: Cell Detection and Classification

Model Description: Given an image patch $i_n \in \mathbb{R}^{H \times W \times D}$, where $I = \{(i_n)\}_{n=1}^{N}$, our model utilizes the deep convolutional features to simultaneously predict the class probabilities c_n^k, where k is the number of classes, and the center location $l_n(x, y)$ of a cell. Figure 1 illustrates the proposed Hydra-Net architecture. The i_n is processed by a stack of convolutional layers (CL) followed by a ReLU activation function. For classification, we use convolutional kernels of relatively small receptive fields including 2×2 and 3×3 kernels, whereas stride for all CLs is adjusted as 1 pixel, preserving the spatial resolution after the convolution operation. The last pooling layer is followed by a spatial dropout layer and the softmax classification layer that predicts the belonging of i_n into c_n^k where $k \in \{1, 2, 3\}$, including background (including the collagen regions), normal and tumor classes. The other head of the Hydra-Net is responsible for predicting the center of each cell $l_n(x, y)$. The intermediate convolutional features are fed into the attention module that enables the model to learn the structural dependencies lie within the provided activation maps. We use a simple yet effective sigmoid (or soft) attention layer, which can be represented as $C_p = f_p(C_{p-1}, w_p)$ and $A = C_p \odot \sigma(C_p)$, where $\odot$ denotes the Hadamard product, A denotes the

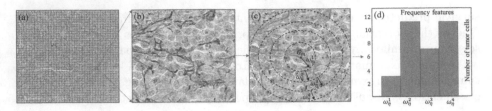

Fig. 2. (a) Given image I with $p \times p$ small grids, (b) a zoomed-in region from I, (c) highlighted region shows collagen segmentation and black-dashed circles represent different proximity regions for DPS, and (d) extracted frequency features. (Color figure online)

output of the attention layer, C_p represents the convolutional features from the pth layer with w_p trainable weights (biases are omitted).

Model Training: The learning mechanism of the Hydra-Net jointly optimizes the combined loss function for multi-class cell classification and regression to predict the location tuple. It optimizes 3 different types of weights $w = (w_c, w_r, w_s)$ including cell classification, regression and shared multi-task learning (MTL) weights, respectively. The parameters w_s are jointly optimized for both the tasks, and the parameters w_c and w_r are optimized by using the combined loss L as defined below,

$$L = L_c(c, c') + \lambda L_r(l(x, y), l'(x, y)) \tag{1}$$

where $L_c(c, c')$ represents log loss for true class c'_i and the second part of the loss function is formulated over the true center location of a cell $l'(x, y)$ and the predicted location $l(x, y)$. The L_r is the l_1 norm between the true and predicted locations, which is more robust to outliers as compared to the l_2 norm. Preferably, we want our model to predict location only for image patches that contains cell, and similarly, for background patches there is no information provided regarding the $l'(x, y)$. Therefore, during training, we introduced a flag λ that is set to 1 for tumor and normal classes and 0 for the background class. During test, each i_n is processed by a multi-stage ensembling predictor (MEP). See Supplementary Material Sect. 2 for the detailed description of the proposed MEP.

3.2   Digital Proximity Signature

Computation of DPS is based on two core components: *(a)* select a set of reference points $G = \{G_m\}_{m=1}^{M}$ within the collagen regions, where M is the number of sampled points, and *(b)* perform proximity analysis between tumor cells and G_m.

Collagen Localization: The main objective of localizing G_m is to select a set of representative points from the collagen regions. We first segmented the collagen regions by performing stain deconvolution separating I into 3 channels, Hematoxylin, Diaminobenzidine (DAB), and background. Collagen VI antibody generally binds with DAB channel having low intensity values and therefore we empirically choose a relatively high threshold $\tau = 0.82$ to binarize the DAB channel I_{DAB}. The highlighted region in Fig. 2(c) (teal color) shows the segmented collagen region. We then compute the medial axis of $I_{DAB}(\tau)$ to retain the connectivity structure of collagen fiber, as defined below

$$Z = (I_{DAB}(\tau) \ominus tS) - (I_{DAB}(\tau) \ominus tS) \circ S \qquad (2)$$

where $\ominus$ and $\circ$ denote the morphological erosion and opening respectively, and S is the structuring element with size t. Further, we split Z into small grids of size $p \times p$, where $Z = \{(z_m)\}_{m=1}^M$ and $p = 256$. The next task is to select a G_m from each z_m, in this regard, we compute the Euclidean distance between the center point $z_m(p/2, p/2)$ and the spatial coordinates of medial axis $z_m(x_\alpha, y_\alpha)$, where α represents the total points in medial axis

$$G_m(x, y) = \min_{x,y} \left(E(z_m(x_\alpha, y_\alpha), z_m(\tfrac{p}{2}, \tfrac{p}{2})) \right) \qquad (3)$$

where $E(.)$ denotes the Euclidean distance. Finally, the collagen region lying close to the center of z_m is selected as the reference point, as shown in Fig. 2(c).

Collagen-Tumor Proximity Analysis: For each G_m, we compute a set of frequency features by counting the number of tumor cells within its vicinity, as shown in Fig. 2(d). Similarly, we compute the features for the entire dataset $\omega = \{(\omega_\eta)\}_{\eta=1}^\nu$, where ν represents the number of collagen reference points from all the WSIs of the dataset. We then perform clustering on the computed features in order to assign labels to the segmented collagen regions.

We use a simple yet effective method, k-means clustering ($k = 4$) to arrange the frequency features into clusters. The algorithm randomly selects the first centroid and the remaining centroids are chosen based on the largest minimum distance to the preceding centroids, as defined below

$$\hat{\eta} = \mathrm{argmax}_\eta \left(\min_\kappa \|\omega_\eta - S_\kappa\|_2^2 \right) \qquad (4)$$

where S_κ denotes the centroid of the κth cluster. The algorithm iteratively updates the cluster centroids by computing the distance between centroids and the data points using the Jensen-Shannon divergence, as defined in (5)

$$JSD(S_\kappa \parallel \omega_\eta) = \frac{1}{2} KLD(S_\kappa \parallel \Omega) + \frac{1}{2} KLD(\omega_\eta \parallel \Omega) \qquad (5)$$

where KLD represents KullbackLeibler divergence and $\Omega = \frac{1}{2}(S_\kappa + \omega_\eta)$. On the basis of clustering results, we assign the clustering labels to the collagen region in the vicinity of G_m. We further normalize the clustering labels to limit their values between 0 and 1. Finally, in order to compute the DPS, we split the normalized clustering labels into 4 categorizes and individually aggregate the statistics. The categories includes weak, moderate, significant, and strong association between tumor and collagen regions. The qualitative results of proximity analysis and its corresponding DPS can be seen in Fig. 3. Our main intuition of identifying DPS into 4 categories is to provide a concise summary of statistics regarding the proximity between tumor and collagen across the WSI.

4   Experimental Results

This study was performed on WSIs of 32 histopathologist-verified cases of DLBCL using immunohistochemistry for collagen VI with a Hematoxylin counterstain to simultaneously detect collagen VI and nuclear morphology. The DLBCL samples included 10 from female patients and 22 from male patients. The age range of the patients was 24 to 90 years, with an average age of 63.6 years. We separately report the results of the Hydra-Net and OS prediction with tumor-collagen DPS.

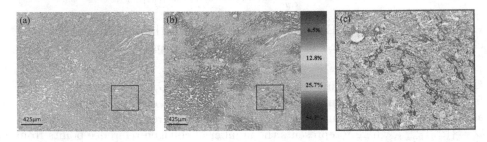

Fig. 3. (a) A visual field extracted from a whole slide image, (b) highlighted collagen regions demonstrate the association between collagen and tumor along with its digital proximity signature, and (c) shows the area marked by rectangles in (a) and (b). (Color figure online)

Cell Detection and Classification: The GT for cell detection and classification was collected on 9 cases and marked by an expert. In total, we get 2,617 annotated cells including 2,039 tumors, 462 normal and 116 macrophages. To mitigate the effect of sparse (and limited) GT, we extensively perform the data augmentation by random rotations, cropping, flipping (horizontal or vertical axis), and perturbing the color distribution, attaining a total of 30,416 patches including 12,100 tumor cells, 9,957 normal cells (including macrophages), and 8,359 randomly selected background patches. Generally, tumor cells and macrophages exhibit a high degree of morphological resemblance, having weakly stained boundaries and hollow structure.

We performed 3-fold cross-validation by selecting 2 folds of the dataset for training and the remaining fold for testing. Table 1(a) & (b) report the quantitative results for cell detection and classification. Overall, the proposed Hydra-Net

Table 1. (a) Comparative analysis for cell detection and classification, (b) Hydra-Net confusion matrix for cell classification.

(a)

Cell Classification			
Methods	Precision	Recall	F1-score
CRImage [7]	0.674	0.689	0.681
Superpixel [8]	0.729	0.708	0.713
SC-CNN [9]	0.834	0.802	0.817
Hydra-Net w/o Att	0.828	0.825	0.826
Hydra-Net	**0.839**	**0.842**	**0.84**

(b)

	Predicted scores		
Background	**89.29%**	4.28%	6.43%
Tumor	4.52%	**84.73%**	10.75%
Normal	9.17%	10.73%	**80.10%**
	Background	Tumor	Normal

(True labels)

Table 2. Contains p-values from overall survival (OS) analysis.

	DPS-3			DPS-4		
	KM p-value	Cox p-value	OS worse in	KM p-value	Cox p-value	OS worse in
Weak	-	-	-	0.39	0.06	High
Moderate	0.05	0.09	High	0.36	0.07	Low
Significant	0.05	0.05	Low	0.08	0.08	Low
Strong	0.03	0.40	Low	0.08	0.30	Low

produces less false negatives as compared to other methods. Table 1(a) also highlights the significance of soft attention layer, which is computationally efficient and enables the model to focus only on a particular element (which in our case is $l_n(x, y)$) within the given input. Besides, the proposed MTL framework offers advantages over single task learning models [7–10]: first, it overcomes the risk of overfitting by increasing the discriminative ability of shared weights. Second, the inference time for the MTL framework is relatively less as it involves single (forward) propagation for handling multiple tasks.

Survival Analysis: To obtain the DPS for a WSI, we computed the average of DPSs obtained from image tiles. The qualitative results along with DPS for a WSI results are shown in Fig S.2. We observed that a large part of the tissue region contains weak association (mainly due to normal regions) between tumor and collagen. Therefore, to avoid the over-localization of weak associations, we separately performed the survival analysis on all 4 values of proximity signature (DPS-4) and the remaining 3 categories excluding the weak associations (DPS-3). It is worth mentioning that we separately performed *sum to unity* scaling on the statistics from DPS-3 and DPS-4. For each DPS category, a Kaplan-Meier (KM) analysis was performed, with patients split into two groups based on the median value of the DPS proportion. Statistical significance of each KM analysis was quantified using the log-rank test. A Cox proportional hazards analysis was also performed for each category of DPS-3 and DPS-4, using the DPS proportion as the explanatory variable, with the Wald test used to determine the statistical significance. For DPS-4, the univariate analysis revealed a non-significant trend for weakly associated tumor-collagen regions with inferior OS (log-rank

$p = 0.39$, Wald $p = 0.06$). Conversely, moderate, significant, and strongly associated regions showed the opposite trend. This might be explained by the fact that weak associations are negatively correlated with the other DPS-4 proportions. Table 2 gives all p-values for DPS associations with survival. Similar results were obtained for DPS-3 (Fig. 4), but associations with survival were statistically significant with p-values of $0.05, 0.05, 0.03$ for moderate, significant, and strongly associated regions, respectively. Our results suggest that DPS-3 is a better predictor of OS than DPS-4 and that using this method, patients whose tumors exhibit strong tumor-collagen associations appear to experience superior OS.

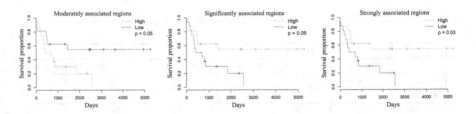

Fig. 4. Kaplan-Meier survival curves from DPS-3 for moderately, significantly and strongly associated tumor-collagen regions. The horizontal axis shows the time in days and the vertical axis represents the probability of overall survival.

Conclusions: In this study, we have described a novel tumor-collagen digital proximity signature (DPS) that can predict overall survival in DLBCL. We proposed computing of the DPS by first detecting and classifying tumor cells using a multi-headed Hydra-Net. Second, we performed tumor-collagen proximity analysis by aggregating tumor cell statistics within the vicinity of collagen regions. Our results show that strong proximity of collagen and tumor cells are linked with better OS in DLBCL patients. We are now exploring the utility of our DPS as a predictor of outcomes in larger cohorts of DLBCL patients.

References

1. Coiffier, B., et al.: CHOP chemotherapy plus rituximab compared with CHOP alone in elderly patients with diffuse large-B-cell lymphoma. New Engl. J. Med. **346**(4), 235–242 (2002)
2. de Jonge, A.V., et al.: Diffuse large B-cell lymphoma with MYC gene rearrangements: current perspective on treatment of diffuse large B-cell lymphoma with MYC gene rearrangements; case series and review of the literature. Eur. J. Cancer **55**, 140–146 (2016)
3. Chen, Z., et al.: Novel risk stratification of de novo diffuse large B cell lymphoma based on tumour-infiltrating T lymphocytes evaluated by flow cytometry. Ann. Hematol. **98**(2), 391–399 (2019)
4. Zhu, X., et al.: Lung cancer survival prediction from pathological images and genetic data—an integration study. In: 2016 IEEE 13th International Symposium on Biomedical Imaging (ISBI). IEEE (2016)

5. Wang, S., Yao, J., Xu, Z., Huang, J.: Subtype cell detection with an accelerated deep convolution neural network. In: Ourselin, S., Joskowicz, L., Sabuncu, M.R., Unal, G., Wells, W. (eds.) MICCAI 2016. LNCS, vol. 9901, pp. 640–648. Springer, Cham (2016). https://doi.org/10.1007/978-3-319-46723-8_74
6. Zhu, X., et al.: WSISA: making survival prediction from whole slide histopathological images. In: IEEE Conference on Computer Vision and Pattern Recognition (2017)
7. Yuan, Y., et al.: Quantitative image analysis of cellular heterogeneity in breast tumors complements genomic profiling. Sci. Transl. Med. 4(157), 157ra143 (2012)
8. Sirinukunwattana, K., et al.: A novel texture descriptor for detection of glandular structures in colon histology images. In: Medical Imaging 2015: Digital Pathology, vol. 9420 (2015)
9. Sirinukunwattana, K., et al.: Locality sensitive deep learning for detection and classification of nuclei in routine colon cancer histology images. IEEE Trans. Med. Imaging 35(5), 1196–1206 (2016)
10. Qaiser, T., et al.: Her 2 challenge contest: a detailed assessment of automated her 2 scoring algorithms in whole slide images of breast cancer tissues. Histopathology 72(2), 227–238 (2018)

An Integrated Multi-scale Model for Breast Cancer Histopathological Image Classification Using CNN-Pooling and Color-Texture Features

Vibha Gupta[✉] and Arnav Bhavsar

Indian Institute of Technology Mandi, Mandi, India
vibha_gupta@students.iitmandi.ac.in, arnav@iitmandi.ac.in

Abstract. Breast cancer is one of the most common human neoplasms in women, commonly diagnosed through histopathological microscopy imaging. The automated classification of histopathology images can relieve some workload of pathologists by triaging the cases. Knowing that histopathological images show a high degree of variability, useful information is often obtained at different optical magnification levels in order to make the correct diagnosis. For automated scoring, if there are differences in the patient's score at each considered magnification, the decision may not be reliable if only one magnification level is taken into consideration. This study proposes an integrated model in which scores across magnifications are combined by weights estimated from the least square methods. Moreover, unlike the existing methods, we consider a novel heterogeneous committee which includes deep and traditional members, to design a system for each magnification. As few studies have shown, such in an ensemble, often only a subset of members is sufficient to provide enough discriminative information. Hence, we use an information theoretic measure (ITS) to select optimal members for each magnification. We use publicly available BreaKHis dataset for the experimentation, and demonstrate that the proposed approach yield comparable or better performance when compared with most CNN based frameworks.

Keywords: Histopathology image analysis · Deep features ·
Color-texture features · Quadratic-SVM ·
Information Theoretic Score (ITS)

1 Introduction

One of the most common human neoplasms is breast cancer (BC), recorded in one quarter of all tumors in females. In all female cancers, breast cancer accounts for 27%, which is more than double the incidence of cancer in women at any other site [1]. This cancer's etiology appears to be multifactorial and involves diet, reproductive factors and associated hormonal imbalances. BC diagnosis typically involves the collection of tissue biopsies from suspected areas, identified

© Springer Nature Switzerland AG 2019
C. C. Reyes-Aldasoro et al. (Eds.): ECDP 2019, LNCS 11435, pp. 172–180, 2019.
https://doi.org/10.1007/978-3-030-23937-4_20

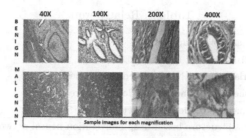

Fig. 1. Sample images correspond to each magnification

using ultrasound imaging or mammography, followed by histopathology image assessment [2]. Visual observation of tissue micro-structures through histopathology is time consuming as well as highly subjective. However, the rates of early diagnosis and treatment have steadily increased in recent years as a result of the development of a more sophisticated computer-aided diagnostic (CAD) systems, which are important to reduce inter-rater variability and also support in reducing the workload of experts.

Tissues typically consist of cells, and different tissues have different cellular properties. Cell shape information is well captured in high-power field microscopic images, but structural information such as a glandular structure which made up of many cells is better seized in a lower-power field. Since cancerous tissues comprise both cellular and structural atypia, information which captured at different magnifications can have important clues while making a decision. As far as diagnosis is concerned, there is lack of consensus about the most informative magnification [3]. Furthermore, in a CAD based scoring system, if there is a significant difference in the patient's score, the decision may not be reliable if only one magnification level is taken into account. Considering improved accuracy can be sometimes achieved by both high and low magnification images. From the Fig. 1, it can be seen that global shapes could be captured by lower magnifications while local by higher magnifications beneficially.

Considering aforementioned points, we believe that an assessment of the overall score which includes multiple magnifications can also provide useful information instead of simply relying on individual scores. With the same spirit, Gupta et al. [4] proposed an integrated model utilizing color-texture feature, where an score over multiple magnifications was calculated as the ratio of total images classified (images of all magnification) to total images of given patient. However, the weightage of individual contribution was ignored. Different from Gupta et al. [4] work, in this study, we combine scores correspond to each magnification through weights estimated using the least square method (see Fig. 3). We hypothesis that weight should be assigned based on accurateness of the model instead of blind or equal assignment. In addition, this work also considers a committee which comprises various deep learning-based members and color-texture feature-based members for classification of breast histopathology images. Learning without considering the color variations could worsen the performance. These color-texture members complement the performance of CNN members as shown by some previous studies [12]. However, we also believe that in such an

Table 1. Related work

Work	Descriptors & approach	Classifiers
Spanhol et al. [5]	CLBP, GLCM, PFTAS, LBP	RF, SVM, QDA
Spanhol et al. [6]	Variant of AlexNet (trained on patches)	
Song et al. [7]	Fisher vector encoding of local features	-
Gupta et al. [8]	Sequential modeling of deep features	XGBoost
Han et al. [9]	Class-structure based deep convolution neural network	-
Nahid et al. [10]	CNN model along with residual block	-
Bardou et al. [11]	Convolution neural network and hand-crafted features	SVM

ensemble, a subset of good members is enough to provide discriminatory information on the relevant categories rather than a large committee. And, therefore, adding a new member to such a subset will not further improve accuracy (or slight improvement) and can sometimes have a negative impact on accuracy. This work explores an information theoretic measure [13] to select optimal committee. Different from traditional methods, it considers both accuracy and diversity.

The effectiveness of proposed framework is evaluated using Break-His [5] dataset. It contains total 7909 images which were collected from 82 patients at four different magnifications. We consider the binary classification task (benign/Malignant). Due to space constraints, we have summarized the related approaches reported in recent years, which also use the above dataset, in Table 1. In our section on experimental results, we also provide comparisons with these.

Summary of Contributions: (1) Propose an integrated model to combine scores from images at different magnification using the least squares method to estimates the combining weights, (2) An ensemble framework which uses both color-texture and CNN members, and shows better generalization (3) An information theoretic approach for diverse member selection, (4) Demonstrate comparable or better performance with various state-of-the-art works.

2   Proposed Approach

The schematic flow of proposed work is shown in Fig. 2. It constitutes basic unit which is shown in Fig. 3. the overall work is divided into the following steps. Due to the lack of space, we only provide short descriptions, and appropriate references are given for further detail.

1. **Building a classifier committee:** The committee is build using the CNN-pooling features from the DenseNet architecture, and color-texture features such as such as Normalized colour space representation [14], Multilayer coordinate clusters representation [15], Opponent colour local binary pattern [16], and Gabor features on Gaussian colour model [17].
   To design deep members, we fine-tune the DenseNet pre-trained on the ImageNet data [18]. As early layers capture the generic low-level features, which are common among pathological images, we frozen the these layers

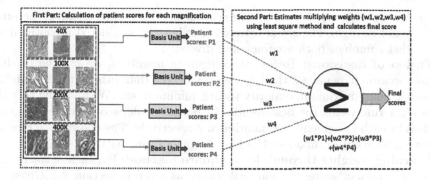

Fig. 2. Schematic digram of proposed approach

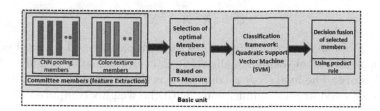

Fig. 3. Basic module of proposed framework

and fine-tuned the remaining network. As this model comprises various layers (165), features can be extracted from convolution and pooling layers. Unlike [8], here, we extract features only from pooling layers as they are fewer, as compared to convolution layers, and yet compasses diverse features also shown in various studies [19].

We employ the popular quadratic SVM classifier with the polynomial kernel of order two for classification with the above features, and consider the output probability scores for further processing.

2. **Selection of optimal members:** Optimal committee corresponds to each magnification is chosen based on information theoretic measure. This measure is summarized below:

   - First select the best individual member:

$$\hat{i_1} = \underset{i=1,2,...,M}{\arg\max}\ I(C_i, C) \tag{1}$$

   Where M is total number of members in committee. C and C_i are true class labels and predicted class labels assigned by member i respectively. I refers to mutual information.

   - Add the member along with above selected member in the new committee for that ITS score [13] between $\hat{i_n}$ and the member is maximized:

$$\hat{i_{n+1}} = \underset{i=1,2,...,M-n}{\arg\max}\ I(C_{\hat{i_n}}, C_i); \quad n = 1.2...M-1 \tag{2}$$

- We iterate step 2 until the improvements by adding member becomes small enough. The set of selected members is considered as optimal set that combines both accuracy and diversity.
3. **Fusion of decisions:** To fuse the output of members, we use the product rule because it penalizes the lower scores better than other fusion strategies such as sum, maximum, majority voting, minimum etc. We observed that the product rule yields the best results. In product rule, score assigned to each class by each base member is multiplied respectively. The class which receives maximum score is announced as final to given input pattern.
5. **Learning weights through least square method:** For each of the magnification, patient scores (PS) are calculated as given in section *3.1*. Given the PS for all magnifications, weights are learned (w_1,w_2,w_3,w_4) using the least square method (as shown below).

$$\hat{\omega} = (X^T X)^{-1} X^T \mathbf{y} \tag{3}$$

Where X is a matrix containing scores for each patient and $\mathbf{y}$ vector contains corresponding label (benign/malignant). $\hat{\omega}$ is an estimated weight vector.
7. **Final score:** The final score is computed as the weighted combination of the scores obtained at all magnifications, with the weights computed as above.

3   Results and Discussion

3.1   Training-Testing Protocol and Evaluation Metric

In our experiments, we randomly selected 58 patients (70%) for training and 24 patients (30%) for testing. This also makes it possible to compare fairly with a state-of-the-art approaches [5–7]. We use data corresponds to 58 patient for training and validation while doing fine-tuning. In order to increase the number of samples, we use data augmentation which involves rotation, flip, height shift, width sift and translation. After augmentation, we have six times the original training data. We use three trails of random selection of training-testing data (based on patine) and show average results.

In order to compare results with the existing approach, we use the patient recognition rate (PRR) and the image recognition rate (IRR). The following definition is given as follows:

$$PRR = \frac{\sum_{i=1}^{N} PS_i}{N} \quad PS = \frac{N_{rec}}{N_P}; \quad IRR = \frac{N_{re}}{N_{all}} \tag{4}$$

where N is the total number of patients (testing), and N_{rec} and N_P are the correctly classified and total cancer image of patient P respectively. N_{all} and N_{re} are the total number of test images and total correctly classified test images.

3.2   Performance Evaluation and Comparison

Tables 2 and 3 illustrate the performance of each individual committee member and with the selection of members based on ITS, respectively. From the tables

Table 2. Evaluation of individual committee members

Extracted features (committee members)	Testing accuracy at patient and image level							
	40X		100X		200X		400X	
	Patient	Image	Patient	Image	Patient	Image	Patient	Image
OLBP (M1)	85.8%	86.5%	87.8%	89.1%	89.3%	91.1%	83.2%	86.0%
NCSR (M2)	85.7%	86.6%	89.6%	90.7%	88.3%	90.1%	84.0%	86.3%
M_CCR_8 (M3)	74.7%	75.5%	81.7%	82.9%	79.3%	80.5%	78.3%	79.3%
M_CCR_64 (M4)	80.1%	81.5%	80.2%	81.5%	85.1%	86.9%	82.3%	85.9%
M_CCR_27 (M5)	77.5%	80.6%	83.3%	83.7%	85.9%	86.9%	79.5%	82.6%
GLCM (M6)	64.8%	62.7%	63.8%	63.2%	66.9%	64.6%	68.3%	67.3%
GCM (M7)	86.2%	87.0%	89.9%	90.9%	88.9%	91.3%	84.5%	86.9%
Pool1 (M8)	79.1%	80.3%	83.8%	84.3%	83.9%	85.2%	84.3%	83.5%
Pool2 (M9)	87.3%	87.8%	87.9%	88.8%	90.2%	90.7%	87.6%	88.0%
Pool3 (M10)	**93.7%**	93.3%	**92.8%**	92.5%	**93.3%**	94.1%	87.0%	88.3%
Pool4 (M11)	91.4%	90.7%	92.4%	92.4%	93.3%	94.2%	**89.7%**	90.3%
Pool5 (M12)	93.4%	93.6%	92.7%	92.6%	92.3%	92.9%	86.8%	88.7%

Table 3. Selected members for each magnification and their combined accuracy

Mag.	M1	M2	M3	M4	M5	M6	M7	M8	M9	M10	M11	M12	Test acc (sel. members)	Test acc (all members)	Best test acc (single member)
40X		*	*			*		*				*	96.43±0.34	91.44±0.48	93.72
100X	*	*	*	*	*	*	*	*		*	*	*	95.79±1.69	93.43±3.33	92.75
200X		*				*		*				*	96.24±1.58	93.64±2.47	93.36
400X			*	*	*	*	*	*			*	*	90.89±4.28	88.26±4.19	89.70
Integrated Model (Patient level)													96.40±0.28	91.62±1.78	-

following can be observed: (1) Best accuracies corresponding to each magnification do not show consistency i.e. different members yield best accuracy for different magnifications. (2) Pooling members perform better than the color texture members. However, from the Table 3, it can be noted that the later compliment the CNN based features, and hence show the improved performance when considered as an ensemble. (3) The accuracy calculated using selected members (with ITS) outperforms the accuracy calculated using all members. (4) The integrated ensemble method shows better accuracy over most of the individual ensemble models, and also shows less variation.

The reason for choosing different features is that the corresponding errors are different. This is indicated in Fig. 4, where we show randomly selected samples on the x-axis, and the corresponding y-axis shows the performance of each member for given sample. Based on this figure it can be noted that errors made by some members can be corrected by the remaining members, therefore the overall framework helps to achieve a more generalized performance.

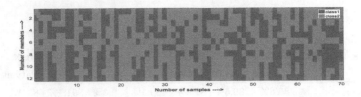

Fig. 4. Diversity among the committee member

Table 4. Performance comparison

Mag./method	Patient-level accuracy comparison						Image-level accuracy comparison		
	[5]	[6]	[7]	[9]	Prop. (Baseline)	Prop. (sel. member)	[10]	[11]	Prop. (sel. member)
40X	83.8	90.0	90.02	97.1	84.72	96.43	94.40	98.33	96.23
100X	82.1	88.4	91.2	95.7	89.44	95.79	95.93	97.12	96.73
200X	85.1	84.6	87.8	96.5	95.65	96.24	97.19	97.85	96.84
400X	82.3	86.10	87.4	95.7	82.65	90.89	96.0	96.15	91.60

Table 4 shows the comparative analysis of the proposed method with various state-of-the-art works. Note that the proposed approach outperforms many recent approaches [5–7]. We also significantly outperform the baseline model. The baseline model is essentially the same fine-tuned Densenet model but used for end-to-end classification.

In some cases, [9–11] shows better performance than the proposed method. In [10,11], some details about training-testing protocol (imagewise or patinetwise) are also not clear. In addition to that, only image level accuracy has been calculated (IRR from Eq. 4) which ignores the patient information. In these works [9–11], a different CNN model is used for end-to-end classification. However, we note that different from these methods, a focus of our work is to demonstrate that the various features including the ones from a CNN framework, when thoughtfully ensembled, can yield much higher results than the baseline CNN (as is observed from the comparison with the baseline model in Table 4). Thus, such an ensembling philosophy can also be applied to the networks in [9–11]. It would be interesting to see if such a strategy can further increase their performance.

4   Conclusion

This study proposes an integrated model utilizing pooled and color-texture features over multiple magnifications for the classification of breast cancer histopathology images. The model proposed shows superior performance when scores are combined using a least square method over individual magnifications. Hence, we conclude that more beneficial decision can be made once we include integrated score. In addition, the selected committee decided on the basis of ITS measures performs better than committee which considers all members.

References

1. Makki, J.: Diversity of breast carcinoma: histological subtypes and clinical relevance. Clin. Med. Insights: Pathol. **8**, CPath-S31563 (2015)
2. Veta, M., Pluim, J.P.W., Van Diest, P.J., Viergever, M.A.: Breast cancer histopathology image analysis: a review. IEEE Trans. Biomed. Eng. **61**(5), 1400–1411 (2014)
3. Wang, D., Khosla, A., Gargeya, R., Irshad, H., Beck, A.H.: Deep learning for identifying metastatic breast cancer. arXiv preprint arXiv:1606.05718 (2016)
4. Gupta, V., Bhavsar, A.: An integrated multi-scale model for breast cancer histopathological image classification with joint colour-texture features. In: Felsberg, M., Heyden, A., Krüger, N. (eds.) CAIP 2017. LNCS, vol. 10425, pp. 354–366. Springer, Cham (2017). https://doi.org/10.1007/978-3-319-64698-5_30
5. Spanhol, F.A., Oliveira, L.S., Petitjean, C., Heutte, L.: A dataset for breast cancer histopathological image classification. IEEE Trans. Biomed. Eng. **63**(7), 1455–1462 (2016)
6. Spanhol, F.A., Oliveira, L.S., Petitjean, C., Heutte, L.: Breast cancer histopathological image classification using convolutional neural networks. In: 2016 International Joint Conference on Neural Networks (IJCNN), pp. 2560–2567. IEEE (2016)
7. Song, Y., Chang, H., Huang, H., Cai, W.: Supervised intra-embedding of fisher vectors for histopathology image classification. In: Descoteaux, M., Maier-Hein, L., Franz, A., Jannin, P., Collins, D.L., Duchesne, S. (eds.) MICCAI 2017. LNCS, vol. 10435, pp. 99–106. Springer, Cham (2017). https://doi.org/10.1007/978-3-319-66179-7_12
8. Gupta, V., Bhavsar, A.: Sequential modeling of deep features for breast cancer histopathological image classification. In: Proceedings of the IEEE Conference on Computer Vision and Pattern Recognition Workshops, pp. 2254–2261 (2018)
9. Han, Z., Wei, B., Zheng, Y., Yin, Y., Li, K., Li, S.: Breast cancer multi-classification from histopathological images with structured deep learning model. Sci. Rep. **7**, 4172 (2017)
10. Nahid, A.-A., Kong, Y.: Histopathological breast-image classification using local and frequency domains by convolutional neural network. Information **9**(1), 19 (2018)
11. Bardou, D., Zhang, K., Ahmad, S.M.: Classification of breast cancer based on histology images using convolutional neural networks. IEEE Access **6**, 24680–24693 (2018)
12. Shen, H., Manivannan, S., Annunziata, R., Wang, R., Zhang, J.: Combination of CNN and hand-crafted feature for ischemic stroke lesion segmentation. Ischemic Stroke Lesion Segment. 1 (2016)
13. Meynet, J., Thiran, J.-P.: Information theoretic combination of pattern classifiers. Pattern Recogn. **43**(10), 3412–3421 (2010)
14. Vertan, C., Boujemaa, N.: Color texture classification by normalized color space representation. In: 2000 Proceedings of the 15th International Conference on Pattern Recognition, vol. 3, pp. 580–583. IEEE (2000)
15. Bianconi, F., Fernández, A., González, E., Caride, D., Calviño, A.: Rotation-invariant colour texture classification through multilayer CCR. Pattern Recogn. Lett. **30**(8), 765–773 (2009)
16. Mäenpää, T., Pietikäinen, M.: Texture analysis with local binary patterns. Handb. Pattern Recogn. Comput. Vis. **3**, 197–216 (2005)

17. Hoang, M.A., Geusebroek, J.-M., Smeulders, A.W.M.: Color texture measurement and segmentation. Signal Process. **85**(2), 265–275 (2005)
18. Huang, G., Liu, Z., van der Maaten, L., Weinberger, K.Q.: Densely connected convolutional networks. In: Proceedings of the IEEE Conference on Computer Vision and Pattern Recognition (2017)
19. Bailer, C., Habtegebrial, T., Stricker, D., et al.: Fast feature extraction with CNNs with pooling layers. arXiv preprint arXiv:1805.03096 (2018)

Icytomine: A User-Friendly Tool for Integrating Workflows on Whole Slide Images

Daniel Felipe Gonzalez Obando, Diana Mandache,
Jean-Christophe Olivo-Marin, and Vannary Meas-Yedid[✉]

Institut Pasteur, Bioimage Analysis Unit-CNRS UMR 3691,
25, rue du Docteur Roux, 75015 Paris, France
vmeasyed@pasteur.fr

Abstract. We present Icytomine, a user-friendly software platform for processing large images from slide scanners. Icytomine integrates in one unique framework the tools and algorithms that were developed independently on Icy and Cytomine platforms to visualise and process digital pathology images. We illustrate the power of this new platform through the design of a dedicated program that uses convolutional neural network to detect and classify glomeruli in kidney biopsies coming from a multicentric clinical study. We show that by streamlining the analytical capabilities of Icy with the AI tools found in Cytomine, we achieved highly promising results.

Keywords: Whole slide imaging · Reproducible research ·
Open-source plugin · Convolutional neural network · Fine-tuning ·
Detection of glomeruli

1 Introduction

The generalization of whole slide imaging (WSI) in pathology services improves Digital Pathology. These high throughput and high resolution images generate large images, called virtual slides offer many outlooks for clinical and research studies. However the clinical analysis doesn't exploit this high potential content and the analysis of virtual slides largely remains the work of human experts. This manual assessment of slides is known to have high variability and limited reproducibility. To fully exploit virtual slides that would improve high-quality reproducibility, we propose a quantitative computing approach. Actually, to process automatically these large images raises many computational challenges [1]: (i) gigapixel images, (ii) high variability of histology images (See Fig. 1). On the other hand, this large amount of data, big data, is particularly adapted to deep learning approaches. Which are known to offer state of the art results in many

We acknowledge the Inception program (Investissement d'Avenir grant ANR-16-CONV-0005) for providing their GPU lab for our research.

C. C. Reyes-Aldasoro et al. (Eds.): ECDP 2019, LNCS 11435, pp. 181–189, 2019.
https://doi.org/10.1007/978-3-030-23937-4_21

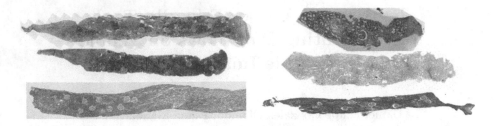

Fig. 1. Color variation in Masson's trichrome staining, due to the muti-centric staining. Even if it is the same staining, the image appearance could vary due to many reasons: (i) the tissue preparation protocol is not exactly the same across pathology services: for example, the resin could be used instead of paraffin, the cut, etc., (ii) image acquisition system and (iii) the age of the slide

imaging applications [2], however it comes with the expense of requiring exhaustive data, accompanied by annotations. In computer vision field, there exist huge databases that contain "cheap" images collected from widely available internet sources and annotations issued from crowd sourced non-expert work. The most pertinent example is ImageNet [3] that contains a number of 2M images belonging to 2K categories. This database powers object recognition methods that manage to outperform the human performance for the object detection task [4].

However building databases of this importance for medical applications is a stringent problem, because the data is not as common as in computer vision field. In particular, the ground truth generation requires interdisciplinary collaboration and specifically expert knowledge. The need for tools that would help minimizing the effort both on the side of the pathologist (providing annotations) and on the side of the computer scientist (image processing), also encouraging an unified workflow.

The present document describes the design, implementation and test for a plugin that deals with WSI applied to the detection of glomeruli, in kidney biopsy.

2   Related Works

In the perspective of collaborative project and open-software for reproducible research, we have only considered the open-source solutions. In fact, the open source packages encourage users to involve in further development and sharing of customized analysis solutions in the form of plugins, scripts, pipelines or workflows. This has offered opportunities for image analysis to contribute considerably to translational research by enabling the development of the adapted analytical methods required to address specific and emerging needs.

Deroulers *et al.* [5] described an open source tool for splitting Hamamatsu digital slides (ndpi format) in tiles, that they could be processed with any tool. In SlideToolkit, Nelissen *et al.* [6] propose a similar workflow based on Cell Profiler. With QuPath [7], the authors propose a bioimage analysis software and high-throughput biomarker evaluation tools. Della Mea *et al.* [8] propose SlideJ a plugin to automatically process digital slides within ImageJ.

3   Our Approach: Icytomine

We have presented in [9] a proof of concept, consisting a in general framework to process the tissue analysis. It combines two softwares: (i) Icy [10] image analysis platform (http://icy.bioimageanalysis.org/) dedicated to bio-image analysis, and (ii) Cytomine [11] the web platform (http://www.cytomine.be/) to store and share the virtual slides and their annotations, for multicentric digital pathology studies.

3.1   Icytomine Features

The plugin Icytomine was created as a bridge between Icy and Cytomine to provide large image and annotation importing, annotation exporting, as well as handling batch processing on these annotations. We propose an intuitive interface that provides a project and image explorer and a low-latency image and annotation viewer, taking advantage of image and data caches to minimize server queries. We also re-engineered available protocols in order to allow for seamless analysis integration and automatic batch processing. We present in the following paragraphs, a brief description of Icytomine and its new features to interact between the Icy software and Cytomine server.

Connecting Two Technologies. In order to provide access for image analysis on large images, Icytomine uses the web communication mechanisms provided by Cytomine. It adapts all incoming data to be compatible with Icy data structures. Among the adapted data we can find project structure, image data, and annotations geometrical data and their labeling. This information is then cached in memory so that it is available for as long as it is needed, or for as long as the memory allows it. This cache enables fast access to data since repeating server request are minimized, and also greedy memory allocation and subsequent out of memory errors are avoided by automatically removing from memory unnecessary data. Finally, data can also be transferred back to Cytomine to update annotation classifications or to send new annotations to the server. For this, Icytomine serves as a translator to adapt data coming from Icy and sending it in the correct format so that Cytomine can subsequently store it (Fig. 2).

Exploring Large Images on Icy. Icytomine allows access to Cytomine servers directly from Icy. Then, user can explore projects or images stored on the server (See Fig. 3). A cached image viewer was developed to provide a responsive user experience when interacting on the image. This viewer let users not only to view annotations made by all the users with access to the image, but also to classify these annotations and review classifications made by other users. A lot of effort was invested on this viewer to compute and show annotations and

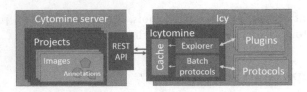

Fig. 2. Icytomine architecture. Icytomine is the communication port with Cytomine on Icy's side

images at different resolution levels while allowing continuous user interaction. To achieve this, annotations are also cached and treated to improve the viewer performance when they are conformed by many control points, in which case a geometry simplification is computed once and then its stored in cache memory. The Table 1 shows the performance in time of Icytomine when loading a slide and its annotations from a remote server. This time depend on the amount of annotations and this time is decreased with the cache: the re-loading is very fast, less than 5ms even with a big amount of annotations.

Table 1. Time to open an image for the first time

Image	Width (px)	Height (px)	Number of annotations	Time in ms (re-load)
ima1	111 145	99 589	0	161 (<1)
ima2	50 603	29 326	35	177 (1)
ima3	134 182	84 480	424	262 (1)
ima4	27 635	34 757	1925	615 (1)
ima5	110 973	108 387	11964	2761 (3)

Batch Processing on Large Images. Automatizing large image analyses can be a challenging task in terms of resource management, even for the easiest analyses. Icytomine address this issue by letting the user work on large images at different resolution scales and processing images by small patches that can be handled by the standard machine. For this, the user designs the analysis as a protocol where boxes represent different processes. Protocol blocks have been developed in Icy for importing images and annotations from the Cytomine server to Icy and exporting annotations to Cytomine server. These blocks can be customized according to the user needs, for example: tile size, tile margin (tile overlapping) and output resolution scale (See Fig. 4).

4   Application to Glomerulus Detection

Glomerulus is a network of capillaries essential to the blood filtration by kidney. Accurate detection of glomeruli is the first important step in many tasks such as

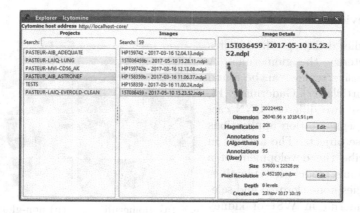

Fig. 3. Icytomine explorer. The first panel shows the list of projects. When the project is selected, the second panel shows the image list within the project. The last panel shows the information related either to the project, either to the selected image. The search bar (project or image) filters the display.

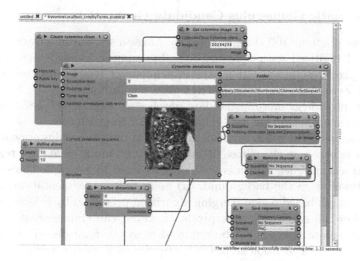

Fig. 4. Batch processing with Icytomine. An image can be processed by tiles that are configured before the batch processing. Extraction of glomeruli within an image o a project

diagnostic, pronostic, or assessment of the kidney quality graft. Due to biological, tissue sample preparation and set-up acquisition variability, the glomerulus appearance could vary in terms of color, size and texture, making automatic recognition of glomeruli challenging as shown in Fig. 5.

4.1   Previous Works

Many studies define specific features to characterize the glomerulus. A comprehensive review can be found in recent article [12]. Gadermayr [13, 14] propose two different CNN cascades for segmentation applications with sparse objects. The authors in [12] describe the development of a deep learning model that identifies and classifies non-sclerosed and sclerosed glomeruli in WSI of kidney frozen section biopsies. This model extends a convolutional neural network (CNN) pre-trained on a large database of digital images.

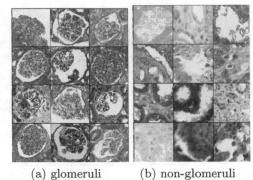

(a) glomeruli   (b) non-glomeruli

Fig. 5. Examples of the two classes stained in Masson's Trichrome

4.2   Automatic Glomerulus Candidate Generation

Our dataset contains 100 slides stained by Masson's trichrome from 7 research centers and digitized with 20X objective by using a Nanozoomer scanner at $0.452\,\mu$m pixel resolution, either Aperio scanner at $0.504\,\mu$m pixel resolution and either Zeiss AxioScan with $0.44\,\mu$m pixel resolution.

Icy can provide glomeruli candidate patches as training set: 5857 glomeruli, 7047 non-glomeruli; test set: 595 glomeruli, 792 non-glomeruli.

As the shape is the solely invariance feature of the glomerulus appearance, its extraction is based on the ellipse fitting [15] of two kinds of feature regions: (i) lumen extraction (when lumen is visible): extracted by a simple threshold that separate tissue from the background, (ii) color texture segmentation (for other cases): the graph based region merging algorithm presented by Felzenszwalb and Huttenlocher [16] generating superpixels. However, this step generates also non-glomerular regions that should be removed from the final detection and could be done with a classification step. CNN appears as a good solution for its high versatility and efficiency.

4.3   Glomerulus CNN Classification

Based on previous works, we chose the classical approach of fine-tuning the state-of-the-art architectures InceptionV3 [17], Resnet50 [18], as well as VGG16 [19]. VGG is characterized by its straightforward construction, with consecutive convolution and spatial reduction blocks which sum up to a large number of parameters i.e. 140M, making it computationally costly. Both ResNet and Inception are based on micro-modules which introduce different pathways in the propagation of information, with the benefit of having dramatically less parameters, $\approx$24M each, while also bringing improved performance.

All architectures were pre-trained on ImageNet and a fully-connected layer of 1024 neurons was added on top as a classifier along with one last neuron as output for binary classification. Fine-tuning was performed by minimizing the cross-entropy loss using stochastic gradient descent on mini-batches of 64 patches with a learning rate of 0.001 and momentum of 0.9. An average of 110 epochs (learning passes on the full training set) was sufficient to reach a stable result for all the architectures.

The architectures were fed with patches of their respective expected input, i.e. 299 × 299 pixels for InceptionV3 and 244 × 244 for ResNet50 and VGG16.

4.4   Glomerulus Segmentation by Mask R-CNN

To go further, we tested Mask R-CNN [20], which is as state-of-the-art instance segmentation architecture, able to achieve pixel accuracy. For the presented work we used the Keras & Tensorflow implementation by [21], with a ResNet50 backbone, also pre-trained on ImageNet.

After fine-tuning the network, we obtained a score of 78% of the mean average precision (mAP). However, the more interesting observations emerged from the visual assessment of the predicted segmentation. We notice that this approach is able to produce a more precise segmentation of the glomeruli borders, while also being robust to the outliers (erroneous ground truth) in the automatic annotation. Studying the cases with null intersection over union (IoU) between the ground truth and prediction, we noticed that Mask R-CNN was able to discover non-annotated positives (both in train and validation set, which is a good indicator for the lack of overfitting). We also observed that this approach is adapted for separating adjacent glomeruli (See Fig. 6).

From these results we deduce that our automatic training set generation method is well suited also for segmentation and what is more, Mask R-CNN can be applied as a last step in refining the annotations.

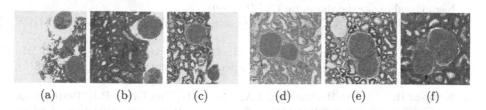

(a)   (b)   (c)   (d)   (e)   (f)

Fig. 6. Examples of Mask R-CNN segmentation results (ground truth in green, prediction in red): glomeruli detection on sample borders in (a) (b) (c), separation of adjacent glomeruli in (d) (e) (f) (color figure online)

5   Results

This framework uses image processing to create candidate patches and need a weak interaction from the user to validate these patches as glomerulus or not. This can be done either with the Cytomine web proofreading tool or the Icytomine viewer, to re-classify manually candidates. Figure 4 shows the Icy protocol that eases the batch processing task. The best results are obtained with the Inception network (See Table 2).

Table 2. Classification accuracy

Method	Accuracy
VGG [19]	0.94375
ResNet50 [18]	0.97188
InceptionV3 [17]	0.975

6   Conclusion

Current research in biology is continuously requiring software capable of supporting high reproducibility of analysis, while offering high performance, re-usability and modularity of available features through plugins. In this work, we proposed a user-friendly framework combining the powerful and complementary tools of Icy and Cytomine open-source softwares to process virtual slides. We have shown by focusing on detection of glomeruli that Icytomine is very well adapted for large-scale, multicentric digital pathology. Moreover this framework eases the generation of datasets to feed deep learning networks.

References

1. Fuchs, T.J., Buhmann, J.M.: Computational pathology: challenges and promises for tissue analysis. Comput. Med. Imaging Graph. **35**(7–8), 515–530 (2011)
2. LeCun, Y., Bengio, Y., Hinton, G.: Deep learning. Nature **521**(7553), 436–444 (2015)
3. Deng, J., Dong, W., Socher, R., Li, L.-J., Li, K., Fei-Fei, L.: ImageNet: a large-scale hierarchical image database. In: CVPR (2009)
4. Russakovsky, O., et al.: ImageNet large scale visual recognition challenge. IJCV **115**(3), 211–252 (2015)
5. Deroulers, C., Ameisen, D., Badoual, M., Gerin, C., Granier, A., Lartaud, M.: Analyzing huge pathology images with open source software. Diagn. Pathol. **8**(1), 1–8 (2013)
6. Nelissen, B.G.L., Van Herwaarden, J.A., Moll, F.L., Van Diest, P.J., Pasterkamp, G.: SlideToolkit: an assistive toolset for the histological quantification of whole slide images. PLoS One **9**(11), e110289 (2014)
7. Bankhead, P., et al.: QuPath: open source software for digital pathology image analysis. Sci. Rep. **7**(1), 16878 (2017)
8. Della Mea, V., Baroni, G.L., Pilutti, D., Di Loreto, C.: SlideJ: an ImageJ plugin for automated processing of whole slide images. PLoS One **12**, e0180540 (2017)
9. Marée, R., Dallongeville, S., Olivo-Marin, J.-C., Meas-Yedid, V.: An approach for detection of glomeruli in multisite digital pathology, pp. 1033–1036, April 2016
10. de Chaumont, F., et al.: ICY: an open bioimage informatics platform for extended reproducible research. Nat. Methods **9**(7), 690–6 (2012)

11. Marée, R., et al.: Collaborative analysis of multi-gigapixel imaging data using cytomine. Bioinformatics **32**(9), 1395–1401 (2016)
12. Marsh, J.N., et al.: Deep learning global glomerulosclerosis in transplant kidney frozen sections. IEEE Trans. Med. Imaging **37**, 1 (2018)
13. Gadermayr, M., Dombrowski, A.-K., Klinkhammer, B.M., Boor, P., Merhof, D.: CNN cascades for segmenting whole slide images of the kidney. CoRR, vol. abs/1708.00251 (2017)
14. Gadermayr, M., Eschweiler, D., Jeevanesan, A., Klinkhammer, B.M., Boor, P.: Segmenting renal whole slide images virtually without training data. Comput. Biol. Med. **90**, 88–97 (2017)
15. Fitzgibbon, A.W., Pilu, M., Fisher, R.B.: Direct least-squares fitting of ellipses. IEEE Trans. PAMI **21**(5), 476–480 (1999). May
16. Felzenszwalb, P.F., Huttenlocher, D.P.: Efficient graph-based image segmentation. IJCV **59**, 2004 (2004)
17. Szegedy, C., Vanhoucke, V., Ioffe, S., Shlens, J., Wojna, Z.: Rethinking the Inception Architecture for Computer Vision. ArXiv e-prints, December 2015
18. He, K., Zhang, X., Ren, S., Sun, J.: Deep residual learning for image recognition. ArXiv e-prints, December 2015
19. Simonyan, K., Zisserman, A.: Very deep convolutional networks for large-scale image recognition. ArXiv e-prints, September 2014
20. He, K., Gkioxari, G., Dollár, P., Girshick, R.B.: Mask R-CNN. In: 2017 IEEE ICCV, pp. 2980–2988 (2017)
21. Abdulla, W.: Mask R-CNN for object detection and instance segmentation on keras and tensorflow (2017). https://github.com/matterport/Mask_RCNN

Author Index

Printed in the United States
By Bookmasters